The Classical Association has a worldwide membership and is open to all who value the study of the languages, literature, and civilizations of ancient Greece and Rome. It creates opportunities for friendly exchange and co-operation among classicists, encourages scholarship through its journals and other publications, and supports classics in schools and universities. Every year it holds an annual conference, and it sponsors branches all over the country which put on programmes of lectures and other activities.

The Classical Association publishes three journals, *Classical Quarterly*, *Classical Review* and *Greece & Rome*. Members may subscribe at substantially reduced cost. Non-members and institutions can subscribe via Cambridge University Press (email journals@cambridge.org).

For more information and a membership application form please contact the Secretary, The Classical Association, Cardinal Point, Park Road, Rickmansworth, Hertfordshire, WD3 1RE. Tel: 07926 632598 (e-mail: office@classicalassociation.org). The Secretary can also give information about the reduced journal subscription rates, and about the Association's other occasional publications.

Greece & Rome

NEW SURVEYS IN THE CLASSICS No. 41

HOMER

BY
RICHARD RUTHERFORD

Second Edition

Published for the Classical Association
CAMBRIDGE UNIVERSITY PRESS
2013

CAMBRIDGE
UNIVERSITY PRESS

University Printing House, Cambridge CB2 8BS, United Kingdom

One Liberty Plaza, 20th Floor, New York, NY 10006, USA

477 Williamstown Road, Port Melbourne, VIC 3207, Australia

314-321, 3rd Floor, Plot 3, Splendor Forum, Jasola District Centre, New Delhi - 110025, India

79 Anson Road, #06-04/06, Singapore 079906

Cambridge University Press is part of the University of Cambridge.

It furthers the University's mission by disseminating knowledge in the pursuit of education, learning and research at the highest international levels of excellence.

www.cambridge.org
Information on this title: www.cambridge.org/9781107670167

First published 1996

Second Edition published 2013 (*Greece & Rome* 58)

A catalogue record for this publication is available from the British Library

ISBN 978-1-107-67016-7 Paperback

CONTENTS

PREFACE

This is a revised and updated version of the Survey I published in this series in 1996. As before, I have attempted to give a reasonably full and wide-ranging account of the Homeric poems and the current state of scholarship on them, with a strong emphasis on interpretation and literary criticism. The intervening period has been a fruitful one, not least in the fundamental areas of text and commentaries: the important work done here is listed in a separate section preceding the main bibliography.

The main changes have been made in the first chapter. Although this book is entitled *Homer*, I have now included a larger discussion of the other early Greek hexameter texts, both extant and fragmentary; given the explosion of work in this field (exemplified in the recent Loeb editions), it seemed useful to provide some orientation. I have somewhat expanded the paragraphs on Near Eastern influences, a subject on which Walter Burkert and Martin West have shed so much light. More has been said on chronology and related issues; some paragraphs on Homeric language have been included; and I have placed more emphasis on the view I have long supported, that the *Iliad* and the *Odyssey* were probably written down by or in the lifetime of their composers. I have also included some comments on traditional referentiality, intertextuality (with or without texts), and allusion. These changes have involved some restructuring of the chapter: I have explained things in a rather different order and sometimes in more detail. Since the chapter is now longer, more subdivisions have been introduced, and these have been numbered throughout the Survey.

The main text of Chapters 2 and 3 has undergone little change. There are some new remarks on the importance of the community in the *Iliad* and of the lower classes in the *Odyssey*. I have modified some formulations and adjusted misleading statements, here and elsewhere. But since on the whole I have not changed my mind about the questions discussed, the modifications to these chapters mainly consist of added references. In Chapter 4 I have added a further 'memorable scene', a discussion of *Iliad* 17.425–56. This is not expansion for its own sake: the passage usefully illustrates some of the issues of allusion now discussed in Chapter 1. Relatively little of the older text has been dropped, though I have removed a few citations where newer work seemed more helpful or more accessible. I have abandoned the distinction between Arabic and minuscule Roman numerals to distinguish citations of the *Iliad* and the *Odyssey*; where there might be ambiguity, the title is now given.

In the first footnote to Chapters 2 and 3 I refer to general studies of the *Iliad* and of the *Odyssey*. Books which deal with both poems are rarer, but there is one that deservedly wins praise for its vigour and readability, Barry Powell's *Homer* (Powell 2004; second edition 2007).[1]

The additions to the bibliography of course represent only a fraction of what has appeared since 1996; much has been omitted, much will no doubt have eluded me. There are very full bibliographical resources elsewhere: in particular, in the recent companions to Homer (Morris and Powell 1997 and R. Fowler 2004) and in the Wiley-Blackwell *Companion to Ancient Epic* (Foley 2005). The third edition of the *Oxford Classical Dictionary* appeared soon after the first edition of this Survey, and an enlarged fourth edition has now been published (ed. S. Hornblower, A. Spawforth, and E. Eidinow, 2012), including a new entry on Homer by Suzanne Said. I also draw attention to another essential reference work, the *Homer Encyclopedia* edited by Margalit Finkelberg (Finkelberg 2011), which again has a massive bibliography and valuable entries on almost every imaginable topic. I seldom refer to this because citations could be provided in every footnote, but any reader of Homer will learn much from it. A third work to which I am much indebted is Gantz 1993, an indispensable guide to Greek mythology in literature and art, and far more reliable than the wayward compilation by Robert Graves.

In the preface to the first edition I thanked Simon Hornblower, Robert Parker, and Peter Parsons for their advice, and Ian McAuslan for his editorial work. Although they have not been involved in this revision, I am happy to repeat my appreciation for their help with the original version. The new edition has similarly benefited from comments by Bruno Currie, Adrian Kelly, and Chris Pelling, as well as from John Taylor, the current series editor. I am grateful to all of them, as also to Philemon Probert (who kindly looked at the section on language), and to many other colleagues who have answered questions or sent me copies of papers.

Constraints of time and space have imposed limits on what could be done, but I hope that in this revised form the volume will continue to be found useful as an introduction to Homeric studies.

RBR
October 2012

---

[1] Latacz 1996 is the work of a distinguished scholar, but less stimulating. Griffin 1980 does deal with both epics, but his emphasis is much more on the *Iliad*.

I INTRODUCTION: BACKGROUND AND PROBLEMS

1. History, myth, poetry

EPIC
I have lived in important places, times
When great events were decided, who owned
That half a rood of rock, a no-man's land
Surrounded by our pitchfork-armed claims.
I heard the Duffys shouting 'Damn your soul'
And old McCabe stripped to the waist, seen
Step the plot defying blue cast-steel—
'Here is the march along these iron stones'
That was the year of the Munich bother. Which
Was more important? I inclined
To lose my faith in Ballyrush and Gortin
Till Homer's ghost came whispering to my mind
He said: I made the *Iliad* from such
A local row. Gods make their own importance.[1]

Patrick Kavanagh's short poem confronts the reader with a number of questions which will preoccupy us in this survey. The Homeric poems show us a world which in many respects seems primitive and remote; even if the expedition of the Greeks against Troy really happened, even if it took place on the scale which the *Iliad* asserts, and lasted the full ten-year span, it would still be 'a local row' compared with later historical conflicts, ancient or modern. Can the bad-tempered disputes of warrior chiefs, the violent revenge of a savage and undisciplined soldier, the lies and posturing of a vagabond rogue, still move or excite an audience today? It will be necessary to show here some of the ways in which Homer gives the conflict at Troy, and the homecoming of Odysseus, a timeless importance, so that these mere episodes in the vanished heroic age – long past even for the poet and his audience – become microcosmic images of human life. The vast subject of Homer's influence upon later western literature cannot be even

---

[1] Kavanagh 1964: 136.

superficially addressed here; but occasional comparisons and illus-trations may help to show how much subsequent poets and artists have found in the *Iliad* and the *Odyssey* to enlighten and inspire their own work.

'I made the *Iliad* from such / a local row.' But what was the local row about, and where and when did it happen? The Greeks always assumed that the war was an authentic historical event, and modern faith in this was strengthened by the landmark excavations in mainland Greece and at Troy by the archaeologist Heinrich Schliemann and his many successors. On the one hand, a glorious civilization had existed in Greece in times far earlier than the classical age; on the other, a city with mighty walls had existed near the Hellespont, had been rebuilt many times, and at some stage had been destroyed by fire. Supporting evidence seemed to appear in Hittite documents, which mentioned a people called the Ahhijawa, a name which could be an earlier or foreign form of 'Achaeans'; and there were other possible correspondences – most intriguingly, evidence of a monarch ruling in 'Wilusa' (Ilium) who bore a name transmitted in documents as Alaksandu, which strongly resembles 'Alexandros', the alternative name for the Trojan Paris. It was tempting to suppose that the legends were substantially true, that a great force of Greek invaders attacked and sacked the city now called 'Troy VIIA', and that some time later the fall of the Mycenaean civilization brought an end to this prosperous era; later mythology saw this in terms of an age of heroes followed by subsequent decline. The discovery that 'Linear B', the language of the Mycenaean age, was in fact an earlier form of Greek, made it poss-ible to hypothesize a continuous tradition of poetic narrative, which preserved a record of these great days through the Dark Ages.[2]

Bold and imaginative reconstruction has continued, with the advance of archaeological and linguistic research. A picture emerges of large-scale conflicts between Mediterranean communities and the societies dominating the eastern seaboard in the late second millen-nium.[3] Yet caution is still in order. If there was a continuous tradition

---

[2] Page 1959 provided a learned and highly readable discussion of the earlier progress of these debates, but is now seriously out of date. For an authoritative account see Latacz 2004 (translated from a 2002 German work; it should be noted that subsequent German editions include updat-ing). The annual journal *Studia Troica* publishes the results of the ongoing excavations at the site of Troy. See also the brief overview in M. L. West 2011b: 97–112.

[3] See especially the collection of essays edited by Foxhall and Davies 1984; also Mellink 1986; Kirk 1990: 36–50. For a penetrating essay which combines archaeological and literary finesse, see

from Mycenaean times, we cannot assume that the tradition was free of distortion or misunderstanding (for instance, those who do not dismiss the Wooden Horse as pure fiction sometimes suppose it to be a confused echo of an Oriental siege engine). Some features of the tradition are, in any case, implausible: the thousand ships, the ten years spent far from home are surely epic exaggeration; nor can even the most romantic of readers suppress doubts about a national campaign fought to recover one leader's wife. Overseas raids and adventures are a familiar part of the epic repertoire and probably of the real-life background, as many passages in the *Odyssey* suggest. In the *Iliad*, Nestor recounts his own exploits as a young man in a cattle-raiding expedition against the people of Elis (11.670–762): as has often been suggested, this may well give a more accurate idea of the scale of warfare in early Greece than the vast assemblage of peoples listed in the Catalogue of Ships.[4] At all events, even if some general account survived from Mycenaean times, it is hardly likely that any details of the course of events were preserved.[5]

Whatever the historical facts behind the *Iliad*, they are separated from the epic itself by a gap of at least four hundred years (the traditional date for the fall of Troy was 1183 BC, and archaeologists currently place the destruction of Troy VIIA not far from that date).[6] The *Odyssey*, being a tale about an individual's fortunes and an island community of little prominence in Mediterranean history, is still less likely to preserve much in the way of historical reality. A great deal of the *Odyssey*, in any case, is set in a world of magic and monsters, remote from authentic history or geography. The poems do contain elements of an older tradition: the wealth of Agamemnon, lord of Mycenae 'rich in gold', Ajax's tower-like shield, and Odysseus' boar's-tusk helmet are examples. Sometimes these memories are blurred or conflated with later conventions: for the most part the warriors carry two thrusting-spears, but the single heavy spear, a Mycenaean weapon, is

Sherratt 1990. A very different approach is adopted by Fehling 1991, who seeks to recover the original core of the *story*, dismissing historicity.

[4] On Nestor's narrative, see Bölte 1934; Hainsworth 1993: 296–8. Frame 2010 is a 600-page monograph on Nestor.

[5] Much historical information is painlessly presented in Morris and Powell 1997 (esp. Bennet 1997 on the Bronze Age; Morris 1997 on the Iron Age is less rewarding).

[6] 1183 is the date accepted by Eratosthenes and Apollodorus, but many other dates were canvassed; it is certainly hard to see how any could have been supported by proof. Burkert 1995 discusses ancient dating-systems and the theories about the Trojan war, concluding that none of the dates suggested has any historical basis.

occasionally recalled, in some passages to arouse awe and a sense of latent power (see *Il.* 16.140–4). Certain verbal phrases and formulae also clearly have a long history, and it has been argued that many of these go back to Mycenaean times or even beyond: this would imply a long and continuous tradition of poetry on heroic themes.[7]

Later ancient criticism assumed that the Greek epics preserved historical tradition, but it was always recognized that the poet had enhanced or embroidered what he inherited: Herodotus remarked that Homer in the story of the abduction of Helen had selected from various versions one which seemed more appropriate to epic storytelling (2.116.1, referring to the *Cypria*), and Thucydides commented that it was natural for a poet to exaggerate the importance of the events he described (1.10). Much has been made of the distinctions between different types of story, such as 'saga', which is conceived as more realistic, though concerned with heroic combat, and 'folk tale', an elusive term often applied to more fantastic or magical narratives; definitions are difficult, and the relation of both terms to 'myth' is unclear.[8] In general it would seem that both Homeric poems include folk-tale or magical elements, but the *Iliad*, with its military theme and firm geographical setting, is more like saga, while the *Odyssey*, especially in its first half, is closer to folk tale.[9] But any strong contrast of this kind swiftly breaks down on closer analysis: the *Iliad* includes a cap of invisibility, a talking horse, a warrior who fights with a river god, and a body magically preserved against decay; the *Odyssey*, in its own way, shows us more of social and domestic 'realities' than the more sombre and dignified *Iliad* will admit. Moreover, the presence of the Olympian gods in both poems, but more prominently in the *Iliad*, makes Homer a peculiarly special case: these colourful and potent figures, intervening freely in mortal affairs for good or ill, seem to belong to neither saga nor folk tale, but transcend such categories.

---

[7] On the cultural amalgam, see Kirk 1962: 179–92; on inherited diction, M. L. West 1988 (earlier Page 1959, ch. 6). On religion, see M. P. Nilsson 1932; Burkert 1985, ch. 1 (but p. 46 offers a warning: 'Startling correspondences with the later Greek [religious] evidence stand side by side with things totally unintelligible. Greek religion is rooted in the Minoan–Mycenaean age and yet not to be equated with it.')

[8] R. Carpenter 1946; Kirk 1970, 1974; Bremmer 1994: 55–7; Hansen 1997, 2002, esp. introduction (10–12 on problems of definition).

[9] Woodhouse 1930; Calhoun 1939; Page 1973a; Hölscher 1989. Csapo 2005 is a sophisticated account of definitions and theories of 'myth', including discussion of folk-tale theory as expounded by Vladimir Propp and adapted by many classical scholars (e.g. Burkert 1979): see e.g. Csapo 2005: 57–67 on the Cyclops in the *Odyssey* and parallel versions.

Comparative studies have shown that, even when narrative poetry of a heroic type deals with events closer in time than the Trojan War, and better documented, startling distortions may be introduced.[10] The Song of Roland recounts an episode in the campaigns of Charlemagne, and a Latin chronicler records the death of 'Hruodlandus' (i.e. Roland) in battle in 778; but the battle in question, an attack by Basques, was of no historical importance. In the heroic style, the poet turns it into a huge conflict between Christian and Infidel, and Roland is slain by a mighty Saracen; the whole poem embodies the spirit of the twelfth-century Crusades.[11] Similar transformations and intermingling of history and imagination can be found in other traditions: the *Nibelungenlied*, for example, or the Serbian epics.[12] The Norse Saga of the Volsungs moves from pure myth – the tale of Sigurd the Dragon-slayer, rich in magic and close to the world of the Norse gods – into a more historical era, with Atli (Attila the Hun) in conflict with the Burgundian Gunnar (Gundaharius); the legends here have connections with those in the *Nibelungenlied*. But even here the saga is demonstrably remote from history, and combines characters who could never have met. Obviously, the fact that modern historians can identify errors does not prove that historical accuracy is impossible in heroic epic. It has been suggested that the broader background may often be more accurate (though less precisely described) than the central incidents;[13] but the probable limitations of this kind of evidence need to be recognized. It may be that the Homeric epics tell us more about the attitudes and outlook of the Ionians of the eighth or seventh century BC than about the actions of the Mycenaeans of the twelfth.

The bards of Homer's age and earlier were concerned to preserve the *klea andrōn*, the 'glorious deeds of men'; it would seem that they believed these men to have existed in time long past, but recognized that they could not guarantee every detail of their accounts. Homer invokes the Muses in terms which admit his dependence on tradition and inspiration: 'you are goddesses, you are present, you know all; we only hear the glorious tale, and have no knowledge' (*Il.* 2.485–6). We may doubt whether Homer had authority in earlier poetry for

---

[10] Vansina 1965, 1985; Henige 1974. For outstanding applications to archaic and classical Greece, see Thomas 1989, esp. chs. 1–2; also O. Murray 2001.

[11] Bowra 1957: 520, 530–7; cf. Finley et al. 1964; Hainsworth 1984, 1993: 32–53. See also Taplin 1992: 26 n. 24.

[12] Finley et al. 1964; cf. Finley 1973, ch. 1, 'Myth, Memory and History'.

[13] Hainsworth 1984, esp. 117, 121.

every warrior whom he names in the *Iliad*; names came into his mind, and seemed to fit – a sign that the Muses were at his side, smiling upon his work. The borderline between adaptation of tradition and creative development, here as elsewhere, is impossible for us to draw, and may have been as hard for the original poet. The poet, then, is not primarily a chronicler. Nor does he attempt to connect the tale he tells with the present day, whether by offering certain characters as exemplary figures for his own age, or more explicitly by tracing the genealogy of royal families or particular patrons back to the heroes of old – a practice easily paralleled in other poetic traditions, and most influentially followed by Virgil in the *Aeneid*. Genealogy is important in the *Iliad* (less so in the more individualist *Odyssey*, where the hero is not competing among equals), but principally in self-assertive speeches, in which the heroes can declare themselves and define their status. There is little sign that Homer's audiences found special satisfaction in the exploits of their supposed ancestors. The most plausible case is the reference to the future destiny of Aeneas' descendants (picked up and developed by Roman readers), which has been read as addressed to self-styled Aeneadae in the Troad.[14] But this example is most notable for its isolation. For Homer and his predecessors, the glorious past mattered more than reflected glory in the present.[15]

2. Poems behind poems

A major issue is whether the Homeric epics are representative or exceptional. The question can also be posed in chronological terms: do they represent the mature and typical form of the epic tradition, or a glorious final flowering? It is at any rate clear that the *Iliad* and the *Odyssey* presuppose, and were preceded by, other poems on a wide range of epic themes.[16] This is evident from references within the poems themselves. We may distinguish references to other episodes in the Trojan War and its aftermath – the abduction of Helen, the wound of Philoctetes, the gathering at Aulis, the first embassy to the Trojans, the death of

---

[14] *Il.* 20.306–8; cf. *h Aphrod.* 196–7; P. M. Smith 1981 (against historical reference) and Faulkner 2008: 3–7 (in favour). Other possible cases are much less plainly marked: see e.g. Janko 1992: 19, 382, etc., arguing for disguised compliments to families claiming heroic descent; M. L. West 1997a: 628–9. On later, similar claims, see Thomas 1989: 100–8, 173–95.

[15] For early genealogies and lists see Jeffery 1961: 59–61; Hornblower 1994: 9–12.

[16] For a survey of these, see now M. L. West 2011c: 28–37.

Achilles, the suicide of Ajax, and so forth – from allusions to other heroic tales which are less closely related to the Trojan War: amongst these are the story of Bellerophon, the wrath of Meleager, the war of the Seven against Thebes, the birth of Heracles and his many labours in service to Eurystheus, and the Argonautic expedition.[17] Within the Trojan saga, it is assumed that the audience knows what the situation is, why the armies are at war (see esp. *Il.* 1.159), and who the characters are: thus Achilles storms away in anger 'with Menoitios' son and his comrades' (1.307), that is, with Patroclus, who is mentioned shortly afterwards without the identification being made explicit.[18]

In a different category come stories about the gods. Again, it is obvious that the Olympians are familiar to the poet's audience, and that this familiarity derives not only from cult worship and visual representations but from previous song. The poems present the divine order as well established, with a clear hierarchy of power and division of provinces (1.533–5, 581; 15.185–217); we see not only from Hesiod's *Theogony* but also from a number of brief allusions in the poems that this was not an eternally fixed condition. There had been wars among the gods in earlier times: the overthrow of Cronos and the destruction of rival powers such as the Titans and Typhon are mentioned, but only in passing: the emphasis is on the security of Zeus's reign. The permanence of the gods in the *Iliad* ('happy and existing forever', 24.99) provides the essential foil to the short-lived and suffering mortals. Elsewhere, in the references to Zeus's adulteries and the complaints of Calypso, we catch hints of a freer intermingling of gods and mortals, with regular amatory encounters involving even the king of the gods (cf. Hes. *Theog.* 535; *Cat.* fr. 1.6–7). Again the Homeric epics are selective: of the leading figures only Achilles is the son of a divinity, and that privilege brings him little advantage: son of a goddess and a mortal, he stands between the two worlds, not wholly belonging to either.

Homer not only cited or alluded to other poems and stories but adapted them to play a part in his own work: for instance, a tale such as the death of Agamemnon, repeatedly cited but never retold at length in the *Odyssey*, is not evoked merely for the sake of digression, or even to advertise the range of the poet's repertoire; it is there to provide a

---

[17] *Il.* 6.155–202; 9.527–99; 4.370–400; 19.95–133 (cf. 14.249–61, etc.); *Od.* 12.69–72 (not an exhaustive list).

[18] But for a different approach to such references, see Scodel 2002: 90–123.

contrast with the central story of Odysseus.[19] Other passages, such as the references in the *Iliad* to Heracles' experiences, can also be ingeniously brought into relation to the larger themes of the poem. Occasionally we may surmise that unusual or obscure versions are the inventions of the poet, to suit the argument of a particular speaker (e.g. *Il.* 1.396–406).[20] Moreover, we can see that the epics make use of a number of themes which might be used elsewhere with other heroes: heroic wrath, the wanderer's return, the descent to the underworld, the forging of divine armour, are all paralleled elsewhere in the Greek tradition, though in some cases the other texts may be echoing Homer. One case in which the borrower seems clearly to be Homer concerns the wanderings of Odysseus, and particularly the perils of the Clashing Rocks. In *Od.* 12.69–70, Circe warns the hero that only one ship has ever passed through these Rocks safely, 'the Argo, known to all men, sailing back from Aeëtes' (70) – known, presumably, through poetry. There is good reason to think that other characters and events in these books of the *Odyssey* have also been taken over from the Argonautic saga: Circe herself, sister of Aeëtes and Medea's aunt, seems to belong to that world.[21] None of this deprives Homer of originality; rather, it shows him as an active participant in a tradition which thrives on competition and constant reworking of well-established themes.

The complexity of Homer's relation to his 'sources' may be illustrated in more detail from the story of Meleager, as told by Phoenix to Achilles in Book 9 of the *Iliad*.[22] Phoenix comments that, until now, no-one could have found fault with Achilles' anger at Agamemnon, but if he still holds out in his refusal to accept the compensation, he may suffer the fate of Meleager, who persisted too long in a similar resentful resignation from war, and lost all chance of gifts in the end. The narrative of Meleager includes a number of parallels with the sequence of events in the *Iliad* itself: in particular, the name of the hero's wife, who eventually persuades him to abandon his wrath, is given as Kleopatra (though reference is also made to another name), apparently an anticipation of the parallel role of Patroclus, who will succeed in persuading Achilles to relent.[23] The motif

[19] *Od.* 1.29–43, 298–300; 3.193–8, 248–312; 4. 512–37; 11.387–434; 24.20–2, 95–7, 198–201; Garvie 1986: ix–xii.

[20] Willcock 1964, 1977; Braswell 1971. This position is opposed by Lang 1983; also by Slatkin 1991, ch. 2, discussing the specific case in Book 1.

[21] See Meuli 1921: 87–115; Page 1955: 2; Braswell 1988: 6–8; M. L. West 2005.

[22] For bibliography on this speech, see Reichel 1994: 111 n. 1; Alden 2000: ch. 7.

[23] J. T. Kakridis 1949: 11–42; March 1987: 27–46.

of Meleager's anger, which is not found in other versions of the tale, appears to be Homer's invention, in order to bring the story into line with the main plot of the epic. A further point is that, in later versions, Meleager dies on the battlefield as a result of his mother's magical revenge for the slaying of her brothers: it is disputed whether Homer suppresses this finale (which would be ill-suited to Phoenix's persuasive task), or whether the version is a later addition to the story.[24] It is, in any case, clear that Phoenix's narrative performs several functions. Like other 'paradigms', it offers an argument to show why the listener, here Achilles, should follow the speaker's advice. But Phoenix's perspective is limited, in two respects. First, he assumes that the worst thing that can happen is for Achilles to lose the chance of the gifts now being offered. In fact, in Book 19, Achilles will receive the gifts anyway, despite his persistence in anger; but they will be meaningless to him because of the far greater anger and grief aroused by the death of Patroclus. Second, in the more theological passage which precedes the Meleager tale, Phoenix advises Achilles to respect the spirits of Prayer, the Litai, or he may suffer the consequences (9.502–14). This simple moralizing has sometimes been taken as endorsed by the poet,[25] but that reading seems to give undue importance to the words of a minor character; nor does Phoenix's ideal picture of divine justice receive much confirmation elsewhere in the poem. If Achilles is 'punished' for excess, it is in a more subtle and less overtly moralizing way. Finally, if the poet is indeed aware of some version in which Meleager's wrath ends in death, it is natural that Phoenix should suppress so grim a conclusion, but it is possible that the audience, alert to the omission, may anticipate the analogous fate of Achilles and relish the irony of the characters' efforts to evade the consequences of this parallel.[26]

3. Poetic language

The traditional nature of Homeric poetry is also clear on the level of language.[27] The poems are composed in a version of Greek which

---

[24] Bacchyl. 5.94–154; Aesch. *Cho.* 594–601; Ov. *Met.* 8. 260–546; Apollod. 1.8.2. Bremmer 1988 argues that this version is post-Homeric.

[25] Bowra 1930: 19–23; similarly Hainsworth 1993: 56–7.

[26] See further Schadewaldt 1938: 139–42; Rosner 1976; Bannert 1981; Swain 1988; Griffin 1995; and Alden 2000, ch. 7.

[27] The standard work is Chantraine 1948–53; see also Monro 1891. More accessible are Palmer 1962, 1980: 83–101; Janko 1992: 8–19; Horrocks 1997; Colvin 2007: 49–53, 192–201; Willi 2011.

was never spoken by a single people or in a single place: it is an amalgam of several dialects. Of these the predominant is Ionic, spoken by
the Greeks of Asia Minor (Turkey), on some of the Aegean islands,
such as Chios, and elsewhere. Second place goes to Aeolic, the form
of Greek spoken by the people of northern Greece (Boeotia,
Thessaly) and on Lesbos. Of lesser importance are the elements of diction perhaps originating in southern Greece in Mycenaean times and
labelled Arcado-Cypriot (because this dialect survived in Arcadia and
Cyprus in historical times).

How, when, and where this amalgam evolved is obscure to us. Its
advantages to the poets are somewhat clearer. Ionic and Aeolic offer
alternative words and morphological forms which coexist in the
Homeric text, and these are usually of differing metrical shape. Thus
we find five metrically differing forms of the verb 'to be' (εἶναι, ἔμεν,
ἔμμεν, ἔμεναι, ἔμμεναι). The poet can employ these different forms
to suit the needs of the metre. The common word for 'ship', ναῦς,
has dative plural ναυσί in Attic, but the epic also uses νηυσί (Ionic),
ναῦφι (an archaic form scarcely found after Homer), and even
νήεσσι, an artificial combination involving Ionic stem and Aeolic ter-
mination. The poems are also inconsistent in using forms which derive
from different periods: for instance, the old genitive in –οιο is found
alongside the later and more familiar –ου. A key discovery in terms of
the 'layering' of Homeric language was Richard Bentley's identification
(1732) of the effects of the consonant 'w', represented in some inscriptions by the letter ϝ, digamma. Digammas do not occur in our manuscripts, because the sound was lost in Ionic at an early date (though it
survived as a numeral). But many Homeric verses will only scan if a
digamma is assumed at the start of a word that in the established
Homeric text begins with a vowel (e.g. ἄναξ, οἶκος). Hence lines or formulae that need a digamma are likely to be older than those which are
composed without respecting its presence. Bentley's detection of this
principle, derided by his contemporaries, is now seen as one of the
most brilliant insights in modern philology.

Metrical needs also explain variation between contracted and uncon-
tracted forms of verbs, addition or omission of augment, and similar
licences. Words can be modified or used where they are linguistically
wrong but poetically convenient (e.g. εὐρύοπα, properly an accusative,
is sometimes treated as nominative or vocative). But metre, however
important, does not explain everything. Sometimes strange words and
exotic forms seem to be used because they have poetic distinction. At

least some of these will be archaisms, and their meaning was unclear to later Greeks, perhaps even to the Homeric poets themselves; misunderstandings sometimes generated fresh usage.[28] The dual form Αἴαντε, 'the two Ajaxes', seems originally to have meant the brothers Ajax and Teucer, but in some passages is reinterpreted to apply to the greater and the lesser Ajax. Cult titles could become fossils (did Argeiphontes really mean 'slayer of Argos', or is this the guesswork of poets and scholars?). In Aristophanes' time the meaning of the expression ἀμενηνὰ κάρηνα was disputed in the schoolroom (*Banqueters* fr. 233 K-A), and Aristotle refers to the so-called 'glosses', words which could not be understood (διάκτορος, μέροψ, ἐριούνιος are examples) (*Poet.* 1459a9–10).

In short, Homer's language was not the Greek spoken by any of his audience. Nor was it unique to Homer, or even to a single region of the Greek world. The linguistic usage of Hesiod and other early hexameter poets closely resembles that of the Homeric poems. Generations of bards had collectively developed a special poetic language which could be modified for different subject matter but which was characterized by archaism and artificiality. Innovations undoubtedly occurred, but they are hard to plot when so much is uncertain about chronology, absolute or relative.[29] What matters is that the epic style maintained a level of dignity and decorum appropriate to the grandeur of its typical subject matter.

4. Light from the East?

The origins of Greek epic may lie further back, and further east, than dark-age Ionia. Near Eastern texts, not least the famous 'Epic of Gilgamesh', yield remarkable parallels or precedents for Homeric conceptions, episodes, and even phraseology.[30] The cosmogony implied in the account of Oceanus and Tethys (*Il.* 14.201, 302) recalls the Babylonian Enuma Elis, the epic of creation.[31] The conception of the

---

[28] Leumann 1950 discusses possible cases. For examples, see Palmer 1962: 104–5: e.g. κύμβαχος, 'helmet' or 'crown', correctly so used at *Il.* 15.536, misused at 5.586 (cf. M. L. West 2011c: 164).

[29] Finkelberg 2012; Wachter 2012.

[30] George 2003 is an important new edition of the Gilgamesh epic; more accessible is his annotated Penguin translation (1999). For discussion, see Burkert 1988 and other important papers collected in Burkert 2001; also M. L. West 1988, 1997a; Burkert 1992, 2004.

[31] Foster 2005: 436–86; see also López-Ruiz 2010.

gods as gathered in assembly is frequent in Akkadian and Hittite. The idea of the fatal letter found in the Bellerophon story is first attested in the story of David and Uriah (*Il.* 6.168–70, 2 Samuel 11); the Old Testament also offers a parallel to the failed seduction and revenge of Sthenoboiia (*Il.* 6.160–66; cf. Potiphar's wife, Genesis 39).[32] Even the supremely Homeric statement of the opposition between god and man has precedent in the heroic realism of Gilgamesh:

The gods, with Shamash [the sun god], they sit forever; as for mankind, numbered are their days. But you here, you fear death? ... I will go ahead of you... If I myself were to fall, let me still set up my name.[33]

Above all, Gilgamesh loses his beloved comrade Enkidu, and grieves for him with Achillean devotion, raging 'like a lioness deprived of her whelps'; elsewhere he journeys to the Underworld, like Heracles and Odysseus in Greek mythology: Gilgamesh, like the Greek heroes, is forced to recognize the limits of mortality.[34] It has long been recognized that prominent features of Hesiod's theology (especially the myth of succession among the gods, and the sequence of the ages of men) are indebted to eastern myth;[35] similarly, the Homeric poems need to be set against a wider background, and recent scholarship has charted some of the channels of communication – migrant craftsmen, diviners, healers, and not least wandering bards.[36]

Yet, for all the gratitude we may feel for this interdisciplinary research, questions and doubts still persist. Though the links with Gilgamesh are generally accepted, many other similarities between the poetry and mythology of the Near East and those of archaic Greece may strike the reader as inconclusive – parallels rather than sources. If warriors in different cultures are compared with wolves or birds of prey, if a king is described as 'like a father to his people', why should we seek a direct connection? Many such resemblances could easily arise independently. Are we dealing with diffusion or

---

[32] Louden 2011 is a detailed study of parallels between the *Odyssey* and the Old Testament, especially Genesis.

[33] Dalley 1989: 144; George 1999: 110; Burkert 1992: 117–18. Cf. *Il.* 12.322–8, Sarpedon's speech (quoted below, pp. 58–9).

[34] Dalley 1989: 93; George 1999: 65 (cf. *Il.* 18.317); Currie 2012: 551. For his journey in search of immortality, see George 1999: 70–99.

[35] M. L. West 1966: 18–31, 1988; see also Walcot 1966; Kirk 1970: 118–31.

[36] M. L. West 1988; Burkert 1992; Penglase 1994. On modes of transmission, see West 1997a: ch. 12 (to my mind the best chapter of the book); Lane Fox 2008: 376–80 tells a very different story.

polygenetic development? More fundamental is the question of the effect of those ideas and details which have been imported. How are they adapted and used in their new context? Do motifs or concepts derived from the Near East delight the audience as exotic novelties, or is the effect one of mystery and awe? Some of the chief advocates of this approach have been content to accumulate material, but the critic needs to look harder at the nature of the resulting compound.[37] Again, what actually happens when the mythic structures and motifs of the Near East are combined with those from the Indo-European tradition? Martin West has produced two extraordinarily rich books on these two streams of influence,[38] but the naïve reader asks how we are to understand the relationship between them, and whether Homer and his fellow poets simply drew on one or other stream unconsciously or according to taste.

One episode in which the connections seem particularly clear and persuasive is the Deception of Zeus (though even here sceptical voices are audible).[39] A cluster of suggestive motifs have been found – the references to the division of the universe among the gods and to the love-making of Oceanus and Tethys, and the magical *kestos* (an ornate and seductive feminine garment) which Aphrodite lends to Hera. If the scene involving Hera and Zeus does indeed owe something to the scene in which Ishtar (the Semitic goddess who corresponds to Aphrodite) attempts to seduce Gilgamesh, then the Homeric version has transformed an episode of antagonism and violent rejection into something more delicate and light-hearted: Gilgamesh's jeering list of Ishtar's former lovers becomes Zeus's fond reminiscences of his own amorous career.[40] The direct connections can be questioned, but the comparison is still a revealing one for the understanding of Homer's divine comedy.

Other questions of influence and development arise with the stories that, like the Cyclops tale, are found frequently in other cultures but only in texts of a later date than Homer: do they all depend ultimately on the story as told in the *Odyssey*, do they emerge independently, or are

---

[37] A point forcibly made by Osborne 1993, reviewing Burkert 1992. See also Dowden 2001, reviewing M. L. West 1997a. Lane Fox 2008 engages polemically with the question of Near Eastern influence, urging the case that Greeks devised many of their myths themselves, partly to account for places and natural features that they encountered in travelling.

[38] M. L. West 1997a, 2007a.

[39] Burkert 1992: 96–8; M. L. West 1997a: 182–4; accepted even by Lane Fox 2008: 353–4. Kelly 2008a denies their conclusions.

[40] *Il.* 14.315–28; Dalley 1989: 77–80; George 1999: 47–50. On this, Kelly 2008a: 289–90 is not entirely persuasive.

Homer and some or all of the later versions dependent on a common source?[41] It is most unlikely that Homer invented the Cyclopes, who are mentioned elsewhere in the *Odyssey* in more incidental contexts; moreover, he fails to make explicit the chief feature of these monsters, and one which is crucial to the plot: that a Cyclops has only one eye (Hes. *Theog.* 143).[42] There are other ways in which the story seems to have been modified or adjusted to increase tension or to suit the ethos of the *Odyssey*. Here and elsewhere, the comparison with other versions, whether older or younger than Homer, serves to bring out the particular qualities and thematic concerns of the Homeric epics.[43] Whether the perennial fascination of these themes depends on their intrinsic merits as material for exciting stories or on some deeper psychological or anthropological roots is a question which goes beyond the province of the literary critic.[44]

5. Early Greek hexameter poetry

However, the *Iliad* and the *Odyssey* did not exist in a vacuum. There were other important poets composing in the epic hexameter around the time of the great epics, and it is time to consider how far we can put the Homeric poems in a specifically Greek context.

To do so means giving more attention to several works which have already been mentioned in passing: Hesiod, the Homeric Hymns, and the Epic Cycle. Traditionally these were all seen as chronologically and generically later than the Homeric poems, but this view, while it may be broadly correct, has been challenged and in any case needs refining. We must distinguish between Hesiod's authentic surviving poems (the *Theogony* and the *Works and Days*) and the many other poems attributed to him in antiquity. Of the so-called Homeric Hymns, none can be ascribed to the same poet as the *Iliad* and the *Odyssey*, and many of the shorter items in the collection are much later. As for the Epic Cycle, none of the poems survive and they are doubtless of very varied dates. Finally, just as the Homeric epics spring

---

[41] Page 1955: ch. 1, 1973a; Fehling 1977: 87–100; Burkert 1979: 156 n. 13.

[42] Page 1955: 14.

[43] See Page 1973a; Griffin 1977; Hansen 1997. See more generally Stanford 1963, on the evolution of the character Odysseus over the centuries.

[44] Burkert 1979: 30–4.

from a tradition, so we must acknowledge that these other works probably had their predecessors, some of which may have predated the *Iliad*. The world of early hexameter poetry was not restricted to heroic epic: there was evidently also a tradition of theogonic poetry, of wisdom poetry, of hymnic narratives, of catalogue poetry. The example of Hesiod shows that one poet could compose in different hexameter genres. The best approach will be to discuss each of the above categories in turn, relating them to Homer.

Authentic Hesiod

Homer is traditionally paired with the Boeotian Hesiod, the first Greek writer to refer to himself by name (*Theog.* 22). Which poet was chronologically earlier was already debated in antiquity, but it is conventional, on no very strong grounds, to put Hesiod later.[45] Partly this is simply because we feel we know him better: in both the *Theogony* and the *Works and Days* Hesiod has things to say about himself, his poetic calling, and his opinions on morality and religion; he does not maintain the epic anonymity and detachment. Hesiod is clearly aware of the epic tales of Thebes and Troy, and has many phrases and formulae in common with Homer, but this only means that heroic narrative and didactic or catalogue poetry are not mutually exclusive genres.[46] Some passages in Homer closely parallel the catalogue-style of Hesiod (especially the list of Nereids in *Iliad* 18 and Odysseus' account of the dead heroines in *Odyssey* 11); at one time these were regarded as interpolations, but they can as easily be seen as a form of homage to an adjacent genre.[47]

Whether or not there is direct interchange between Hesiod and the Homeric poems, the comparison of their works is enlightening in many ways. Both have a sense of the history of the cosmos, in which the present state of Zeus's reign did not prevail from the beginning: Homer alludes to conflicts among the gods and the imprisonment of Cronos and the Titans, whereas Hesiod presents a detailed narrative

---

[45] This view has been repeatedly challenged by M. L. West, e.g. 1966: 40–8; 2011b: 194–5, 212–26; and now 2012: 226, with list in n. 3 of passages in which he thinks Homer imitates Hesiod (some of these are very unpersuasive, though I agree that the light-hearted theomachy of the *Iliad* presupposes an earlier and more serious treatment – not necessarily by Hesiod).

[46] M. L. West 1973a: 191–2; G. P. Edwards 1971, ch. 8. More generally on Hesiod in comparison with Homer see Wade-Gery 1959; O. Murray 1980, chs. 3–4; Millett 1984; Rosen 1997; Clay 2003; for many aspects, see Montanari et al. 2009.

[47] So e.g. Danek 1998: 231.

of the wars which end with the supremacy of Zeus. The *Works and Days* also contributes to an understanding of mythical chronology (the Myth of Ages); on another front, the stern moralism and stress on Dike (Justice) and hard work has some affinity with aspects of the *Odyssey*, notably the peasant wisdom of Eumaeus.

The Hymns[48]

The collection of so-called 'Homeric' hymns includes considerable variety. Some are very short, some are clearly very much later than the archaic age. The most important are also the longest and probably the earliest – hymns to Demeter (2), Aphrodite (5), Apollo (3; widely believed to be a combination of two hymns), and Hermes (4).[49] Of these the first two are influenced by the Homeric epics or closely related poems; all four are composed in a comparable epic style. The chief difference between these and Homeric epic is that the gods, not mankind, are at the centre of the stage (as the hymnic form makes natural): their birth, youth, powers, and characteristic activities are recounted and celebrated. In the hymns, the realities of cult action and worship in specific shrines are much more prominent: Eleusis for Demeter, Delphi and Delos for Apollo. Aetiology of cultic ritual practice is prominent, and, in general, interaction between gods and mortals is important in all but one of the poems. The hymn to Aphrodite describes the liaison between the goddess and Anchises, from which sprang the line of Aeneas; the hymn to Demeter shows the goddess journeying in disguise among humankind and provides the aetiology (tale of origin) explaining how the Eleusinian mysteries were established; the hymn to Apollo similarly explains the aetiology of the major shrines at which the god was worshipped in historical times. The exception is the hymn to Hermes, which is concerned with the apportionment of privileges between Apollo and Hermes; it is much more light-hearted than the others.[50]

---

[48] M. L. West has provided an admirable Loeb edition (M. L. West 2003b). For commentaries on the whole collection, see Allen, Halliday, and Sikes 1936 and Càssola 1975.

[49] The fragmentary hymn to Dionysus (1) may be among the earliest, though, because so much is lost, much is uncertain. Like the hymn to Hermes, it presents the resolution of conflicts among the gods (in this case Dionysus and Hera). Recent papyrus publications mean that older editions of this hymn are out of date: see M. L. West 2001a, 2011a.

[50] On the hymn to Demeter, see N. J. Richardson 1974 and H. Foley 1994; on the hymn to Aphrodite, Faulkner 2008; on the hymn to Hermes, a commentary is in preparation by Oliver

The Cycle and pre-Cyclic material

The Epic Cycle is the collective name which designates the known epic poems recounting heroic myth from early Greece. Apart from the *Iliad* and the *Odyssey* they survive only in fragments.[51] They were not originally composed to form part of a sequence, but were apparently arranged in sequence (probably with some editorial modifications) at a much later date, perhaps in Hellenistic times. The known titles may be grouped in three categories: poems about Thebes and the Theban wars, poems about the Trojan War, and poems about heroes such as Heracles and Theseus (a relative latecomer to mythology). The evidence is most abundant for the second category, because Hellenistic and later scholars often referred to these poems in commenting on the *Iliad* and the *Odyssey*, and because an important outline of their content by a scholar called Proclus has been preserved in summary form (it was included as part of the introductory material in our earliest complete manuscript of the *Iliad*, Venetus A, in the tenth century); no such summary survives for the other poems.[52] The summary tells us the number of books into which these poems were later divided; this gives us at least a very rough impression of their scale.[53] In the list below, book numbers or total line numbers, where known, are given in brackets.

Theban poems:
Oedipodeia (allegedly 6,600 lines), Thebaid (7,000 lines), Epigoni ('The sons who came after'; 7,000 lines), Alcmaeonis.
Poems about the Trojan War:
Cypria (11 books), Aethiopis (5 books), The Little *Iliad* (4 books), The Sack of Ilion (2 books), The Nostoi ('Homecomings'; 5 books), Telegony (2 books).
Poems about other heroes:
The Capture of Oechalia, Heracleia (possibly two poems), Theseis.

Thomas. N. J. Richardson 2010 is briefer (covering the hymns to Apollo, Hermes, Aphrodite). More discursive treatments: Janko 1982 (very technical); Thalmann 1984; Clay 1989, 1997; and Parker 1991. A new collection of essays is Faulkner 2011 (note esp. the editor's review of scholarship, 1–25). See also N. J. Richardson 2007 on *Hermes*.

[51] Editions include Bernabé 1987; Davies 1988; and especially M. L. West 2003a (Loeb). See Griffin 1977; Davies 1989; Burgess 2001; Dowden 2004; M. L. West 2013.

[52] Apart from West's Loeb, the summary is translated in Burgess 2001: 177–80, and paraphrased in Dowden 2004: 198–200.

[53] But note that Burgess 2001: ch. 1 argues in detail that the poems as read by Proclus (in the fifth century AD?) may have been significantly shorter than the originals. Proof is lacking, but a case for caution has been well made.

Aristotle drew a clear distinction between the quality of the two epics which we now ascribe to Homer and that of the rest; thereafter the term 'cyclic' was attached to the other poems and acquired a pejorative sense, almost equivalent to 'second rate'.[54] Traditionally, scholars have considered these poems to be later than Homer, at least partly dependent on his work, and less ambitious in scope and inferior in quality. It was also believed that the Trojan poems were created to fill in the gaps and supplement the *Iliad* and the *Odyssey*. More recent work has shown that these conclusions are far from certain. Although it is probably right that these epics were mostly later than the Homeric epics, it is clear that they draw on earlier myth and poetry which was also available to Homer.

The Cyclic material gives us precious insight into the broader mythological and poetic tradition. We can recognize motifs and episodes which are comparable or parallel with Homeric examples; but the Cyclic poets also included many events, characters, and motifs which the poets of the *Iliad* and the *Odyssey* played down or excluded (though they may well have known about them): for instance, cannibalism, pollution, curses, human sacrifice (Iphigenia, Polyxena), or various types of magical devices and exotic creatures. It is clear that the poems of the Cycle strongly influenced visual artists in various media, lyric poets such as Pindar, and the fifth-century tragedians; they drew on them as readily as on the two great epics. Indeed, most of these poems were ascribed indiscriminately to 'Homer' until the fifth century, when Herodotus expressed doubts about their authorship (2.116–17; 4.32). We would be unwise to make assertions about the merits of lost poems; what matters is that they existed, and that they were part of the tradition of tales about the heroic age.

Pseudo-Hesiod

Just as poems of heroic mythology tended to be ascribed to Homer, hexameter works on mythical genealogy were often attributed to Hesiod. These are now lost, but substantial papyrus finds have given us a much clearer picture of some of them. Of these the most important (and clearly the most popular) is the *Catalogue of Women*, also known as the *Ehoiai* (from the recurrent phrase ἢ οἵη, 'or such as she...', which

---

[54] Callim. *Epigr.* 28 Pfeiffer; Hor. *Ars P.* 132, 136; Pfeiffer 1968: 227–30.

introduced new sections).[55] This poem, in five books, was constructed to serve as a continuation of the *Theogony*. The latter ends with a catalogue of liaisons between gods and mortals, listing their offspring; the *Ehoiai* recounted a long series of heroic mortal marriages and the resulting off-spring. The work had an elaborate structure mapping out the different lines of descent and ethnic groupings in the Greek world, though it clearly did not bring the story down to the poet's own time. Rather, it described the heroic age, which was said to come to an end with the Trojan War (the marriage of Helen and a catalogue of her suitors formed a prominent part of the last book). The *Catalogue* is usually considered the work of an imitator, composing much later than Hesiod (West puts it in the late sixth century), although Janko has argued on linguistic grounds that it may indeed be Hesiod's own work.[56] Even if late, it obviously makes use of older material and may indeed have evolved gradually. Other pseudo-Hesiodic works circulated, some of them very substantial (the so-called *Megalai Ehoiai* must have been a work longer than the Catalogue), but we know much less about them and most of them are not very relevant to Homer.

The *Shield of Heracles* is in a different category, both as a narrative poem and because it survives complete.[57] It begins with the transitional formula 'or such as she...' (introducing an account of Alcmena), and so at least affects to be a portion or offshoot of the *Catalogue*; but the main part of the poem is a duel between Heracles (with his squire Iolaus) and Cycnus, supported by his father Ares. The centrepiece, occu-pying half the poem, is an extended description of Heracles' shield, which is clearly indebted to the Shield of Achilles but goes beyond it in length, as also in macabre and bizarre detail. With its eccentric form and central ecphrasis, the poem prefigures such later 'epyllia' as Catullus 64.

6. Dating the poems

In discussion of all these texts, chronology presents severe problems. Modern readers do not always realize just how fragile and approximate

---

[55] West 1985; R. L. Fowler 1998; Hunter 2005; Hirschberger 2004 (reviewed in West 2007b); Janko 2012; I. C. Rutherford 2012.

[56] Janko 1982: 221–5, 1992: 14.

[57] The only modern commentary is Russo 1965. The date of the work is unknown: it is gener-ally put *c.*570 or somewhat earlier (see Janko 1986). For a lively essay on the *Shield*, see Martin 2005.

the arguments for dating ancient texts usually are. Ancient testimony seldom helps, partly because of the lack of any universal dating system. In the late fifth century the Athenians recorded the victories at the dramatic festivals year by year in inscriptions, and these lists were used by later scholars and editors; hence we have reliable dates for many of the surviving plays. This is altogether exceptional, and nothing like this existed in earlier centuries. For the most part, modern scholarship has constructed a chronology based either on internal evidence – for instance, references to events, practices, or institutions which can be given an approximate date – or on the assumption that one work is definitely later than another (so that even if an absolute chronology cannot be established, some clarity is achieved in relative chronology).

Neither of these approaches is free of difficulties. Hesiod is traditionally dated by his participation (mentioned in *Works and Days* 650–9) in the funeral games for Amphidamas, a warrior of Chalcis in Euboea, which most interpreters associate with the Lelantine War of the late eighth or early seventh century, but we know so little about this war that some scholars have even questioned whether it really took place.[58] It is essentially this datum that leads to Hesiod being given a date in most reference works around 700, and Homer is placed *c.*750–700 because he is generally thought of as being earlier than Hesiod. Our total ignorance of Homer's identity and origins may seem to justify an earlier date, although this largely arises from the anonymity of epic narrative style: how much would we know of Hesiod if he did not talk about himself? Current scholarship divides between those who hold to a date in the eighth century for the *Iliad* (whether *c.*750 or elsewhere) and those who see no obstacle to downdating that poem to the first quarter of the seventh century or even later.

Archaeological evidence is also invoked, though this is treacherous ground.[59] Agamemnon wields a Gorgon-shield, and the figure of the Gorgon is not found in Greek art before 700, and not used on shields until *c.*680; therefore, it is argued, the *Iliad* must be later than 680. Clearly this is an argument from silence; if another, earlier Gorgon-shield were to be found, its value would be nullified. Some of the other arguments for dating sections of the poem are

---

[58] Hes. *Op.* 650–9; M. L. West 1995: 218–19 with Janko 1982: 94–8 and Janko 2012: 37. For doubts about the war, see e.g. J. Hall 2007: 1–8, 20–1.

[59] Crielaard 1995.

unsound[60] or more speculative, but we should attach some weight to the judgement of archaeologists that Achilles' reference to the wealth of Delphi would be improbable much before c.700.[61]

An important test case in the argument is the famous cup discovered on Pithecusae (Ischia), off the west coast of Italy, an early Greek colonial site. This cup is inscribed with verses which use formulae from epic: 'I am the cup of Nestor, good to drink from; whoever drinks from this cup, straight away he will be filled with longing for Aphrodite of the lovely garland.' The cup is currently dated c.740 BC.[62] We naturally think of the scene in *Iliad* 11.632–7, where Nestor's bond-slave prepares a cup of refreshment, and both the drink and the cup are described in some detail. If the inscription does indeed allude to this scene, the prior date of the *Iliad* is settled; but it can of course be argued that Nestor and his cup may have had a place in much earlier poetry, and that the scene in Book 11 draws on those earlier works.

The arguments for relative dating depend on our ability to detect the influence of one poem on another. Older discussions tended to assume that Homer was the earliest surviving Greek poet, and therefore all later resemblances were imitations of passages in Homer. But 'echoes' of Homeric scenes and lines are often illusory, since the imitation may be of epic material in general, and not of what we think of as 'Homer'. Imitation may indeed be the wrong term, since we are often dealing with 'typical' scenes or sequences, part of the repertoire of bards in general. The very idea of 'quotation' or 'allusion' has been judged invalid by those who prefer to speak in terms of 'traditional referentiality' or 'resonance'.[63] On this model the poet does not refer to other poetic texts but to the poetic tradition in general: no poem has privileged status as a source. There are problems with this position, which seems to assume a steady state, a wonderfully huge and coherent body of tradition, while leaving little room for innovation and diversification. Some parallels and correspondences between extant texts do

---

[60] For example, the long-standing debate over the presence of hoplite tactics in the *Iliad*, on which see van Wees 1994 (pro) and Janko 1992 on 13.126–35 (contra). See generally Kirk 1960.

[61] *Il.* 9.404–5, with Morgan 1990: ch. 4. The arguments of Burkert 1976 that the *Iliad* must postdate 715 or even 663, based on the reference to Egyptian Thebes in the same speech, are rejected by Janko 1992: 14 n. 20 and by Kelly 2006.

[62] ML no. 1 = *CEG* 1.454 (date misprinted; see corrections in the editor's second volume), with discussions e.g. in Powell 1991: 163–8; Lane Fox 2008: 157–8.

[63] See pp. 30–1 below.

seem more specific and significant. The *Odyssey* surely does follow and imitate or echo the *Iliad*; the Hymn to Demeter seems influenced by both the *Odyssey* and the Hymn to Aphrodite.[64] Similarities may cluster or cohere in such a way that it is hyper-sceptical to question a direct relationship; but this is a matter of scholarly judgement, and in an area where so little is known for certain, different scholars may legitimately differ in their view of the probabilities.

Richard Janko has scrutinized the language of Homer, Hesiod, and the Homeric Hymns from the standpoint of philology: applying a number of criteria of linguistic change (observance of digamma is one of the more readily understood), he finds confirmation of the 'traditional' sequence of relative dates, with *Iliad* first, then *Odyssey*, then Hesiod's *Theogony* and *Works and Days*, and later still the Hymns.[65] This is reassuringly close to what might be considered likely on other grounds: Hesiod himself in the *Works and Days* refers back to a passage in the *Theogony*, and we shall see that there is good reason to believe the *Odyssey* a later poem than the *Iliad*.

Janko also offered some hypothetical 'absolute' dates, though strictly as illustrative possibilities. That is, if the *Iliad* were dated to 750–725, he believed that his findings would establish, within a margin for error, secure 'absolute' datings for each later work. Unfortunately this argument has been misunderstood as a claim that these dates were indeed established as the definite dates of composition.[66] But even relative datings are valuable, if these statistical arguments are accepted as decisive. Not all have agreed that they are. It is objected that statistics take insufficient account of differences between poets and between different types of passage; that poets of different age or working in different local traditions may have different preferences in the epic linguistic repertoire, regardless of their chronological position.[67] The field divides between those who treat Janko's linguistic arguments with particular respect and those who prefer to give greater weight to other criteria of dating.

---

[64] Details in N. J. Richardson 1974; see also Faulkner 2008: 38–40.

[65] Janko 1982: 195–6, 200, 228–32.

[66] See Janko 2012, esp. 34–5. In the first edition of this Survey I was one of those who thus misrepresented his position. It must be said that the presentation in his 1982 book does not make the hypothetical nature of the argument wholly clear.

[67] E.g. M. L. West 1995, 2012; Janko replies in Janko 2012: 36–8.

7. The debate on the oral epic tradition: Milman Parry and his followers

The Homeric epics, whatever their actual date of composition, were at some stage committed to the written form in which they have come down to us. But did the original poets make use of writing, or are we dealing with a purely oral tradition, oral not only in terms of practice and performance but also in the process of transmission? This has been the predominant theme of Homeric scholarly debate through much of the last century.

The Homeric poems themselves portray heroes singing, and poets performing at feasts: Phemius at the court of Odysseus, Demodocus in the land of the Phaeacians. These bards seem not to need written texts: they perform with instrument in hand, a *kitharis* or a *phorminx*, conventionally translated 'lyre', and are probably imagined as chanting rather than singing throughout. They follow the directions of their aristocratic patrons: Penelope asks Phemius to choose another song, and the disguised Odysseus calls for a laudatory narrative of his own exploits in the sack of Troy. Telemachus mentions the attraction of a new song, and Demodocus is described as singing 'the lay whose renown reached as far as broad heaven at that time' (*Od.* 8.74). Fluency and sound organization are admired, in poetry as in rhetoric (*Od.* 8.489; contrast *Il.* 2.213, 246); still higher praise is given for the vividness of the narrative.[68] Odysseus tells Demodocus that he has given a marvellous account of the sufferings of the Achaeans at Troy, 'as though you yourself had been present, or heard it from another' (*Od.* 8.491). Poetry gives delight and enchants: the audience sit spellbound (*Od.* 1.325–6; 17.518–20). It can also arouse grief and pain, particularly when it calls to mind past suffering (1.337–42, 8.521–31); at the same time, the listener should be strong enough to endure this sadness and reflect on the meaning of that suffering (1.353–5). The scenes involving bards and song can be combined to yield a coherent and subtle conception of poetry and its function.[69] These representations of singers at work, honoured in their society and rewarded with a good cut of meat, may well bear some similarity to the situation of

[68] Minchin 2001 explores the storytelling and structural techniques by which the oral poet gives his song an organized form and compelling power.

[69] Marg 1956; Maehler 1963; Griffin 1980: 100–2; Macleod 1983; Ford 1992; Halliwell 2012: ch. 2.

Homer himself. Ancient readers already made this assumption, suggesting that the blind Demodocus was a mirror image of Homer.[70] Without embracing the biographical approach, modern scholars naturally scrutinize these scenes in the hope of recovering some picture of the poet's original setting. By combining the slender indications of the poems with later Greek texts on music, imaginative scholarship has even offered a reconstruction of the original 'tune' with which the poet accompanied his song.[71]

All of this may be justifiable, but we should remember that Homer's bards are performing in a heroic world, and that the *Odyssey* in particular seems deliberately to elevate the status of the poet (e.g. *Od.* 22.344–9; cf. 17.383–5). These are idealized images of the poet and his audience, particularly the picture of Demodocus in the fairyland world of Scheria. We should not draw too close a connection between the poet himself and the singers in his poem. To take only the most prominent difference, the songs of the bards in the *Odyssey* are very short; Demodocus sings three in the course of a crowded day and still leaves plenty of time for Odysseus' own tale. By contrast, it is hard, perhaps impossible, to find an occasion on which the *Iliad* or the *Odyssey* could actually have been performed: even in an age which was accustomed to long poetic recitations and appreciated the singer's art, how could such lengthy works ever have been heard in their complete form? A major festival event, perhaps the Panionia at Mount Mycale near Ephesus, could have provided a suitably grand occasion,[72] but even this context hardly explains the sheer size of the epics. Yet the cumulative evidence for close integration and careful planning of both epics as monumental unified works compels us to accept that the ideal performance context would be one which allowed for total recitation of the entire poem.

We do not know who Homer was, and ancient biographies, largely fanciful in the manner of the genre, are no help; the fact that there was even speculation as to the origin of the name proves that antiquity was no wiser than we are about the man behind it.[73] In the early period,

---

[70] See e.g. schol. EV on *Od.* 8.63; Hardie 1986: 54–5.

[71] M. L. West 1981.

[72] Wade-Gery 1952: ch. 1; Webster 1958: 267–75. Cf. Taplin 1992: 39–41.

[73] Fairweather 1974; Lefkowitz 1981: 12–24. On the traditions about the poet's name and career, see Allen 1924: 11–41; Schwartz 1940; and other material cited in Burkert 1987: 57 n. 1. M. L. West 1999 has argued that the name is a fiction, derived from a word referring to 'an assembly of the people with which poetic contests were associated, a sort of eisteddfod' (375). The traditions about Homer are discussed in detail by Graziosi 2002.

as we saw, many other poems were attributed to Homer (even Thucydides assumes his authorship of the Hymn to Apollo), and it may be that the name was simply applied to all or most of the songs preserved by the group known as the Homeridae ('sons of Homer'), who claimed descent from the great bard.[74] Later readers became more discriminating; by the fourth century it could at least be asserted that he had composed only the *Iliad* and the *Odyssey* (Xen. *Symp.* 3.5). This became the standard view, although the so-called 'separatists' had their doubts.[75] It remains convenient to use the name 'Homer' as shorthand for the creator of both epics, even if one supposes that the *Odyssey* is in fact by a later imitator.

Equal darkness covers the place and date of composition of the epics. Notoriously, different cities and islands of the eastern Mediterranean competed for the honour of being Homer's birthplace (this dispute is the subject of various epigrams in *Anth. Pal.* 16.293–99). The Ionian coastline or the island of Chios, with its later association with the 'Homeridae', have strong claims; by the time of Simonides (early fifth century BC), Homer could be cited as 'the Chian' (fr. 19 West[2]). Some of the descriptive passages in the *Iliad* concerning places near Troy probably rest on first-hand experience: in particular, the poet knows that Poseidon could have seen Troy from the topmost peak of Samothrace, though the island of Tenedos might have been thought to obstruct his view.[76] That the *Odyssey* poet had similar knowledge of Odysseus' kingdom, the island of Ithaca, is less likely, given the geographical difficulties; and his acquaintance with remoter regions such as Egypt, important though these are in the *Odyssey*, was extremely hazy.[77]

The question of the date of composition of the *Iliad* and *Odyssey* is bound up with the problem of the process of creation and transmission.[78] In antiquity the Homeric poems were seen as literary creations: that is, readers supposed that they had been created with the aid of writing, as was the work of later poets. Although the Jew Josephus declared that Homer was illiterate, this was for no good critical reason but formed part of a polemic in which he denigrated the

---

[74] On Homeridai, see Pind. *Nem.* 2.1–5 and scholia; Pl. *Ion* 530d, *Resp.* 10.599e. See further Allen 1924: 42–50; Burkert 1972; Fehling 1979 (total scepticism); Graziosi 2002: 201–17.

[75] Kohl 1917.

[76] *Il.* 13.11–14; cf. Janko's note in Janko 1992; Kirk 1962: 273.

[77] M. M. Austin 1970; Braun 1982; S. West 1988: 65; Boardman 1999: ch. 4.

[78] See Dodds 1968; Myres 1958; Davison 1962b; Hainsworth 1969: *passim*; A. Parry 1971; Heubeck 1974; H. W. Clarke 1981.

classic texts of paganism in contrast with the authority and dignity of the scriptures (*Against Apion* 1.12). In modern times it was F. A. Wolf in his *Prolegomena* (1795)[79] who set forth the fundamental objections to the hypothesis that Homer wrote his poems down, in the way in which we normally imagine a poet at work in a study. The arguments partly concerned the history of writing in early Greece – how early was the technique available, and how readily would the necessary materials come to hand? – and partly exploited the inconsistencies of language, style, and construction which Wolf and his successors believed that they could detect in both epics. Hence arose the long-standing conflict between the 'analysts' (those who cut up or separated the poems into layers or independent lays) and the 'unitarians' (those critics who opposed this procedure and insisted on the fundamental unity and quality of both epics).[80]

Although the concept of oral composition was current from the time of Wolf,[81] it was the work of Milman Parry which gave this notion a central place in the interpretation and study of Homer.[82] He addressed the question of what made Homer's poems so different from later epic, and his answer was that these poems were not simply the creations of an individual but the poems of a people, in that they were oral creations, drawing on a poetic tradition which went back over several lifetimes, even centuries. The evidence for this was above all linguistic, and Parry's most important work focused on the repetitions and variations in linguistic phrases or repeated 'formulae' which recur in the Homeric texts. 'Much-enduring godlike Odysseus' is an obvious example, tied to a particular character; another, which can be used in contexts involving many characters, is 'He, wishing them well, addressed them and declared...' (*Il.* 1.253, etc.). These recurring formulae most commonly

---

[79] Wolf 1985. Wolf was partly anticipated by Robert Wood (1769) and others: see A. Parry 1971: x–xiv.

[80] I intend to say little about the problems or objections raised by the hardline analysts, many of which now seem pedantic and trivial. Some cases which remain problematic are discussed in later chapters. For a pre-Parryist treatment, see Bowra 1930: ch. 5; Page 1955: *passim*; and a more recent survey by H. W. Clarke 1981: ch. 4. Van Thiel 1982 and 1988 document analytic criticism exhaustively; Dawe 1993 also maintains an analytic position with reference to the *Odyssey*. West 2011c and elsewhere argues that the analysts correctly identified problems but erred in explaining these by multiple authorship rather than gradual revision and rewriting by the master poet.

[81] A. Parry 1971: x–xxi.

[82] M. Parry 1971 (Milman Parry's collected papers, with invaluable introduction by Adam Parry) remains fundamental. His followers are too numerous to list here, but see the bibliography in J. M. Foley 1988. For clear summaries of his theories, see Page 1959: 222–5; Hainsworth 1968: ch. 1.

consist of whole hexameter lines, or of half-lines beginning or ending at the 'caesura' or pause point in mid-line. In other words, they are phrases created to ease the task of a poet composing in hexameter verse.[83] Homer has often been described as an improviser, a misleading term. On the level of metrical technique and formulaic vocabulary he does indeed work with tools which were devised to ease the process of oral composition; but the *Iliad* and the *Odyssey* could not have been produced without long preparation and premeditation. A corollary of this is that the formulae, besides being useful as building blocks, can also have an aesthetic contribution to make: 'what is technically convenient can also be poetically effective'.[84]

The systems of formulaic phrases which Parry analysed were so numerous and showed such economy (in the sense that superfluous or duplicated phrases were kept to a minimum) that it became impossible to suppose that this was merely one poet's linguistic repertoire, all devised for his own use: it could only have been built up gradually by generations of bards. This conclusion was confirmed by philology. The language of Homer is an artificial tongue, never spoken by a single race or state at a given period; it is an amalgam of elements from different dialects and periods. Such a linguistic mixture could not have evolved in a single poet's lifetime; the poetic language was developed by poets over a period of generations. Rather than being the first and greatest of poets, Homer was shown to have composed with a long line of predecessors behind him, all of whom had contributed to the subject matter and diction of his own work. Some have rebelled against Parry's conclusions, feeling that they deny Homer any claim to originality or invention; but this is to misconceive the debate. Any artist imitates or makes use of his predecessors; the relation between tradition and innovation is a subtle and fruitful one, for the literate and for the oral poet.[85] Nevertheless, the Homeric epics, though created in a tradition, stood out even in antiquity as exceptional in quality; this was, after all, the verdict of Aristotle and of Horace.[86]

Parry's researches were published gradually rather than being brought together in a book, and his untimely death in 1935 meant that some time

---

[83] For more detail on Homer's metre, see M. L. West 1982: 35–9, abridged as M. L. West 1987: 19–23; also M. L. West 1997b (with more emphasis on aesthetic aspects). See also Hainsworth 1969: 27–8; Kirk 1985: 17–37; R. B. Rutherford 1992: 78–85. A readable essay on the subject is provided by Bowra 1962.

[84] Macleod 1982: 38.

[85] Eliot 1932, a classic statement which still demands close attention.

[86] Arist. *Poet.* 23, 24; Hor. *Ars P.* 136f.; but note Garvie 1994: 10–11.

elapsed before his ideas had their full impact. Nor have they ever influenced continental scholarship as much as they have Anglo-American work on Homer, though there are signs that things are changing. Much has been done to extend and develop his ideas, particularly in the analysis of formulaic systems. Parry was mainly concerned with the noun-epithet formulae ('much-enduring godlike Odysseus' and the like), but made some moves towards the examination of larger sequences in terms of recurrent patterns: motifs, themes, typical scenes, and so forth.[87] Subsequent work in this area, notably by Fenik, has been especially valuable.[88] By comparing a set of arming scenes or scenes in which a stranger arrives and is given welcome, episodes which occur in comparable form in different parts of Homer's work, we can see some of the poet's repertoire and observe how he plays variations on a 'standard' sequence; the overall similarity highlights differences which are often significant.[89] Sometimes we may suspect that the poet is adopting a standard sequence in order to introduce a new or unexpected element, surprising his audience. In general, Parry's methods help to make us more alert to Homer's craft as a storyteller.

In the initial excitement arising from Parry's work large claims were sometimes made about the consequences for criticism: for instance, that the Homeric poems were entirely composed of formulae (a claim that can only be sustained by unacceptably expanding the concept of a formula); that Homer, composing orally and improvising, was incapable of advance preparation or subtlety of design; that oral poetry in any case did not seek the same effects as literary poetry, and could not be judged by the same criteria; that, indeed, a whole new form of 'oral poetics' is required.[90]

There has also inevitably been a reaction.[91] Some of Parry's formulations were clearly vulnerable, and some of his followers went too far in ruling out any kind of traditional 'literary' criticism. On the other

---

[87] See Arend 1933, with Parry's review, reprinted in M. Parry 1971: 404–7; Hainsworth 1969: 25–6; bibliography given in Schwinge 1991: 485.

[88] Fenik 1968, 1974; also e.g. Krischer 1971, and M. W. Edwards in a series of papers (e.g. 1966, 1968, 1975, 1980, 1987b; also his survey article in 1992). For hospitality scenes see now Reece 1993.

[89] Armstrong 1958; for another aspect see Segal 1971a.

[90] See e.g. Notopoulos 1949, 1950, 1964; Lord 1953, and other paper collected or cited in Lord 1991. A more moderate position is adopted by Hainsworth 1970. For valuable surveys of work on formulae, see M. W. Edwards 1986, 1988.

[91] Note Pope 1963; Hoekstra 1965: ch. 1; Young 1967; Whallon 1969: A. Parry 1972; N. Austin 1975: ch. 1; N. J. Richardson 1987; Shive 1987. See also the discussions cited in A. Parry 1971: xxxiii and xlix n. 3.

hand, it is evident that the formulaic style, and other features of Homeric poetry which distinguish it from the epics of Apollonius or Virgil or Milton, do need to be taken into account in criticism. At the very least, Parryism can explain the frequency with which lines or phrases are repeated in the poems. It is surely necessary to go further, and to see Homer's narratives as composed for performance. Sometimes inconsistencies and oddities can be explained or excused by this assumption, though perfectionist critics may still be irked when 'Homer nods'.[92] 'Schedios is killed by Hector not once but twice; we do not weep for him. Chromios is killed three times, and innumerable eyes are dry.'[93] Again, if the poets are using traditional plot lines and motifs, the problems or obscurities may sometimes be explained by the blending or juxtaposition of slightly different motifs (the difficulties in *Iliad* 2 concerning Agamemnon's testing of the troops may be an example of this, though characterization also plays a part). Both analysts and oralists should bear in mind that there are many anomalies and inconsistencies in works certainly composed with the aid of writing.[94]

On a verbal level, the analysts had complained that Homer often used language inappropriately, for instance in applying 'stock' epithets where they did not fit (Penelope's 'fat' hand in *Od.* 21.6 was a notorious example), and here the oral theory offered an answer, but an unsatisfying one for many readers. Parry went so far as to claim that the poet used these phrases so automatically that they no longer possessed a real meaning for him. What needs saying here is that the cases of inept use are remarkably rare, and need to be balanced against examples of Homer's conscious and tactful adjustment of formulae to suit a particular situation. A small but telling instance occurs at *Iliad* 16.298, when Zeus, who is often given the epithet 'gatherer of the clouds' (*nephelēgereta*), is described instead as 'gatherer of the lightning' (*steropēgereta*), a variant which is found only here. The reason is clear: the

---

[92] The expression derives from a famous line in Horace's *Ars Poetica*, in which the Roman poet admits that literary perfection, however desirable, is not always attainable: *et idem / indignor quandoque bonus dormitat Homerus, / verum operi longo fas est obrepere somnum* (*Ars P.* 358–60: 'I even feel aggrieved, when good Homer nods; but when a work is long, a drowsy mood is understandable'). Pope's riposte to this tag should be taken seriously by critics: 'Those oft are stratagems which error seem, / nor is it Homer nods, but we that dream' (*An Essay on Criticism*, 179–80).

[93] Page 1959: 305.

[94] Scodel 1999 is a stimulating account of the question of inconsistency in literature, especially epic and tragedy.

poet is describing how Zeus *disperses* the clouds, and the normal epithet would naturally jar.[95]

Parry stressed the element of tradition in the Homeric epics, while others have sought to isolate particularly creative uses or modifications of traditional material, or have even maintained that Homer is working against or remoulding the tradition.[96] Another fruitful line of research is to explore the complexity of Homer's diction and styles: whereas Parryism seemed to imply a monolithic formulaic style, recent work has made clear that there are important distinctions between the style of the speeches and that of the narrative; moreover, different speakers may be characterized by different styles.[97] In all these areas, what matters is to recognize that tradition and originality are combined, even if there are limits to how far we can define the relationship between the two.

A different approach, again seeking to vindicate the aesthetic as well as the functional qualities of the formulaic language, makes the traditional nature of that language a major resource for the poet. By using phraseology and typical episodes which he and others have used elsewhere, he evokes these other uses, recalling for the audience a world that they intuitively recognize. 'Traditional referentiality', to quote its chief exponent, 'entails the invoking of a context that is enormously larger and more echoic than the text or work itself, that brings the lifeblood of generations of poems and performances to the individual performance or text.'[98] Formulae and themes metonymically draw on a larger world: '*pars pro toto*' is an expression that Foley has used repeatedly.[99] The approach allows for variation and distortion of the

---

[95] For Parry's fullest defence of the statement that the meaning of the epithets was unimportant, see M. Parry 1971: 118–72; see also the briefer account at 1971: 304–7. But Parry himself allowed for some cases of deliberate choice or adjustment (1971: 156–61), and the argument is taken further by Hainsworth 1969: 29–30; Macleod 1982: 35–42; R. B. Rutherford 1992: 49–57. For Penelope's fat hand, see Woodhouse 1930: 200–1, who wails 'Oh Homer! How could you?'; defended by N. Austin 1975: 73.

[96] Sale 1963; Russo 1968; Tsagarakis 1982, esp. 32 ff.; cf. Taplin 1992. On technical aspects of the evolution of the formulaic system, see Hainsworth 1962, 1978; and especially the magisterial account in Hainsworth 1993: 1–31; also Finkelberg 1989. For a range of approaches, see Visser 1987, 1988; Russo 1997; Bakker 2005.

[97] Griffin 1986, with de Jong 1988; de Jong 1987a; Martin 1989; Mackie 1996 (on differentiation of Trojan speech); Finkelberg 2012.

[98] J. M. Foley 1991: 7; brief account of his views in Foley 1997; for detailed readings see J. M. Foley 1991: 135–89 (on *Iliad* 24), 1999: 241–62 (on *Odyssey* 23). Kelly 2007b systematically applies this method to *Iliad* 8; for good examples of his method see pp. 183–4 (imagined third-person speakers), 205–8 (on *nēpioi*), 250–3 (prayers).

[99] E.g. J. M. Foley 1997: 168. See also Graziosi and Haubold 2005, esp. 49–60, on 'resonance'.

norms; audiences are experienced enough to detect such abnormal usage. This is a very suggestive approach, though problems remain (such as how far different bards might differ in their styles and subjects, and how to allow for the evolution and invention within the tradition).

The other aspect of Parry's work which particularly caught the imagination of his followers was the comparative approach, pursued through fieldwork on existing oral poetic traditions, above all in Yugoslavia in the 1930s.[100] There it proved possible to hear, record, and question bards composing without literacy, and to test the reliability of their memories of previous songs. Through this fieldwork, so Parry believed, a poetic tradition comparable with that of Homer could be observed and preserved. Fascinating though the comparison has proved, subsequent scholarship has been cautious in making deductions about the consequences for Homer. In quality and metrical subtlety the Yugoslav poems seem to fall short of Homer's; nor do these bards generally compose on such a large scale, except on special request.[101] The differences between ancient Ionia and modern Europe mean that special caution is needed in tracing the development or degeneration of an oral poetic tradition.[102] These analogies can only be suggestive, not probative. In the end, Parry's work on modern traditions may be found less valuable for Homeric studies than his analysis of Homer's own style and formulae.

8. But could Homer write?

Milman Parry tended to say or imply that his researches had 'proved' that Homer was an oral poet, in the sense of one who not only performed orally but made no use of writing in the composition of his works or at any stage. Modern readers of Homer – 'readers' is the key word – find it almost impossible to imagine the effort of memory involved in preserving long poetic texts such as these without any aide-mémoire. True, actors and operatic singers achieve feats scarcely less miraculous even in our own time, but they have a written text to memorize.

---

[100] M. Parry 1971: chs. 13–17 (17 by A. B. Lord), with A. Parry 1971: xxxiv–xli, xlvii–xlviii; Lord 1960. See further Finnegan 1977; Hainsworth 1993: 32–53 (a valuable essay on 'The *Iliad* as heroic poetry'); and, for broadening of the comparative picture, e.g. Hatto 1980; J. M. Foley 1991, 2005.

[101] But important new work on the South Slavic traditions may require modification of current assumptions: see Danek 1998: 7–23; Danek 2010; and esp. Čolaković 2006.

[102] As is too eagerly attempted by Kirk 1962: 95–8. Contrast Thomas 1993: ch. 3.

It can be argued, however, that this is the wrong model. According to Parry, and to many who have studied oral poetic traditions more widely than he, the singer is not memorizing and reproducing, but composing afresh, re-creating; each new performance is in a sense a new song, and tape recorders will show differences of some significance even when a singer does claim to be repeating 'the same' song. According to this view, the poet is in large part 'improvising', a word with disturbing implications. Did the *Iliad*, or parts thereof, go through this process in Homer's lifetime, being re-created many times? In that case, we may well suspect that the poet refined his work and added fresh beauties, rather than simply starting afresh each time; but how can we be sure that we have the 'best' version? The problem becomes greater when a different poet takes over the song, and remakes it anew. If a period of several generations intervenes before the poem is committed to writing, it may undergo extensive changes. In a way, it is not 'Homer's' poem. We may think of the paradox of the axe hanging on the wall for generations: if the blade has been replaced twice, the handle once, is it still 'grandfather's axe'? Hence the attractions of assuming a literate Homer; a written text may be subject to the normal mishaps of miscopying but at least imposes some fixity. Lord and others have supposed that Homer himself was illiterate but dictated his works to willing disciples or scribes, so making it possible for the master's works to live on.[103] Others have wished to go a step further and cut out the middleman: could not Homer himself have learned to write and used this opportunity to preserve, perhaps to enhance and enlarge, his greatest poem? It is an intriguing proposal that the discovery of writing itself could have been the stimulus which prompted a poet of exceptional gifts to create or develop a poem of extraordinary scope and length, in the knowledge that the instrument now existed to ensure his work's survival.[104] More far-fetched is the hypothesis that the alphabet was itself devised specifically as a means of preserving epic poetry.[105]

Current orthodoxy places the introduction of the alphabet from the Phoenician into the Greek world in the late ninth or early eighth century: the earliest known Greek inscriptions come from

---

[103] Lord 1953, and elsewhere; accepted e.g. by Janko 1992: 37–8, and re-argued in Janko 1998.

[104] A view championed by Bowra 1930, and by Adam Parry in an important paper (A. Parry 1966); contrast e.g. Taplin 1992: 8–9, 35–7. My own preference has always been for this theory; for others of the same opinion, see Garvie 1994: 16 n. 51, and now West 2011c, esp. 10–14.

[105] Powell 1991; for criticism see Woodard 1997.

*c.*770–750 BC.[106] Whether we suppose that an alphabet, if available, would have been utilized to put Homer's poetry in a permanent form, or whether suitable writing materials could be obtained at this date, will partly depend on the importance which we suppose was attached to poetry in this period. Papyrus was an expensive import even in fifth-century Athens; leather has also been suggested.[107] The difficulties are formidable, but the notion that the *Iliad* was consigned to writing from the start, at a date in the late eighth or early seventh century, is not a physical impossibility. The special attraction of this theory is that it explains the composition of so massive an epic, which would hardly have been composed for performance alone. Alternatively, some look hopefully to the so-called Homeridae, who, if they recognized the stature of their poet, may perhaps have sought to memorize rather than re-create.

My own view, then, would be that the seventh-century date, while possible, is not proven, and I am content to see the *Iliad* as reaching something very like its final form towards the end of the eighth century, and quite possibly being committed to writing within the poet's own lifetime. The *Odyssey*, whoever its author may be, follows in its wake, after an interval of at least a decade. Only gradually would the two poems become known beyond the region (wherever that was) in which they were created and recorded, and it would be a long time before they became 'classic' texts to which other poets and artists might consciously allude.[108] The sheer length of these poems may have meant that they were at first actually *less* popular and would certainly have meant that most audiences would only have heard parts; geographical distance must also be taken into account (wherever they were composed, the process of diffusion would be different from modern 'publication' and far slower). Advocates of a seventh-century date point to the startling fact that Alcman, Stesichorus, and the Lesbian poets (*c.*600) are the earliest certain instances of allusion,[109] but the

---

[106] Jeffery 1961: 1–42 with addenda on pp. 425–7 in 1990 edition by Johnston, against the early dating proposed by Near Eastern experts such as J. Naveh; Burkert 1992: 25–33. See also Heubeck 1979.

[107] Cost: *IG* i^3 476.289–90; cf. Jeffery 1961: 56–7; Jensen 1980: 92–5. Burkert 1992 supports leather.

[108] This was a slow process, as shown by the paucity of representations in art and certain echoes in literature. See Burkert 1987; Snodgrass 1998; Burgess 2001: ch. 2.

[109] Alcman *PMG* 77 and 80; Alcaeus F 44 Lobel-Page; Stesich. *SLG*, esp. S11, revised in Davies, *PMGF* I; cf. Page 1973b. On the dating of Stesichorus, see D. A. Campbell 1991: 2–4; see further Burkert 1987.

yawning absence of early Greek poetry outside the hexameter tradition deprives that argument of a great deal of its force.

9. Sixth-century Athens

According to later sources it was in the sixth century, during the reign of the Athenian tyrant Pisistratus (d. 527) and his sons, that an authoritative written text of Homer was prepared, for use by rhapsodes who recited the epics at the great festival of the Panathenaea.[110] These sources are not only much later but mutually contradictory, and there have been attempts to dismiss the whole 'Pisistratean recension' as a fiction; but, although we should not envisage anything like a scholarly publication, it seems likely that some such centralized text was established, and that this stage in the tradition accounts for some of the 'Atticisms' or traces of Attic dialect in our texts of Homer. The idea that before this date no coherent epic songs existed, and that it was Pisistratus who brought various songs together and created 'Homer', was brilliantly asserted by Wolf and has been re-argued since,[111] but seems fundamentally implausible: the Greeks thought of Homer as an older figure, and did not associate him with Athens; the Athenians themselves make a poor showing in the *Iliad*, which makes it unlikely that the poem was radically modified in that city; the assertions that the Athenians did in fact interpolate certain passages presupposes a pre-existing text; and the theory contradicts the chronological arguments of Janko. It is much more likely that Pisistratus or his sons 'procured the first complete set of rolls to cross the Aegean',[112] and that their contribution was later exaggerated.

The earliest testimony to this activity by the Pisistratid family ascribes it to Hipparchus, his son: 'he first conveyed the poems of Homer to this country, and made the rhapsodes go through them in order at the Panathenaia, taking turns at the task, as they still do today' (Pl. *Hipparch.* 228b). These rhapsodes ('weavers of song'), professional reciters of poetry which is not their own, are often seen as a new

---

[110] Pl. *Hipparch.* 228b; Isoc. *Paneg.* 159; Lycurg. 1.102; Cic. *De or.* 3.137; Merkelbach 1952; Davison 1955; Janko 1992: 29–32; Lewis 1988: 292. For a different approach see Nagy 1995; he sees the story of the Pisistratean recension as in effect a myth describing a gradual process by which the text became fixed.

[111] Jensen 1980, esp. ch. 7.

[112] Janko 1992: 37.

phenomenon, distinct from the genuine oral poet; the dividing line may not be quite so sharp.[113] Our view of them is biased by Plato, who satirizes the pretensions of one such figure, the complacent Ion, who can perform Homer to perfection but cannot explain him. The poets and their kinsmen no longer have a special authority over their poetry; by becoming a classic, Homer has entered the public domain.[114]

A more specific allegation in antiquity, preserved in the Homeric scholia, was that Book 10 of the *Iliad*, often called the *Doloneia*, was not part of the original poem, but was separately composed and incorporated in the epic by Pisistratus (schol T. 10.1). The association of the change with Pisistratus may be merely the result of the earlier stories about his involvement with the Homeric text, but the suggestion that Book 10 is a later addition gains some support from the linguistic, structural, and ethical peculiarities of that book, as well as from the lack of cross-references to it in the rest of the *Iliad*. Although the tenth book presupposes the *Iliad*, the *Iliad* does not need the *Doloneia*.[115]

This leads on to the general question of addition to and subtraction from the Homeric text during the course of its transmission.[116] If a whole book has been interpolated, what other changes may have been made at different times? Other cases were indeed cited, or at least problems were identified, by ancient critics: most alarmingly, the conclusion of the *Odyssey* (see below, p. 98).[117]

[113] Hes. fr. 357 M-W seems to anticipate the image, but applying it to the bard; contrast Pind. *Nem.* 2.2. See Patzer 1952; Sealey 1957; Herington 1985: 167–76; Burkert 1987; M. L. West 2010.

[114] For the emergence of interpretation of Homer by non-poets, see Theagenes of Rhegium (fragments in Diels–Kranz 8), esp. B2, discussing the battle of the gods in *Iliad* 20; later, e.g. Ar. *Banqueters* fr. 233 K-A; Prt. 80A29, 30; Plut. *Vit. Alc.* 7.1. See N. J. Richardson 1975. On the origins of criticism, see Ford 2002.

[115] See esp. Hainsworth's 1993 commentary and the earlier bibliography on his p. 155, esp. Klingner 1940; Danek 1988 (with Danek 2012, in English).

[116] Gregory Nagy in a long series of publications (e.g. Nagy 1996, 2003, 2010) has argued that a creative performance tradition for Homer continued long after Pisistratus, and that many differing versions of the epics existed, so that modern attempts to establish or reconstruct an early fixed text are misguided. This argument has found little support: see the criticisms by Finkelberg 2000, with Nagy's reply in Nagy 2001. The tradition of Homer is far less 'multiform' than some other oral traditions (examples in M. L. West 2001b: 11).

[117] Other cases are for the most part much shorter. In antiquity there were controversies about so-called Athenian interpolations (Arist. *Rh.* 1375b30, Dieuchidas *FGrH* 485F6 = D. L. i.57; cf. Allen 1924: 241 ff.), but the Athenians makes so small a showing in the *Iliad* that it is hard to suppose that much was added. Suspect passages on this score include 1.265, 2.553–5, 11.602–4. On manuscript evidence for interpolation see Bolling 1925 and Apthorp 1980a: the problems are too complex to discuss here. M. L. West 2001b: 12–14, with wonderful confidence, sets out a catalogue of Iliadic interpolations grouped in categories.

10. Text and scholars

It hardly needs saying that commitment of the epics to writing, and even the possible establishment of an 'authorized' text for the Panathenaic recitations, did not ensure a calm and straightforward transmission of the text from that point to the present day. In virtually all textual traditions, the work comes down to us by various routes, and is recopied many times; even setting aside deliberate interference, it is an established fact that new errors will occur at every stage.[118] Although there is much that we cannot reconstruct, it seems clear that Homer circulated in many versions which differed significantly from one another during the centuries after Pisistratus: the evidence comes partly from quotations in other literary sources, partly from the early papyri, which often deviate from the text that later became 'standard', in particular including additional lines. The divergences are sometimes so marked that scholars refer to early extracts as the 'wild' papyri.[119] Alexandrian scholars did much work identifying possibly spurious lines and deciding between variant readings; after the third century BC the text seems to have settled into more or less the form which we have inherited, and it is usual to associate this development with the name of Aristarchus, one of the most distinguished scholars of Alexandria.[120]

In modern times, the analysts claimed that they had identified many later additions, and sought to reduce the poem to its earliest and purest state by purging it of such intrusions. This practice is misguided and in any case fruitless: even supposing that all such cases were objectively identified, we cannot assume that they have been simply added to a core which remains uncontaminated. If that assumption is not made,

---

[118] On textual criticism in general see M. L. West 1973b; Reynolds and Wilson 1991: ch. 6. For more detail on the Homeric tradition, see Davison 1962a; M. L. West 2001b; Haslam 1997, 2011. On the *Odyssey*, see S. West 1988: 33–48.

[119] The 'wild papyri' are edited by S. West 1967; for a brief account, see E. J. Turner 1968: 106–12. D. Sutton n.d. is an online database 'Homer and the Papyri', now overseen by G. Nagy.

[120] Besides the variations in manuscript evidence, there is the supplementary testimony of ancient quotations: for a conspicuous case of a passage preserved only in one source, not represented in manuscripts or papyri, see 9.458–61, quoted by Plutarch as excised by Aristarchus; these lines may well be authentic (cf. Janko 1992: 27–8; Hainsworth 1993: ad loc.). On the Alexandrian scholars, see Fraser 1972: 447–79; Davison 1962a: 222–6; Pfeiffer 1968: part 2, esp. chs. 2 and 6; Janko 1992: 22–9 (with invaluable bibliography and lists of examples of their judgements); M. L. West 2001b: 33–85; F. Schironi, entries in Finkelberg 2011, under 'Alexandrian scholarship' and the names of scholars.

then the supposed original is irrecoverable. But in an oral tradition the very concept of an 'original' version may in any case be a chimaera. Nevertheless, many critics have continued to build up counter-arguments to the more drastic version of analytic criticism, showing how well integrated and intricately structured both epics in fact are. Scenes are demonstrably connected, later events are foreshadowed, explicit anticipation is common, and the poet has a firm control over an extended but carefully organized plot. Against those who maintained that oral composition must be loose and 'paratactic', this new wave of unitarians insists on the subtlety and complexity of Homer's art. This is a version of the argument from design: random combination or cumulative addition could not have resulted in this satisfyingly ordered microcosm. Schadewaldt and Reinhardt, Bannert and Reichel in German, Macleod and Taplin in English, have charted an impressive range of connections and cross-references which surely imply the master hand of a 'monumental poet' who planned the *Iliad* as a whole. Similar arguments have been applied to the *Odyssey* by Garvie and myself, among others. It remains true that some of these intricate structures are more visible and significant than others; some, it may be said, are perceptible only to the eye of faith. More disquieting is the argument that many of the thematic echoes and links which the unitarians detect can equally be explained by the conscious development of the poem by a succession of bards; to seek a single poet of surpassing genius is merely romantic misunderstanding of the nature of an oral tradition.[121] Such a hypothesis offers one possible explanation for the problems at the conclusion of the *Odyssey*.

11. Reception and interpretation

From the beginning following Homer, because all have learned [from him?]...
(Xenophanes B10)

It is they [Homer and Hesiod] who by their poetry gave the Greeks a theogony and gave the gods their titles; they who assigned to them their statuses and skills and gave an indication of their appearance. (Hdt. 2.53).[122]

---

[121] Nagy 1992, esp. 30–1; Seaford 1994,:144–54, part of a complex argument, many stages of which I cannot accept. Griffin 1995: 8 attempts a brief response to Seaford. See also Sourvinou-Inwood 1995: 94–103.

[122] Burkert 1985, 119–25; Gould 1994.

Consequently, Glaucon, when you encounter admirers of Homer who assert that this poet has been the educator of Greece, and that...one should organise and lead one's whole life in accordance with this poet's work...   (Pl. *Resp.* 10.606e)

These and many other passages attest the special prestige of Homer in the classical period. Simonides could refer to him as 'the Chian' (fr. 19), but in time he became simply 'the poet' – no ambiguity was possible. Aristophanes' Aeschylus calls him 'divine' (*Ran.* 1034); the real Aeschylus was said to have declared his tragedies 'fish-slices from the banquet of Homer' (Ath. 8.347c). The highest praise for a later poet was to call him 'Homeric' (D. L. 4.20, on Sophocles). Prose writers were praised in the same terms ('Longinus' 13.3 on Herodotus; *SEG* 48.1330). Homer was not the pathfinder of tragedy alone; he can also be seen as the inspiration for historiography, which shares his concern to preserve the 'glorious deeds of men', for rhetoric, even for New Comedy. The ancient novel, with its parted lovers wandering in strange foreign lands but eventually reunited, is another obvious descendant.[123] Quintilian and others compared Homer with the Ocean, which encircled the world and flowed into every lesser river.[124]

Homer has indeed been called 'the Bible of the Greeks', but this description requires some important qualifications. At no stage were the epics sacred texts: they were not kept in temples or interpreted by priests; although Homer was gaining pre-eminence by the end of the sixth century, other early texts were quoted and cited to illustrate mythical 'facts' or to back up an argument; as we have seen, Herodotus paired Homer with Hesiod as a formative influence on the Greeks' conception of the gods. Above all, Homer was not venerated without question. 'Poets tell many a lie', said the Athenian Solon, echoing Hesiod.[125] The Pre-Socratic thinker Xenophanes was more specific: 'Homer and Hesiod attributed to the gods all the things which bring reproach and disgrace among men – theft, adultery, deceit' (B11). Heraclitus was more forthright: 'Homer deserves to be thrown out of the public contests and given a beating' (B42). Pindar expressed reservations as to the reliability of Homer's testimony about Odysseus: 'I

---

[123] E.g. Hägg 1983; for tales of the ends of the earth see also Romm 1992.

[124] See Hornblower 1994: 7–13 for historiography, with Marincola 2007; Radermacher 1951: 1–10 for rhetoric. Satyrus, *Life of Euripides* fr. 39, col. vii, 23 ff. Arrighetti, comments on the line of descent from Homer to New Comedy. Homer as Ocean: Quint. 10.1.46; F. Williams 1978: 98–9.

[125] Solon F 29 West; Hes. *Theog.* 27–8; Thalmann 1984: 147–9; Pratt 1993.

hold that the renown of Odysseus is more than his sufferings, because of Homer's sweet singing... Art beguiles and cheats with its tales' (*Nem.* 7.20–3). Plato refers in the *Republic* to 'an ancient quarrel between poetry and philosophy' (10.607bc),[126] and excises offending passages, particularly those which show gods or heroes in an ignoble light. The controversy over the immorality of Homer's gods continued throughout antiquity.[127] But the morality of the heroes, the impetuous Achilles and the devious Odysseus, also aroused strong feelings. The tragic dramas of fifth-century Athens constantly rework Homeric themes and scrutinize epic values from the standpoint of a later age: enthusiastic admiration is mingled with questioning and even protest.[128]

Interpretation arises out of competition and polemic, for later poets sought to compete with or surpass the epic master. Hesiod, elaborating on the function of Strife in the community, speaks of competition between potters, carpenters, beggars, and bards (*Op.* 25–6).[129] Hesiod's own reference to the Muses' lies has sometimes been taken as a jibe at epic narrative, probably wrongly; but Stesichorus revised Homer's mythology and his own, rejecting the tale that Helen went to Troy with Paris (*PMG* 192). In the sixth century Theagenes allegorized Homer; in the fifth Protagoras criticized his grammar. We recognize the beginnings of scholarly commentary.[130] Many passages of Homer are quoted and discussed, not always in negative vein, by speakers in Plato's dialogues or the works of Xenophon. Although interpretation was often whimsical – selecting passages to prove a point without considering context, applying anachronistic criteria, or finding fault in order to show off – the eventual effect was to generate a rich and varied body of critical discussion.

The special importance of Homer meant that his poems, and especially the *Iliad*, were more closely studied than any other works of pagan antiquity. Historians debated the date of the fall of Troy, parodists spoofed epic phraseology, rhetoricians analysed the forms of argument employed in the speeches, students of mythology sought to

---

[126] Cf. Curtius 1953: ch. 11.

[127] Pease 1955–8 on Cic. *Nat. D.* 1.42.

[128] Cf. Easterling 1984; Goldhill 1986, esp. ch. 6.

[129] For mutual rivalry and criticism among poets see e.g. Simonides on Pittacus, *PMG* 542, and on Cleobulus, ibid. 581; also the stories of a contest between Homer and Hesiod. See further Griffith 1990; Buxton 1994: 31.

[130] Pfeiffer 1968 is the fundamental reference work, supplemented by N. J. Richardson 1975 and esp. 1993: 25–49. See also Lamberton and Keaney 1992.

reconcile or relate different legends, and grammarians puzzled over linguistic forms, tried to explain difficult words, and assessed the merits of
variant readings. One work which would have shed much light on the
state of interpretation in classical times was Aristotle's *Homeric
Problems*, now lost except for a few extremely suggestive fragments;
the much more sketchy treatment of some Homeric topics in a chapter
of the *Poetics* gives an idea of the acumen with which Aristotle must
have cut through much arid or ill-conceived argument.[131] After the
lengthy complaints in Plato and others about the unworthy behaviour
of Homeric gods and men, there is something refreshing about the
curt response of Aristotle:

Correctness in poetry is not the same as correctness in morals, nor yet is it the same as
correctness in any other art. ... If an error arises through the poet's setting out to represent something incorrectly, and that is the reason why we find in the poem a mistake
concerning, say, medicine or some other art,...this does not involve the essential nature
of poetry.   (Arist. *Poet.* 25.1460b13–21)[132]

Above all, the ancient commentaries on Homer, which digest and pass
on many of the observations of the great Hellenistic editors, provide not
only precious mythological data and testimony to the textual tradition
of the poems, but literary comment which may sometimes appear
naïve, but retains interest and value.[133] It is mere arrogance to suppose
that only the most recent critical methods and concepts can offer any
insight to the modern reader.[134] Similarly, reception studies have
brought home to many readers how much can be learned from the
responses of earlier generations, whether amateurs or professionals
and whether they came to Homer in the original or through the count-
less translations.[135]

---

[131] *Hom. Probl.*: frr. 142–79 Rose; *Poet.* 25, with commentaries; Carroll 1895.

[132] Translation from Hubbard 1972 (slightly modified). See further Halliwell 1986: 10–17 and
ch. 7.

[133] For the Hellenistic critics whose views are quoted by the scholia, see the works cited in
n. 114 above; also Kirk 1985: 38–43; Meijering 1987; Nünlist 2010.

[134] The monumental edition of most of the scholia to the *Iliad* is Erbse 1969–88, supplemented
for the D scholia by van Thiel 2000. A new edition of the *Odyssey* scholia has begun to appear
(Pontani 2007; for books not yet covered one must still go back to Dindorf 1855). For guidance
on this and other editions, see Dickey 2007: 18–28. On their critical criteria and preoccupations
N. J. Richardson 1980 is invaluable. Cf. Snipes 1988 (similes); N. J. Richardson 1993: 35–40; see
also Heath 1989: ch. 8. Griffin 1980 also makes use of the scholia, but tends to praise or damn
them according to the extent that they confirm his views.

[135] No attempt can be made here to survey the history of Homeric reception, which would
embrace much of the history of western literature. Helpful starting points include Thomson
1962; F. M. Turner 1981; France 2000; Graziosi and Greenwood 2007; Grafton, Most, and

Many of the topics considered by scholars and students of Homer today were pioneered by the ancient critics: the study of plot construction, characterization, rhetorical techniques, decorum and generic convention, preparation, foreshadowing, retardation, ironic double meanings – the list could be extended. The ancients were also more alert to matters of metre and audible effects, an area much neglected in our post-oral culture.[136] Thucydides and Aristotle formulated the principle of poetic licence (Thuc. 1.10.3; Arist. *Poet.* 25); Longinus, in a brilliant paragraph, summed up unforgettably the differences between the *Iliad* and the *Odyssey* (*On the Sublime,* 9.11–15). We need not be too modest: some advances in critical understanding have become possible because we know more about philology and linguistic development than ancient scholars did; scientific archaeology has given us a far clearer insight into the dark ages and the earlier era of Mycenae than was available to Thucydides. Other improvements are technical. We have more readable printed texts, supplemented by systematic grammars, Homeric lexica, and computerized concordances: the study of Homeric vocabulary and formulaic diction is far more straightforward for us today than it was for Aristarchus or even for Wolf and his followers.

Some modern approaches, although perhaps anticipated in earlier times in certain specific observations or insights, do seem to represent fresh steps towards a deeper understanding. One which has already been mentioned is the study of creative or imaginative development of 'stock' formulae and themes. Another is the application of a sociological or anthropological approach to Homeric society, scrutinizing the institutions, the structures of the community, and above all the values and morality which motivate the characters in the epics.[137] Closely related to this is the study of Homeric religion in relation to worship and cult in historical times: in one way this is the hardest of all tasks for modern readers, brought up in a completely different religious tradition (or in none), but there is another sense in which we have an advantage over the Greeks, since we are viewing the subject from outside, with a quite different perspective. After much ground-breaking

---

Settis 2010; Hardwick and Stray 2008; also, on the *Odyssey,* E. Hall 2008. Eight of the essays in R. L. Fowler 2004 deal with Homeric reception. For translations, see pp. 134–5.

[136] N. J. Richardson 1980: 283–7; M. W. Edwards 1987a: ch. 15.

[137] Finley 1954 (rev. 1978) and Redfield 1975 are particularly important works in this area; more recently, van Wees 1992b; Raaflaub 1991, 1993; D. Cairns 1993 (and more recent articles, e.g. 2003, 2011); Osborne 2004.

and original research we may now hope that we have a better understanding of the relation between Homer's poetic presentation of the
gods and the historical realities of ritual and cult.[138] Valuable work
has been done on the use of imagery, metaphor, and even symbolism
(in the sense of poetic representation of physical objects which also con-
veys a deeper meaning), matters which at one time seemed too fanciful
or sophisticated for Homer.[139] The extended simile is not the only way
in which Homer adorns and obliquely sheds light on his narrative.

Modern Homeric scholarship has also welcomed the advent of narratology – again, the systematic development of an insight already explicitly discussed in ancient texts. Narratology examines the sequence and
emphases of a narrative: not just 'what happens?' but 'how is it
described?'.[140] It also stresses the distinction between the poet's author-
ial viewpoint and that of his characters, and pays special attention to the
passages in which the distinction is blurred or ambiguous. Instead of
taking the story for granted, we are encouraged to look more closely
at the way in which it is told. This has already had beneficial effect,
not least in demonstrating the futility of the old debate as to whether
Homer is 'objective' or not; the terminology of former discussion is
seen to be hopelessly over-simplified.[141] A related enquiry is to examine
the defining structures of Homer's plots, seminal for so many later
works. A bold and intellectually demanding attempt to do just this
has been made by Nick Lowe, drawing not only on narratology but
on cognitive science and game theory: the contrasts he draws between
the *Iliad* and the *Odyssey* as models for later plots in tragedy, comedy,
and the novel are illuminating for the original poems and for later literature as well.[142]

---

[138] Burkert 1985 (English translation of his 1977 book) is a rich store of insights. See also Parker
1983: 66–70, 130–43, etc.; Griffin 1980: chs. 5–6; new ch. in Redfield 1975 (1994 edition);
Bremmer 1994, Versnel 2011 (very wide-ranging; for Homer see esp. ch. 2). See further
Kearns 2004, 2011; and pp. 64–70 below.

[139] M. W. Edwards 1987a: chs. 11–14; Griffin 1980: ch. 1. Rather differently Lynn-George
1988, e.g. 252–72 on grave mounds and monuments. On metaphor, see M. Parry 1971: 365–
75, 414–18; Moulton 1979; M. W. Edwards 1991: 48–53. For gesture, facial expression, and
related matters, see Lateiner 1995; D. Cairns 2005.

[140] Genette 1980; Bal 1985; de Jong 1987a introduced this approach to Homeric studies (also
in many other papers, some listed in the bibliography); the method is applied on a grand scale to
the *Odyssey* in de Jong 2001.

[141] Pragmatic treatment in Griffin 1986; more theoretically grounded, de Jong 1987a;
S. Richardson 1990; di Benedetto 1994, part 1. See also M. W. Edwards 1991: introduction,
1–10.

[142] Lowe 2000.

These and other critical techniques cannot be adequately explored in the abstract; they need to be illustrated through examples drawn from the epics themselves. In the pages which follow only a few instances can be provided from the abundance of Homer's store. As Dryden wrote of Chaucer, 'here is God's plenty'.

II THE *ILIAD*[1]

1. Structure, Characterization, Themes

The *Iliad* is not an *Achilleid*, although Achilles is the most important character in the epic. One of the most striking features of the poem is the way in which it embraces the action of the whole Trojan War by retrospective and prospective references, rather than by narrating the events in full. In this, as is evident from ancient testimony, the *Iliad* was markedly different from the 'cyclic' epics (see esp. Hor. *Ars P.* 136–7). The human characters refer to the abduction of Helen, the initial embassy to the Trojans, the mustering at Aulis, the earlier campaigns and clashes; the prophecies and comments of the gods, particularly Zeus and Thetis, anticipate the doom of Achilles and the ultimate fall of Troy, also grimly foreshadowed in other ways.[2] In an important passage which seems to be deliberately reserved for a late stage in the poem, Homer himself looks back to the origin of the whole conflict, the judgement of Paris which aroused the implacable anger of Athena and Hera against Troy.[3]

Another remarkable feature is the intensity of the action of the poem. In terms of time, the whole poem occupies some forty days, of which only fourteen include narrated events, and three in particular are the subject of fourteen books.[4] As for place, the human action is virtually confined to three areas: the camp of the Greeks, the city of Troy, and

[1] The commentary by Kirk and others (1985–93) is now the first resource; see also Latacz et al. 2000 - (in progress); Macleod 1982 on Book 24; Griffin 1995 on Book 9; Graziosi and Haubold 2010 on Book 6; and de Jong 2012 on Book 22. For general books on the *Iliad* in English, see also Bowra 1930; Redfield 1975; Mueller 1984; Schein 1984 (useful but rather derivative); M. W. Edwards 1987a; Silk 1987 (short but acute); Taplin 1992; Louden 2006. In German, Reinhardt 1961 and Schadewaldt 1938 are fundamental. Stanley 1993 is extremely useful for book-by-book bibliography even if one finds his analyses over-schematic. M. L. West 2011c is highly selective but has many interesting observations. More specific studies are mentioned below.

[2] 3.443–6; 3.204–24; 2.301–30; for references to earlier campaigning, see e.g. 2.688–93; 9.128–30, 328–33, 663–8; 19.295–6. For anticipation of the fall of Troy, see e.g. 4.163–5 = 6.447–9; 15.69–71; 18.207–13; 22.410–11, etc. For the death of Achilles see below, p. 118. In general, see e.g. Kullmann 1960: ch. 5; Griffin 1980: 1; Mueller 1984: 66–7; Dowden 1996: 55–6.

[3] See esp. Reinhardt 1938; Griffin 1980: 195 n. 49; Richardson 1993: 276–8 (a very careful discussion). M. L. West 2011c: 412 regards this passage as a 'rhapsodic interpolation'.

[4] Taplin 1992, 14–22, with earlier references.

the plain of battle which lies between. The scenes involving the Olympians are more various and provide a broader perspective, but their attention too is generally focused on the human suffering on the battlefield. Consequently, the *Iliad* gains in emotional power what it lacks in diversity of scene and situation. A third feature, already implied, is the prominence of the Trojans in the poem. The very title *Iliad*, though probably not original, reminds us that this is no jingoistic or 'pan-Hellenic' epic; despite the claims of some ancient commentators, the Trojans are treated by Homer with great sympathy and generosity.[5] That is not to deny the fundamental guilt of Paris or to assert that the Achaean victory is undeserved.

The main subject of the poem is proclaimed as the wrath of Achilles. Much remains undisclosed by the opening lines in which the poet states his theme. In particular, we are given no hint that the anger of the hero will change direction: having first been directed against Agamemnon and his fellow-Greeks, it will be turned after Patroclus' death far more savagely against the Trojans and above all against Hector. Moreover, the way in which the hero's wrath ends proves to be as important as the punishment of his enemies. Rather than making Achilles relent as a result of compensation or apology, Homer allows violent revenge to give way to pity and magnanimity. Heroic wrath itself is clearly a traditional theme,[6] and on the evidence of the formulaic system it is likely that Achilles and Hector had both figured in epic for a long period before the *Iliad*,[7] but it is not so clear whether the tale of Achilles' anger had been narrated before Homer. Whatever the truth about his predecessors, Homer's conception of Achilles as a proud, intransigent, yet ultimately noble figure is central to the plot. In the *Iliad* Achilles is not just a rebellious chief but a tragic figure, remote

[5] G. Nagy, in a series of studies, has described the Homeric epics as 'pan-Hellenic' in a different sense, following use of the term by A. Snodgrass: see e.g. Nagy 1990: 70–1, 1995. By this he means that the epic spread widely, and that a common tradition of heroic song was swiftly established throughout the Greek world. It is certainly remarkable that the epic assumes that characters and readers are familiar with place-names and peoples throughout the Greek mainland and islands. This use of 'pan-Hellenism', however, would not affect the point made in my text, that the epic is not obviously nationalistic.

[6] As the Meleager tale especially makes clear (9.524–99); see also 13.460; 20.178–86; 6.326, 335. Cairns 2003 has a broader discussion of the significance of anger; see also van Wees 1992b: 126–38; Harris 2001; Most 2003.

[7] See Page 1959, ch. 6, esp. 248–51, 286–8; Combellack 1944. But see Kullmann 1960: 182–8 on Homer's enlargement of Hector's role. As for Patroclus, Schadewaldt 1965: 178–81 thought it conceivable that he was invented by Homer; Kullmann 1960: 44–5 prefers to think that Homer significantly enhanced his role.

from his fellow-heroes and mysterious to them, caught halfway between divinity and humanity, doomed to an early end, hungry for glory yet seeing at times its elusiveness and even its futility.

The main plotline of the *Iliad*, then, is inevitably the sequence involving Achilles' withdrawal from the war and his reactions to the Greeks' overtures and subsequent events. At least the first half of the poem is dominated by his absence; in Book 9 the Greeks unsuccessfully beg him to return; in Book 11 a long and intricate process begins which culminates in Patroclus' more successful appeal in Book 16, an appeal which leads to the latter's death. Thereafter, Achilles' return to battle is inevitable, but characteristically delayed (the well-known Homeric fondness for 'retardation') – first by the time-lapse until he receives the news, then by the need for fresh armour, then by the formal reconciliation with Agamemnon. From that point, the spotlight is on Achilles, who on re-entering the battle carries all before him, and who dominates the last six books of the poem. Heroic revenge is achieved in Book 22, with the slaying of Hector. It has often been maintained that the poem could have ended at this point, with the hero triumphant and the Greeks certain of their future victory. Whatever the truth about earlier versions of the tale, it is difficult to believe that the poet who has throughout shown Hector and his fellow-Trojans in such an attractive light would have abandoned the Trojan hero to the atrocities of Achilles and denied him burial. A further argument comes from the character of Achilles himself. The friend of Patroclus, the man who showed respect for the father of Andromache, the sparer of suppliants in earlier times, the most emotional and articulate, yet most impulsive speaker in the poem is no mere killing machine. The final scenes of the poem including the hero – those between Achilles and Priam – allow gentler feelings to surface and provide a foil to the savagery which has gone before. Verbal and thematic echoes seem to confirm that the twenty-fourth book is a carefully integrated conclusion to the *Iliad*.[8]

Much that is contained in the *Iliad* is only tangentially connected with the main storyline. Hence the analysts sought to identify an 'original' wrath-poem, usually regarding certain books as essential to this narrative (especially 1, 16 and 22),[9] while rejecting others as later

---

[8] Beck 1964; Macleod 1982, esp. 32–5; N. J. Richardson 1993: 1–14. Contrast Seaford 1994: ch. 5 (hardly tenable).

[9] In all this discussion it must be borne in mind that the book divisions are unlikely to be the work of the poet. They are first attested in Alexandrian times, and may well be the work of the

additions. The alternative model, now more fashionable, regards the *Iliad* as a creative synthesis, drawing on material which had been previously separate but combining episodes and sequences of events into a greater whole. On this assumption, we may accept that some planks in the structure were originally independent, but we may still see the new combination as harmonious and effective. The adaptation is not always perfect: it is fairly clear that the Catalogue of Achaean forces in Book 2 has been adapted from a poem in which it featured at the beginning of the expedition: in particular, whereas a catalogue of ships makes sense at that earlier point, when the fleet assembled at Aulis, there is little point in listing the number of ships so late in the war, without considering the number of men who survive. The editorial hand is particularly clear in the short passages which adapt the catalogue to changed circumstances, explaining the death of Protesilaus and the absence of Philoctetes.[10]

This approach seems preferable in considering, for example, the early books, in which the Greeks try to maintain their superiority without Achilles. In the hero's absence, other characters (Menelaus, Nestor, Odysseus) take the limelight: in particular, Homer gives special prominence to Diomedes, a hero of great courage and energy, but one who lacks the hot temper and self-destructive tendencies of Achilles, and who functions as a foil to the greater hero. Diomedes enjoys an *aristeia* in Books 5 and 6: that is, a period in battle in which he shows himself to be 'best' (*aristos*) and fights with exceptional success. Much that he says and does there, interesting and exciting in itself, stands in contrast with Achilles' behaviour in his later and more extraordinary *aristeia*, in Books 20 to 22.[11] This is characteristic of Homer's technique: the heroes do not exist in isolation, but are regularly compared or contrasted with one another. Achilles and Patroclus (Book 16), Hector and Paris (Books 3 and 6), Hector and Polydamas (18.249–314), Odysseus and Menelaus (3.205–24), and Odysseus and Achilles (19.145–37) are a few examples.

In the course of the *Iliad*, Homer includes many other heroes and gives them their share of glory. Diomedes has already been mentioned;

---

school of Aristarchus (Janko 1992: 37; for an earlier date, S. West 1967: 18–25; cf. S. West 1988: 39–40). Their inadequacy has been strenuously asserted by Taplin 1992; Heiden 2008 (and in earlier work cited there) tries to defend them and use them for interpretation. It is a major defect of Stanley 1993 that so many of his analyses assume the division goes back to the poet. On the ancient titles given to books or episodes, see Stanley 1993: 418 n. 133.

[10] 2.699, 721–6, cf. 686–94. In general on the Catalogue, see Kirk 1985:168–87, 237–40; Visser 1997; Sammons 2010; Kullmann 2012.

[11] Andersen 1978 is a detailed study of Diomedes' role. See also Reichel 1994: 217–30.

the Cretan heroes Idomeneus and Meriones are prominent in Book 13; Patroclus has his brief hour of glory in Book 16; and the greater Ajax, typically excelling in defence, plays a key part in blocking the Trojan onslaught on the ships (Books 15 and 16). Even Agamemnon, though shown in no very favourable light by Homer, has a somewhat abbreviated *aristeia* in Book 11 until he is wounded. Defenders of Book 10 might wish to see it as an atypical *aristeia* (at night, and involving spying and trickery), suitable for the crafty Odysseus.[12] After the fighting of the *Iliad* has come to an end, the funeral games held by Achilles for Patroclus are used by the poet to show the various heroes in action once more, but in lighter vein: Taplin has described the episode as a 'curtain-call'. The contests of the games show the Greeks contending with each other, in pursuit of honour and prizes as on the battlefield, but with less deadly consequences.[13] All of this implies an audience familiar with these characters and eager to see them play their part in an unusually ambitious epic.

Not much has been said so far about the Trojans and the scenes within the city (especially Books 3, 6, 22, 24); yet these are among the most memorable aspects of the poem.[14] While it was natural that in a poem of this scale much should be seen of the warriors on both sides, it was not inevitable that the Trojans, particularly Hector, should be portrayed with such sympathy. Indeed, there are indications that the earlier epic tradition may have treated the opposing side in more negative terms. Even in Homer the advance of the Trojans and their allies is described as a noisy, undisciplined movement (3.2–13, 4.428–38). Trojans slain greatly outnumber the Greek dead (189 versus 54). Trojan heroes propose duels they are unlikely to win. Most significantly, there are a number of typical patterns on the battlefield which discredit the Trojans: they need to be whisked away from death by divine protectors (3.379–80, 5.445, etc.); the most gruesome wounds tend to be inflicted on Trojans and their allies; and all those who supplicate and beg for their lives to be spared are Trojans.[15]

---

[12] Dué and Ebbott 2010; Fantuzzi 2005.

[13] The quotation is from Taplin 1992: 253. See further Redfield 1975: 206–12; Macleod 1982: 28–32. Postlethwaite 1995 (correcting a rare error of Macleod's regarding 23.891) argues that tensions among the Greeks remain even at the end of Book 23.

[14] J. T. Kakridis 1971, 54–67 rejects simple assertions of Homeric philhellenism; see also E. Hall 1989: ch. 1. Sale 1989 argues that Homer greatly expanded the role of the Trojans.

[15] See further Stoevesandt 2004 (there is a useful review of this book by M. Willcock in *BMCRev* 2006).

But if the tradition did indeed have a pro-Hellenic bias, the *Iliad* shows far more generosity. In Book 24 Helen stresses Hector's gentleness, and that of his father Priam: it is obvious that these qualities, illustrated in Books 3 and 6, were important to the poet's conception of these major characters.[16] The household of Hector, with loving wife and infant son for whom his father hopes for so much in vain, epitomizes the civilized life of the city which the Greeks will destroy; moreover, the family life of Hector stands in contrast with the isolated individualism of Achilles, whose son Neoptolemus is mentioned only once, as the son of a war-bride being brought up far away, and whose feelings for Briseis, the cause of the quarrel, veer from possessiveness to exaggerated affection and later to animosity. If Achilles shows us what a supreme hero, son of a goddess, is like, Hector embodies a more human ideal: a warrior who fights not just for glory but to protect his family and his fellow-citizens.[17] The frivolity and vanity of Paris, an archer and generally an unheroic figure, is perfectly contrasted with the more sombre and serious Hector; the adverse judgement and taunting comments of Helen reveal the disharmony that reigns in their household, where there is no child and no true marriage. Yet Paris can rally and behave well when rebuked by his brother, and is later prominent in battle: he has been disparagingly described as 'the archetypal Trojan', but this is unfair both to him and to his countrymen.[18] Finally, Priam, who is too old to fight and in some episodes cuts a curiously ineffective figure, rises to a genuinely heroic level of determination and courage when he journeys by night, at the risk of his life, to beg Achilles for Hector's corpse. The wonder and compassion which Achilles feels, and the way in which the two men sit gazing in admiration at one another, guide the audience's response (24.483, 516, 628–34). Suffering and endurance of loss are part of the heroic life as well as victory and slaughter.[19]

Returning to principles of structure, some generalizations may be offered, most of which will recur at a later stage. We have seen that Homeric poetry is characterized by repetition on both a verbal and a

---

[16] 24.762–75, esp. 767, 771–2.

[17] Other ways in which Hector and Achilles are contrasted are discussed below, pp. 71–5.

[18] Griffin 1980: 3–6 and 23 overstates the case against Paris. On p. 23 he is mistaken in saying that the wound Paris inflicts on Diomedes is 'superficial': Diomedes' heated response is mere bluff, and he is incapacitated for the remainder of the fighting (see 19.48–9). Collins 1988: 27–39 makes a case for Paris as representing an alternative 'ethic of Aphrodite'.

[19] Macleod 1982: 22 n. 2.

thematic level; situations recur, on both large and small scales, and are described in the same or comparable ways. If variations are introduced, these are often important. One striking case of a small-scale episode which provides a parallel to the main plot of the poem concerns a minor character, Euchenor, the son of a prophet. He was warned by his father that he had a choice of lives: either he could die of a slow and cruel disease at home, or else in battle at Troy. He chose the latter, and is slain by Paris in Book 13 (660–72). The motif of the choice of lives is used on a grander scale with Achilles, especially in Book 9; since the choice of a long illness is an easier one to reject, the poet makes the alternative more tempting: a long life of prosperity and comfort in his native land – but without glory (9.410–16).

Another case concerns the origins of the quarrel and of the war itself. The Greeks have come to Troy because of the abduction of a woman, Helen, after peaceful efforts have failed to recover her; the priest Chryses calls down Apollo's retribution on the Greeks because Agamemnon has seized his daughter Chryseis, after his own efforts to reclaim her have failed; and Achilles denounces Agamemnon and withdraws from the war because the king has deprived him of his prize, Briseis. The analogy between the two slave-girls is particularly clear from the parallelism of name. The poet composed naturally in such patterns.[20]

The *Iliad* achieves its vast length partly by elaboration of episodes, partly by retardation. On the whole, the more important an episode, the more fully it is narrated, usually with the addition of speeches and similes. Thus the advance of the Achaean forces in Book 2 is adorned with no fewer than four similes. When an important warrior is about to embark on an *aristeia*, he is often given an arming scene; the most extensive such scene is that of Achilles, for whom new armour is actually manufactured by the gods. When a major duel is to be fought, the gods observe and comment; their attention enhances the significance of an event. Often a less significant or less emotional incident will precede and prepare for a greater: thus the attack by Diomedes on Aphrodite can be seen as a more humorous, less formidable anticipation

---

[20] See further Schadewaldt 1938: 148; Reinhardt 1961: 63–8; Rabel 1988. Fenik 1974: 172–207 discusses the *Odyssey*'s fondness for 'character doublets' (e.g. Eurycleia and Eurynome), and illustrates this tendency also from the *Iliad*; cf. Fenik 1968: 147–50. On Briseis, see further Dué 2002.

of the attack on Ares.[21] On a larger scale, the whole episode of Diomedes' attack on the gods is a prefiguration of the more momentous battle between Achilles and the River-god. From one point of view these sequences show the poet manipulating formulaic or traditional material, but he is in control of his techniques and resources, not deploying them at random.

As for retardation, this is conspicuous in both epics on both a large and a small scale. The promise of Zeus to Thetis in Book 1 is not even referred to again for several books, and he only begins to go to work in Book 8; the return of Achilles to the field is anticipated as early as Book 9 and becomes imminent in Book 16, but does not actually take place until Book 20. The urgent message of Nestor to Achilles is delayed while Patroclus pauses to tend Eurypylus (11.809–48, taken up at 15.390–404). Similarly in specific episodes: in Book 16 the narrator has made clear that Patroclus is doomed, and we are shown Zeus looking down on the combat, pondering over the hero's fate: will he strike him down now, or allow him a little longer, a few more moments of deluded triumph? The god, here a mirror image of the poet, chooses the latter. As in Attic tragedy, the audience relishes the suspense while aware of the inevitable outcome; what is in doubt is not so much what will happen, but when and how it will happen.[22]

As the last example suggests, Homer makes extensive use of foreshadowing, whether explicit (as in the prophecy of a god or a comment by the omniscient narrator) or implicit (as in the symbolic moment when Patroclus must leave behind Achilles' spear, which he cannot lift: like other details in that scene, this suggests that he is no adequate substitute for Achilles).[23] Major prophecies by Zeus foretell subsequent events and map out the course of the poem (8.470–7; 15.49–77); narrative commentary on misguided hopes or unfulfilled prayers provide irony and poignancy (e.g. 2.419–20; 16.249–52). Other forms of intervention by the narrator include invocations (usually at powerful

---

[21] 5.318–52, 792–865. For another case, see Patroclus' assault on the wall, 16.698–711 (where he yields ground before Apollo), and his renewed onslaught at 782–804 (where Apollo strikes him down). On the principle see esp. Fenik 1974: 180–7; also M. W. Edwards 1991: 13, 19–21.

[22] 16.644–55. On retardation in general, see Reichel 1990; also Bremer 1987: 33–7. A related technique, misdirection (that is, leading the audience to expect one development and then surprising them), is also present in Homer, though less important: on this see Morrison 1992 (confined to the *Iliad*).

[23] 16.140–2. See further, for explicit cases, e.g. 2.35–40, 419–20; 11.604; 16.46–7; for implicit, e.g. 18.22–7 (pp. 117–18 below); 18.207–13 and 219–22; 22.420–2 (similes which anticipate the sack of Troy). On this whole topic, see Duckworth 1933, Reichel 1994.

moments) and résumés; also noteworthy are the frequent occasions where we are told that an event *nearly* happened, but, for example, a quick intervention by a god averted this outcome.[24] But at this point study of narrative technique merges into more detailed analysis of style, which cannot be attempted here.

Major episodes in the Homeric poems are frequently linked in some way other than by explicit cross-reference. Important parallels connect the parting of Hector and Andromache, and other moments in Book 6, with the passage in Book 22 in which Andromache learns of her husband's death. Similarly, Thetis' appearance in Book 18 in response to her son's grief is a mirror scene, a repetition of the moment in which she came to comfort him for a far less important loss in Book 1; verbal parallels reinforce the connection. The analogies between the death scenes of Patroclus and Hector are well known: the parallels are too prominent, the occasions too important, for these to be coincidental.[25] The sequence of scenes involving exchanges between Hector and Polydamas leads up to the climactic moment of wise advice ignored in Book 18.[26] Above all, the scene in Book 24 in which Priam successfully appeals to Achilles seems to cap and surpass the embassy scene in Book 9. In both, Achilles receives an unexpected visitor or visitors by night; in both, he is offered rich compensation; in both, food and drink are consumed (though in Book 24 only after the appeal has succeeded); and in both Achilles gives a passionate statement of his disillusionment. The differences are of course equally significant: Priam, a king, has come face to face with Achilles as Agamemnon did not (cf. esp. 9.372–3, 387, with 24.519–20); he has brought the treasure with him, rather than merely sending a catalogue; he humbles himself far more than the Greek ambassadors, and approaches Achilles at far greater risk.[27] As for Achilles, his self-centred eloquence in Book 9 has given way to a more sombre and compassionate mood in Book 24, and, although still bitter and quick to anger, he is able to see the parallels between his own and Priam's situations.[28]

[24] E.g. 2. 155; 8. 217; 16.698–701; see further Reinhardt 1961: 107–13; de Jong 1987a: 68–81; Nesselrath 1992; Kelly 2007b: 128–32.

[25] For detailed analysis, see Fenik 1968: 217; Janko 1992 on 16.830–63; N. J. Richardson 1993 on 22.330–67.

[26] 12.60–80, 210–50; 13.725–53; 18.249–313. See Schadewaldt 1938: 104–6; Redfield 1975: 272–7; Bannert 1988: 71–81; Reichel 1994: 175–82.

[27] The simile applied to Priam at 24.480–4 brings out the extraordinary nature of his situation: see the note in Macleod 1982.

[28] For further analysis of corresponding scenes of this type, see Schadewaldt 1938; Taplin 1992.

Something has been said about structure and characterization. A more nebulous concept is that of the poem's 'theme' or themes, as distinct from the plot. The term is sometimes used for the recurring motifs or typical episodes in Homeric epic (thus an arming scene might be an instance of a theme),[29] but here I use it in a different sense, found in analysis of literary as well as oral texts. In this context, the term refers to the larger abstract, moral, or metaphysical issues which seem to be implied or to arise out of the text. With a work as long and complex as the *Iliad*, this raises problems: must we insist on specifying a single theme for the whole, and, if not, how many themes are to be allowed? The late G. S. Kirk voiced reservations about 'single-minded interpretations in terms of tragic essence or human predicament',[30] and there are indeed dangers in losing contact with the particularities of the poem. Nevertheless, it is natural to want to go beyond mere retelling of the story, and we are on relatively safe ground in considering the issues which seem to matter most to, and to be most extensively debated by, the characters themselves. Conduct in war, the winning of honour, the rights and wrongs of the quarrel and of the war itself, the justice of the gods, and the morality of victory matter greatly to Homer's heroes and presumably to the poet and his society. The privileged access which the audience is allowed to the counsels of the gods also helps us to assess the overall import of the story, though the divine perspective raises questions as well as answering them. In the sections which follow I shall discuss three major topics: warfare, men's relation to the gods, and human error or folly. I shall try to describe the way in which the poet presents these themes and to draw out some of the possible implications for an Iliadic view of the world.[31]

2. War and the hero

In the proem we are already told that we must expect violent death in battle; the Achaean and Trojan hosts are marshalled for combat in Book 2; wholehearted conflict begins at the close of Book 4; and

[29] See further Lord 1960: 68–98; Powell 1977; M. W. Edwards 1991: 11–23 (contrast N. J. Richardson 1993: 14–24).

[30] Kirk 1985: ix – though he goes on to allow that 'such dimensions undeniably exist'.

[31] I say 'Iliadic' deliberately, since it is not necessarily the case that Homer the man held precisely these views in his everyday life: not only are literature and life distinct, but the *Iliad* itself clearly represents a deliberately selective vision of the heroic world.

warfare dominates most of the poem up to the climax of Hector's death in Book 22. Even the most memorable scenes off the battlefield – the meeting of Hector and Andromache, the embassy, the Olympian episodes, Nestor's lecture to Patroclus – are overshadowed by the war and their outcome often influences its progress. The fighting of the *Iliad* has been much studied: some of this work has concentrated on the formulaic and thematic construction of the battle scenes, while other scholars have discussed the relation of this poetic fighting to real-life tactics and warfare of the Dark Age. Finally, there has been intense discussion of the ideology of war in the *Iliad*, and of the attitudes of the poet and his characters to the slaughter which the poem relentlessly narrates.

The fighting in the *Iliad* involves large forces on both sides, but the focus is constantly narrowing to describe the exploits of individuals, usually in one-to-one combat. The leaders organize formal duels in Books 3 and 7 (Menelaus vs. Paris, Ajax vs. Hector), and in Book 22 Achilles will permit no-one else to share his revenge upon Hector; but even in books which represent a general battle scene the poet normally prefers to follow the progress of particular heroes, whether major figures of the poem or lesser characters temporarily given the limelight. True, there are passages which take a broader view, and similes sometimes describe the clash of opposing armies, but the main narrative focuses on individuals. Moreover, this is aristocratic combat: the common man is almost invisible.[32] In Book 2, Odysseus rebukes any noisy slacker of the lower ranks: 'you are of no account in war or in counsel' (202). Thersites, their clownish spokesman, gets a beating for daring to question his betters.[33] Although numerous characters are introduced, and no doubt often invented, to die in battle, the poet in his introductions usually makes them of at least respectable birth. In a bizarre passage, Thoas even recommends that the Achaeans send the common troops back to the ships, 'and let us, who can claim to be the best men among the host, stand firm' (15.294–9). His advice is followed: in a crisis, it seems, one is actually better off without the lower ranks.

There are many other respects in which the warfare of the *Iliad* is highly unrealistic, even if we set aside the numerous interventions by

---

[32] Morris 1986 and van Wees 1992b: 78–89 argue that the epics serve to 'legitimize' kingly rule (similarly Janko 1992: 38). This works well with the Thersites episode, but surely does not represent the primary purpose of the poems.

[33] See further Thalmann 1988; Reichel 1994: 106 n. 9; Halliwell 2008: 69–77. It is astonishing that Thersites figures only in a single nugatory footnote in Haubold 2000.

the gods for later discussion. The army of the Achaeans has been at Troy
for nine years, yet only after a setback in Book 7 of the poem is a defen-
sive wall constructed around the camp (this aspect also perplexed
Thucydides, who gave a different account of events on *a priori* grounds,
1.11).[34] The sources of supplies for so vast an army are never fully clari-
fied: the most explicit hint is the arrival late in Book 7 of a fleet of ships
from Lemnos bringing fresh wine.[35] There seems to be no concept of a
supporting staff of carpenters, smiths, oarsmen, or other camp-followers
to handle practical matters: the heroes themselves perform all such tasks,
and the army apparently contains no non-combatants. The physician
Machaon is wounded in 11.504–15, and, in the absence of his fellow-
doctor Podalirius, he has to be treated by amateurs (11.618–43; cf.
Eurypylus, 11.828–36). Even the aged Nestor is still active at least in
advising the charioteers on tactics, and sometimes even participates in
the fighting (4.322–3; cf. 8.80–159; 11.500–1); still more surprising is
the appearance of old Phoenix as commander of one of the columns
of the Myrmidons (16.196).[36] There are no slaves except for those
(mostly female) taken in war. Little is said about the discomfort of life
in camp (though Odysseus allows that separation from their families
for so long is indeed hard to bear; 2.289–97). The weather never varies
(except in similes), and the heroes suffer neither privation nor natural
diseases – the exception is, of course, the plague imposed on them as
divine punishment in Book 1. The heroes have horses and chariots,
which could hardly have been brought *en masse* from mainland Greece
by sea; perhaps they are thought to be part of the loot from raids in
the Troad mentioned by Achilles and others, for Diomedes captures
Aeneas' horses within the poem itself. But the chariots themselves are
mysterious vehicles: the poet seems not entirely to grasp their possible
function in war, and the heroes use them merely to ride to the battlefield,
whereupon they dismount and fight on their feet. Sometimes the concept
of chariot transport and horse-riding are confused: in one notorious passage the Trojan forces try to leap across the Achaean trench, horses, chariots, and all! (16.364–76, cf. 380).[37]

---

[34] Against Page 1959: 315–24, who argued from Thucydides for late interpolation of the passages concerning the wall, see M. L. West 1969 and Tsagarakis 1969.

[35] In the Cycle the solution was magical: *Cypria* fr. 26; cf. Griffin 1977, 40–1. On the passage in
Iliad 7 (466–82) see Finglass 2006, with the reply by Kelly 2008b.

[36] In general on the problems concerning Phoenix, see pp. 108–10 below.

[37] Janko 1992 ad loc. defends Hector's success in crossing the ditch by appealing to an earlier
passage where Apollo opened the way for the Trojan attack (15.358–9), but the lines still seem

More striking still are the actual clashes between warriors.[38] These follow regular patterns: a common sequence is for a hero to cast a spear, which misses his opponent, and for the opponent to respond with fatal effect. Alternatively, the first shot may miss its intended target but kill another hero close at hand. A chain of killings regularly develops, with a friend of the slain man rallying to avenge his comrade by attacking the slayer. The weapons used are the throwing spear, the thrusting spear and the sword; archery, though practised by certain individuals such as Paris and Teucer, is as far as possible marginalized, and the term 'archer' can even be used as an insult (11.385). Apart from the *Doloneia*, the poem almost entirely excludes any kind of fighting that would involve deception or devices other than hand-to-hand combat.[39] This partly explains the curious way in which the 'disguise' of Patroclus in Achilles' armour is handled: Patroclus is quite clear that the object is 'to make them think I am you' (16.41) but, although this is indeed the initial effect, it is not long before Sarpedon suspects an impostor (423–5), and thereafter the idea is dropped: by line 543 Glaucus is in no doubt that the new arrival is Patroclus.[40]

There is a recognized hierarchy of heroes on both sides, though a particular hero's status may be questioned or mockingly challenged in moments of anger. Major heroes slay more people than minor figures; moreover, it is virtually impossible for a minor hero to kill a major figure, and this can only be achieved with the aid of a god (as Apollo will aid Paris in slaying Achilles, 22.359–60). Success is swift once a hero actually confronts his foe: duels are rarely prolonged beyond a single exchange of shots. If a man is wounded, he either dies at once or is rescued by his allies and recovers. Pain is real but short-lived: the hero may groan deeply, but Homer does not show his characters delirious or raving in pain (contrast Soph. *Phil.* 730–806).

difficult. However, van Wees 2004 (and earlier articles) argues that modern scholarship has been over-sceptical about the presentation of chariots in Homer.

[38] Fundamental treatment by Fenik 1968; see also Strasburger 1954; W. H. Friedrich 1956; Krischer 1971; Kirk 1976: ch. 3; Latacz 1977; Mueller 1984: ch. 3 (a very useful brief account); Kirk 1990: 15–27; van Wees 1992a, 1992b, 2004: ch. 11. Willcock 1983b compares Homeric and Virgilian battle scenes.

[39] The brief reference to ambushes by Idomeneus in 13.279–87 (cf. 1.226–7) is abnormal. Contrast the *Odyssey*, and see further A. T. Edwards 1985: ch. 1. Deception and treachery were more prominent in the Cyclic poems: e.g. Odysseus and Diomedes murdered Palamedes in the *Cypria* (fr. 27); the same heroes sneaked into Troy and stole the Palladium in the *Little Iliad* (fr. 11).

[40] For another reason for the dropping of this motif, see M. W. Edwards 1987a: 57. Ibid. 261 thinks even Sarpedon's uncertainty is a stock motif, cf. 5.175–6.

If the wound is not severe, careful medical treatment (occasionally with divine intervention) restores him to unblemished health. Only in exceptional cases – Sarpedon, Patroclus, and Hector – can the dying man even speak a few words before the end. Perhaps most strikingly of all, there are no walking wounded: on neither side do we see cripples or other permanently maimed warriors. After battle has ended, the bodies must be recovered and burned with honours: this procedure is carried out with dignity and without gruesome descriptions of the condition of the dead.

All of these conventions serve to create a highly artificial yet curiously convincing world, in which warfare is straightforward and noble.[41] Naturally victory in the war remains the ultimate goal, but in the day-to-day action of the battlefield the most important challenge for each warrior is to face the foe courageously, and if necessary to meet a heroic death. Individual achievement is of greater moment than overall strategy or united planning. Despite the occasional wise pronouncement by Nestor, there is little in the way of tactical discussion before the battle, and next to none when actually on the field. Obligations and duties are conceived on a personal level: naturally one rallies to the aid of a friend or a brother in danger. But the immediate aim is simple: to kill one's opponents until the enemy are put to flight. Beyond that, the Achaeans are fighting for glory and booty, as well as to win back Helen and avenge the insult to Menelaus' honour. The Trojans, whom many modern readers find more sympathetic, are fighting for their city's survival and for their wives and children (15.494–9); the scenes in Troy in Book 6 show us something of what this means. Hence the Trojans, a threatened community, have no choice but to fight. Whether the war is worth fighting, whether the suffering is justified, is something which can only be considered by those on the Achaean side, and in the *Iliad* only Achilles has the leisure and the insight to ask such questions.

At the heart of the value system of the Homeric heroes is honour, *timē*, expressed through the respect of one's peers and embodied in tangible forms – treasure, gifts, women, an honourable place at the feast. In time of war it is inevitable that honour be won above all through prowess in battle, ability as a leader and a fighter. Other qualities are also admired – ability as a speaker, piety, sound judgement and

---

[41] See Griffin 1980, *passim*, e.g. 48–9.

advice, loyalty, hospitality, gentleness, but these are secondary and the last would indeed be out of place in combat. The crisis of the *Iliad* arises because the greatest of the Greek warriors is not given the honour (both prizes and respect) which he feels to be his due. Because he is a hero, and quick to anger, he will not tolerate this treatment. The situation is worsened by the tactless and injudicious aggressiveness of Agamemnon, and there are no constitutional procedures which can defuse the dispute. It has been plausibly argued that Agamemnon has no clearly defined authority over his fellow-kings, but acts as *de facto* overlord because of the size of his forces (100 ships) and his relationship to the wronged Menelaus.[42] A further contributing factor is Achilles' bitterness at the prospect of a short life: in his knowledge of his own future he differs from all other major characters in the poem (1. 352; 9.410–16, etc.). Despite his passionate account of his own motives in Book 9, his fellow-Greeks cannot understand the depth of his feelings.

The heroic outlook on life, above all as expressed in the speeches of Achilles, is one of the great contributions of the *Iliad* to western literature.[43] Modern discussions have perhaps tended to schematize 'heroic ethics' too rigidly. A few memorable lines are naturally prominent in these discussions: 'always to excel, and to be superior to other men' (6.208 = 11.783); 'one omen is best, to fight for one's native land' (12.243); 'I feel terrible shame before the Trojans and the Trojan women with their trailing robes, if like a base man I hang back and skulk away from the war' (6.441–3). Most famous of all, justly, is Sarpedon's speech to Glaucus in Book 12, which sums up the hero's credo with moving simplicity and realism (12.310–28):

'Glaucus, why is it that we two are held in the highest honour in Lycia, with pride of place, the best of the meat, the wine-cup always full, and all look on us like gods, and we have for our own use a great cut of the finest land by the banks of the Xanthos...? That is why we should now be taking our stand at the front of the Lycian lines and facing the blaze of battle.... Dear friend, if we were going to live for ever, ageless and immortal, if we survived this war, then I would not be fighting in the front ranks myself or urging you into the battle where men win glory. But as it is, whatever we do the fates of death stand over us in a thousand forms, and no mortal can run from them or escape them – so let us go, and either give his triumph to another man, or he to us.'[44]

[42] Taplin 1990; Reichel 1994: 198–203.

[43] Bowra 1957: ch. 2 and 1961: ch. 3; also Bowra 1964. More recently, see e.g. van Wees 1992b: 64–5, 69–77, 107–25.

[44] Translation from Hammond 1987, slightly modified.

Things are not as simple as Sarpedon's account suggests. There is a potential conflict between the striving for individual excellence and the collaborative effort to achieve an end in unison: the individual may pursue his own prestige to the detriment of the army as a whole, as happens when Achilles dismisses his fellow-Greeks and allows them to die.[45] In the end, Achilles bitterly reproaches himself not only for the death of Patroclus but for many others' as well (18.102–3; 19.61–2) – because of his insistence that he receive the honour he believes he is due. The complexities are differently illuminated by the case of Hector. Unlike Achilles and unlike his self-centred brother Paris, Hector has played the very role that Sarpedon envisages, as a king who fights among the foremost, inspires his men, defends his fatherland. But his very devotion to this task, his own prowess and success as a fighter, carries him too far, bringing both leader and army to the brink of disaster. Standing outside Troy and facing defeat, Hector dreads the accusation, partly justified, that in his pride and self-confidence he has destroyed the host (22.107).

'The host', the people (normally *laos*), have become more prominent in some recent discussions of Homer.[46] The leaders of the armies may be superior in birth, status, and wealth than the rank and file, but they cannot entirely ignore the common soldier. The very first scene of the *Iliad* highlights the fact that Agamemnon, in rejecting Chryses' appeal, is ignoring the will of the people in assembly (1.22–3), and it is the people who suffer in consequence (51–2). The assembly scenes of Books 2 and 19 in particular remind us of the role of the masses, and the need for the rulers to sustain their authority and retain the loyalty of the people. Even Achilles is conscious of the discontent among his Myrmidon followers while he abstains from battle (16.200–7). Along with much else, the *Iliad* is an early exploration of community politics. It is of course possible to overstate this element; the populace has little power to do more than express its dissatisfaction. Horace sardonically commented: *quidquid delirant reges, plectuntur Achivi* ('whatever lunacy the kings get up to, the Greek army takes the knocks') (*Epist.* 1.2.14; he obviously has the beating up of Thersites in mind). Nevertheless, the origins of Greek political discourse are clearly visible in Homer, as in Hesiod, and the conflict of interest between personal honour and civic responsibility is at the heart of the main plot. This would remain

---

[45] See Irwin 1989: ch. 2.
[46] For what follows see especially Hammer 2002; Haubold 2000; Barker 2009; Allan and Cairns 2011.

a key issue in Greek society: in the fifth century, the *Ajax* of Sophocles memorably developed the theme.[47]

The special status of Achilles makes him an exceptional case: a more 'normal' hero – Diomedes, for instance – would not react so tempestuously to an insult as Achilles, nor hold out so long against Agamemnon's overtures.[48] Moreover, though all heroes value honour and respond to challenges, different heroes excel in different fields: thus Odysseus is superior at stratagem and counsel, Achilles in combat. Paris, archer and sensualist, seems only to be a hero on a part-time basis, though it is true that he responds readily enough to protests from Hector. Taplin has argued that the whole conception of a 'heroic code' should be abandoned as over-simplifying; in particular, he rejects the assertion by Finley (in one of the weakest sections of a valuable book), that 'The heroic code was complete and unambiguous, so much so that neither the poet nor his characters ever had occasion to debate it.'[49] In this emphatic form, such a view is clearly untenable: the characters of the epic regularly hold rational as well as heated discussions of proper conduct, though it is of course true that they do not debate abstractions in the manner of speakers in Plato's dialogues. Patroclus faces a conflict of loyalties, between his friend Achilles and the rest of the Greeks. Nestor, Odysseus, and Diomedes in various scenes recall Agamemnon to the demands of his position and correct his misguided suggestions. In Book 19, the argument between Odysseus and Achilles about whether the army should eat is a dispute between passion and expediency. Sound advice and good judgement are valued, and Achilles himself ruefully admits that others are superior to him in these areas.[50] But it remains true that, apart from Achilles, few of the heroes in the *Iliad* have cause or opportunity to question the values by which they live or the justification for their own behaviour.

In an influential discussion, E. R. Dodds described Homeric society as a 'shame-culture' rather than a 'guilt-culture'; that is, the primary source of morality in that society was what others said and thought about you, rather than a self-conscious assessment of the moral rightness and wrongness of one's actions, irrespective of others'

---

[47] Goldhill 1986: 154–61; note also Arist., *An. Post.* 97b15, identifying Achilles, Ajax, and Alcibiades as men characterized by pride.

[48] Andersen 1978; Griffin 1980: 74; Macleod 1982: 25 n. 1.

[49] Taplin 1992, 6–7, 50–1, 71–2, 166 against Finley 1979: 113, cf. 115.

[50] See 18.105–6, and further Schofield 1986; also Greenhalgh 1972.

opinions.[51] Homer's heroes are indeed alert to potential loss of face, and this motivates many of the most important decisions of the poem. 'I would be called a coward and a good-for-nothing, if I am to yield to you in whatever you say', declares Achilles to Agamemnon (1.293–4). 'I feel shame before the Trojans,' says Hector, and remains on the field to face his death (22.105, echoing 6.442). Subsequent interpretation has sometimes taken this insight so far as virtually to deny any other moral force in the Homeric universe: Homeric society is, it is claimed, a 'results-culture', where only success counts.[52] Competitive values must overwhelm gentler attitudes and cooperative ethics.[53] Moreover, the inner man – the sense of obligation, responsibility, or conscience – is virtually eradicated. Here moral and psychological analysis meet, since it has also been maintained that 'Homeric man has no unified concept of what we call "soul" or "personality"'.[54]

A moderate version of this argument now prevails. As Dodds himself allowed, shame and guilt are not mutually exclusive motivations, in an individual or a society, and Homer's characters do show themselves affected by other considerations besides loss of face.[55] Indeed, *aidōs* itself, the term commonly rendered as 'shame', is a concept which covers more than the English term might imply: it also includes embarrassment, a sense of inhibition, and respect, including self-respect.[56] Important passages can be cited in which other moral or emotional factors override the simple consideration of 'what people will say'. Achilles did not strip Andromache's father of his armour, 'for he felt awe at that in his heart' (*sebassato*; 6.417). Achilles' grief and self-reproach at the harm he has brought upon Patroclus (and, indeed, his other friends) also go beyond any sense of loss of prestige (18.102–4; 21.134–5). *Aidōs* is felt towards the suppliant in the case of Priam in Book 24, yet many suppliants are slain elsewhere in the poem, and there is no

---

[51] Dodds 1951: chs. 1–2, esp. 17–18, 28, 47–50. For modern studies of honour and shame, see e.g. J. K. Campbell 1964; Peristiany 1965; also Lloyd-Jones 1990; Scodel 2008. Recent approaches are surveyed by Cairns 2011.

[52] Adkins 1960, and many subsequent articles. For criticism, see Long 1970 (contrast Adkins 1971); Lloyd-Jones 1971: ch. 1; Dover 1983; B. Williams 1993; Zanker 1994, esp. ch. 1. A polemical exchange between Adkins, Gagarin, and Lloyd-Jones may be found in Adkins 1987; Gagarin 1987; and Lloyd-Jones 1987. Rowe 1983 is a review of the issues. Yamagata 1994 retraces the ground at book length.

[53] Again the terminology derives from Adkins, e.g. 1960, 31–46.

[54] Dodds 1951: 15. Cf. Snell 1953: ch. 1, esp. 17–20; Fränkel 1975: 75–80. Contrast B. Williams 1993: ch. 1; also Fenik 1978b, and the works cited in n. 89 below.

[55] Lloyd-Jones 1971; Dover 1983.

[56] Cairns 1993, an exhaustive treatment; see also B. Williams 1993: ch. 4.

implication that Achilles would have been regarded with disapproval by
his peers if he had struck down the aged king. It is not loss of face he
fears but (if anything) the anger of the gods; even that motive is overwhelmed by fellow-feeling and pity for a weak old man.

What of heroic morality in the context of the battlefield?[57] That men
die in war is a truism (calculations differ, but one scholar counts 318
deaths in the *Iliad*); but the *way* in which Homer's characters kill, the
fervour of bloodlust and the viciousness of some of the wounds, have
disturbed many readers in recent times. There is a certain taste for
gruesome descriptions, and some of the wounds, though occasionally
impossible, are ghoulishly narrated.[58] The spear lodged in a dying
man's heart still vibrates in the air with the desperate efforts of the
heart's final beating (13.441–4); a man's eyeballs fall to the earth at
his feet (13.616–7; 16.741–2); the brain comes oozing out from the
eyeholes along the spear (17.296). Agamemnon, in a scene which
sets the pattern for denial of supplications in the poem, urges
Menelaus to kill the helpless Adrastus: let no Trojan escape, not even
the child still slumbering in the mother's womb (6.57–60).[59] Dead
men are decapitated, their heads sent rolling through the crowd of
the battlefield (11.146, 261; 13.203). Hector threatens to stick the
head of Patroclus upon a stake (17.126 and 18.175), and the related
threats of denial of burial and permanent mutilation of the corpse
gain prominence by increasingly frequent repetition in the last third
of the epic.[60] That threat is finally perpetrated by Achilles upon
Hector; his revenge for Patroclus also extends to the unique horror of
human sacrifice, passed over hastily and perhaps uneasily by the
poet.[61] The ultimate barbarity of cannibalism does not go beyond a
threat, though uttered with appalling force: 'If only the strength and
the heart within me might drive me to hack off your limbs and eat
them raw, such harm you have done me.'[62]

---

[57] See further Segal 1971b; Vermeule 1979: ch. 3; Parker 1985.

[58] The standard instance of an impossible wound is 13.545–9. For gruesomeness, see W. H.
Friedrich 1956; Griffin 1980: 91; Mueller 1984: 82–6. Saunders 1999 (not for the squeamish) presents the medical facts.

[59] On supplication, see above all Gould 1973 (80 n. 39 for a full list) (= Gould 2001: 32 n. 39);
also Thornton 1984; Goldhill 1990; Crotty 1994; Naiden 2006.

[60] Segal 1971b: 18–47. See also Griffin 1980: 44–6, for Eastern parallels and contrasts.

[61] Threatened at 21.27–31, fulfilled at 23.175–83. Cf. G. Murray 1934: ch. 5.

[62] Achilles to Hector, 22.346–7; cf. 4.34–6, Zeus to Hera on her hatred for the Trojans; also
24.212–13, Hecuba on Achilles. See Redfield 1975: 197–9; Griffin 1980: 20.

How are we to regard these endlessly brutal slayings? Is this the inevitable content of a battle epic, which Homer would avoid if he could?
That view would be hard to sustain, given the fullness of the description
and the length at which Homer narrates these conflicts. When a hero
launches upon an *aristeia*, the audience is surely meant to sympathize
with his energy and to relish the excitement of the battlefield, to
enjoy the cruel wit of the taunts directed at his opponents; the analogies
drawn with the modern western or war film are not unreasonable.[63] It
does not follow, however, that Homer is merely a glorious primitive,
revelling in the savagery of an age in which violence came naturally.[64]
We must distinguish the poet from his characters, and also between
the characters in the heat of battle and in calmer or more reflective
moments. The violence of the slaughter is balanced by the sympathetic
treatments of the victims, whose deaths are often softened with a beautiful simile or dignified with one of the famous epitaphs or 'necrolo-
gues'.[65] Besides the similes, the extended description of the scenes on
Achilles' shield reminds us of other aspects of life, far from the horrors:
there we find scenes of marriage and celebration, ploughing and har-
vesting, within the framework of earth, sea, and sky. War is on the
shield too, but it is a more 'normal', local kind of warfare, seen as a
part of the larger world of human existence.[66]

The anger and distress of the survivors in the war, and still more the
moving portrayal of the non-combatants such as the women of Troy or
Briseis in the Greek camp, make sufficiently clear that dismay at the
savagery and grief for those who have fallen are not inappropriate or
anachronistic reactions. As for Achilles' mutilation of Hector, it
seems important that this is a repeated action, prolonged artificially
for days after the actual slaying; in this it differs from the decapitations
and other violent wounds perpetrated by Agamemnon and Meriones.[67]

---

[63] See Vermeule 1979, esp. 99–103; Parks 1990.

[64] A memorable essay by S. Weil, 'The *Iliad* as a Poem of Force' (Weil 1940–1), emphasizes
both the pity and the horror of Homeric warfare; the horror is more cheerfully accepted by
Finley 1979: 118 ('The poet and his audience lingered lovingly over every act of slaughter') and
by Vermeule 1979: 84, 85, 96, 99, 114 (who speaks of 'wit' and 'ballet' in the battle scenes).

[65] E.g. 4.473–89 (well discussed by Schein 1984: 73–6), 5.152–8 (the bereaved father), 11.241–
7 (the bride left behind); more examples in Strasburger 1954; Griffin 1980: ch. 4. For similes used
to enhance the pathos of death, see e.g. 8.306–7; Porter 1972.

[66] On the shield, see Schadewaldt 1965: 352–74; Reinhardt 1961: 401–11; Taplin 1980. There
has been much interest in the shield among students of *ecphrasis* (the formal description of a work
of art in literature): e.g. Becker 1995, with earlier bibliography.

[67] It is misguided to lay too much stress on the phrases 'unseemly acts' and 'harsh deeds'
(22.395; 23.24, 176), used to describe Achilles' actions (as is done by e.g. Bowra 1930: 21;

The continuous victimization of Hector represents an impossible wish on Achilles' part to extend his revenge indefinitely; it would not even be possible if the gods were not preserving Hector's corpse from decay, and in the scene on Olympus in Book 24 we see that the gods themselves, prompted by Apollo, view Achilles' excesses with displeasure. To deny that Homer treats death in war as both glorious and tragic is to deny something vital to the greatness of the *Iliad*.

3. Gods and men[68]

It is obvious that the gods are fundamental to the nature of the *Iliad*. Not only do their activities underlie the action and provide its premises (the Judgement of Paris, the abduction of Helen), and not only do they regularly intervene in the events narrated in the poem; the poet also allows his audience to observe the life of the gods, which becomes an essential foil or contrast to the existence of men. 'Thus the gods have woven destiny for unhappy mortals, for them to live in misery. But they themselves are free of cares' (24.525–6). The most important aspect of the gods in the *Iliad* is the way in which they help to define the human condition.

Immortal themselves, the gods are involved in various ways in the world of mortals. They depend on them for sacrifice and regard this and the other honours which humans pay them as their due.[69] Divinities may also be the parents of mortals through brief liaisons with human lovers: Aphrodite and Aeneas, Zeus and Sarpedon, and above all Thetis and Achilles: her marriage to Peleus seems to be an unusual case of a longer relationship, but by the time of the *Iliad* she has returned to the sea and Peleus lives alone. Gods may also have particular favourites among mortals, without any kinship between them: Aphrodite cares for Paris, Athena for Odysseus. More broadly, this favouritism extends to cities and their peoples: although the gods receive worship from all, they may have special affection for certain places: thus Hera cares most for Argos, Sparta, and Mycenae, while

---

Segal 1971b: 13); they do not necessarily convey moral criticisms. See Griffin 1980: 85; Vermeule 1979: 234 n. 11; Hainsworth 1993: 49–50; N. J. Richardson 1993; and de Jong 2012, ad loc.
    [68] See esp. Griffin 1980: chs. 5–6; Erbse 1986; M. W. Edwards 1987a: ch. 17; Kirk 1990: 1–14; Janko 1992: 1–7. On religion more generally, see above all Burkert 1985 and Bremmer 1994. For illustrations of the gods in art, see Simon 1985.
    [69] For various consequences of this see Parker 1998.

Zeus admits to particular affection for Troy (4.44–52). In the *Iliad*, the gods are thoroughly involved in the war, often fighting in disguise on one side or the other. Athena, Hera, and Poseidon have a special hatred for Troy: in vain the Trojan women convey rich offerings to Athena's temple in an attempt to win her over (6.237–311). It is a striking example of Homer's sympathy with the Trojans that they are not represented as worshipping some separate pantheon of barbarian gods (contrast Virgil, *Aeneid,* 8.698–700).[70]

As in other areas, we must distinguish between what the characters know of the gods and what the poet tells or represents.[71] The mortals in the Homeric poems generally regard the gods as powerful supporters; in particular, they regularly assume that they will reward piety and uphold justice. Thus, in Book 4, Agamemnon declares that the Trojans, who have broken the truce, will receive certain punishment as oath-breakers should; similarly Menelaus declares that Paris and the other Trojans will be punished in the end for their offences against Zeus, god of hospitality (4.155–68; 13.620–7). The reality is more complex and disturbing, for the gods as shown in their own habitat display little concern for justice as humans understand it. Zeus yields to Thetis' importuning out of reluctance to reject her request (and perhaps from gratitude for past favours), even though it will mean the death of many Greeks. The gods themselves plot to disrupt the truce sworn in their name. Apollo strikes Patroclus down and renders him helpless, as later Athena lures Hector to his doom. The favouritism shown by Aphrodite to Paris is even less defensible on moral grounds: having aided him in his seduction of Helen, she whisks him away from deserved retribution. Although gods do sometimes respond to human prayers, their response is swiftest when their own honour is involved, as when Apollo sends plague to punish the Greek army for spurning his priest.[72] The heartfelt prayer of Hector, that his son may grow up to be a great fighter and bring joy to his mother, receives no reply (6.476–81).[73]

This contrast between human and divine perspective permits much irony and pathos. Human hopes and fears are prompted by their lack

---

[70] E. Hall 1989, 43–5.

[71] Jörgensen 1904.

[72] Cf. the stories of Niobe (24.602–9) and of Meleager's father (9.533–7); Page 1973a: 79–83; Weiler 1974.

[73] On this case, and on prayers in Homer more generally, see Macleod 1982: 42; more bibliography in Reichel 1994: 73; Pulleyn 1997.

of knowledge of the future; even Achilles understands only in part what his own future involves, and is crucially blind to the significance of a divine warning (18.6–14). Agamemnon is deluded by a false dream, and supposes he will sack Troy on the very next day (2.35–9). Patroclus asks Achilles to send him forth to battle, 'in his great folly, for he was praying for evil death and doom for himself' (16.46–7); much is made in Book 16 of the fact that Patroclus is fighting, so to speak, on borrowed time. Even when a divine message grants a mortal some insight, it is partial and often misunderstood or neglected: thus Hector forgets the limitations set on his success, and anticipates further victories beyond the day that Zeus promised him (11.193–4; 17.453–5; 18.293–5).[74] The gods themselves feel the pity of the situation: rather than presenting them solely as capricious or sadistic gamesters, Homer often shows Zeus in particular observing events with concern and compassion (15.12; 16.644–55; 17.198–208). Yet the essence of the divine is that it is separate from the human: the gods can always turn away and rest their eyes from combat, which man cannot escape (13.1–7). For this reason mankind and its concerns can be regarded as trivial: 'you would not call me sensible if I were to fight with you over wretched mortals', comments Apollo to Poseidon (21.462–4; cf. 1.574, 8.428). The exception is Thetis: once married to a mortal, devoted to her mortal son, she is bound up with the human world as the other gods are not.[75]

The paradigm case of the contrast between human and divine spheres is the first book of the *Iliad*, in which the disagreements on Olympus, arising from Hera's suspicion of Zeus, mirror the human quarrel between Achilles and Agamemnon. The uncertain authority of Agamemnon is contrasted with the unchallengeable supremacy of Zeus, king of the gods; the comical figure of Hephaestus, the peacemaker, is a light-hearted reflection of Nestor, who intervenes without success in an effort to calm the heroes. Detailed verbal connections confirm the parallel. But the scene on earth ends with the angry departure of Achilles, which will bring 'innumerable woes'; on Olympus, although bitterness remains, the quarrel is temporarily suspended as the gods laugh at Hephaestus' antics; forgetting the affairs of mortals, they turn to enjoy the feast and the song of Apollo and the Muses. Human beings cannot be important enough to spoil the festivities.[76]

---

[74] R. B. Rutherford 1982: 156–7, with other examples.
[75] In general on Thetis' role in the *Iliad*, see Slatkin 1991.
[76] The scene is discussed in detail by Halliwell 2008: 77–86.

This opposition, between tragically serious mortals and frivolous divinities, is one of the most brilliant creative strokes of the epic tradition. The 'divine comedy' can, however, be overstated: it is always possible for the gods to reassert their authority and their dignity, as Zeus does in this book. Yet total seriousness is denied them, for they are immortal and cannot suffer or perish. Hence Longinus' famous paradox: 'Homer, it seems to me, has done his best to make the men of the Trojan War gods, and the gods men' (*On the Sublime*, 9.7).

Despite the frequency with which the gods appear and the apparent abundance of detail in their treatment, the *Iliad* is extremely selective in its presentation of the divine. The focus is mainly on a few major divinities (Zeus, Apollo, Hera, Athena, Aphrodite, Poseidon; more rarely Hephaestus, Hermes, Iris, and others). The earlier background of wars among the gods, including the overthrow of Cronos, is taken for granted but only mentioned in vague terms. There are passing references to Demeter, Dionysus, Hades, Persephone, the Erinyes, and other powers, but these do not play speaking roles. The exclusion of Demeter and Dionysus has sometimes been explained on the grounds that they are less aristocratic, more popular gods; it may be more plausible to maintain that they are benefactors of all humanity, and so not easily fitted in to the partisan line-up of deities in the Trojan War. The powers of the underworld are more easily explained, since the *Iliad* is clearly averse to this more uncanny side of the supernatural; we hear almost nothing of what Hades' realm is like, and the finality of death is a central fact of the *Iliad*, an essential premise of the heroic outlook. There are no exceptions: 'even Heracles died', says Achilles as he accepts his own fate; and Castor and Pollux both lie under the soil in their homeland. The *Odyssey*, by contrast, allows Menelaus immortality together with Helen, daughter of Zeus, and seems also to be aware of the legend that Castor and Pollux enjoyed immortality day and day about. Later poetry was still more accommodating.[77]

Those gods who do appear are presented as an extended family, mostly resident together on Olympus; like any family, they have their disagreements and their changing moods. Zeus is affectionate towards both Aphrodite and Athena; Hera uses her feminine charms to try to get her way; Aphrodite is sometimes at odds with Hera, sometimes willing to help her. In other scenes the appropriate human parallel may be rather

---

[77] *Il.* 18.117; 3.243–4; *Od.* 4.561–69; cf. *Od.* 11.299–304, on Castor and Pollux. See M. L. West 1978 on Hes. *Op.* 166–7; Griffin 1977: 42.

the court of a king and his fellow-nobles: we have seen that Zeus possesses the authority that Agamemnon would like to have. In Book 15,
Poseidon asserts his status like a blustering aristocrat, but eventually
yields to the threat of Zeus's superior power (185–217, esp. 185–6,
206–10). Yet Zeus sometimes faces determined opposition (as at the
opening of Book 4) and occasionally he must allow an outcome which
he does not himself want, as when his son Sarpedon must die in Book 16.

Some at least of Homer's conception of the gods is 'poetic' in the
sense that it probably lacks any basis in cult. Homeric religion is both
selective and creative. The detailed description of scenes on Olympus,
such as the cloud garage in which Hera keeps her chariot; the robots
of Hephaestus; Poseidon's chariot ride, with the sea creatures gambolling
in his wake; the mysterious ichor which runs in the gods' veins – all of
these are surely colourful elaborations. The idea of a god intervening
in human disguise is closer to everyday belief,[78] but the forms which
that belief is given in epic spring from a poetic imagination: Athena seizing Achilles by the hair from behind, whereupon he spins round and
recognizes her, though for others she is invisible (1.194–200); Apollo
smashing through the Achaean wall like a playful child destroying a sandcastle (15.360–6); Zeus brandishing the aegis high upon Mount Ida,
while thunder shakes the mountain (17.591–6). Images such as these
influenced all later Greek poetic presentation of the gods and much of
Greek art.[79] The pre-eminent example is Pheidias' statue of Zeus at
Olympia, one of the wonders of the ancient world: the artist is said to
have modelled it on the majestic lines in which Zeus nods his head in
promise to Thetis (1.528–30, with Dio Chrys. 12.25, etc.).

I have implicitly assumed that one form of interpretation, which sees the
gods as symbols of natural forces or human psychological impulses, is mistaken. Such an approach not only makes nonsense of the scenes in which
gods are represented on their own, talking, fighting, or making love; it also
runs into difficulties even with the scenes such as Athena's restraint of
Achilles, or Helen's exchange with Aphrodite, which the approach was
devised to explain. For the purposes of the poem, the gods are real and
play a physical part in the poem; they are part of the natural world, though
existing on a higher plane than mortals. As we have seen, the poet embroiders their life and personalities imaginatively (unexceptionable in a society
which lacked a formal creed limiting the options of believers); he

---

[78] Cf. *Od.* 17.483–7; Kearns 1982; Lane Fox 1986: ch. 4.
[79] Burkert 1985: 119–25.

sometimes introduces characters who are indeed personifications (Fear and Panic, companions of Ares, for example). But to suggest that the gods were fictions or symbols to the poet or his audience is perverse.

The precise relationship of divine influence and human response is more difficult: sometimes we seem to have 'double motivation', where the divine prompting duplicates the natural reaction of the mortal character, but in certain cases the god's influence seems more compelling (as perhaps in 16.684–91). Even then, however, the gods seem to work on what they find in the human heart: it is predictable, for instance, that the resourceful Odysseus should be the one whom Athena prompts to stop the rout in Book 2 (167–82).[80] Naturally enough, mortals are often confused or uncertain in these cases; in some circumstances tact or self-defensiveness may cause one of them to emphasize the divine role unjustifiably.[81] Some of the characters refer to the malign influence of 'Atē', often rendered 'madness' but probably better interpreted as 'affliction' or 'harm'. Whatever the exact sense, Atē is a divine force or personification, which characters can blame for their own errors or blindness. She is prominent in Agamemnon's famously awkward apology in Book 19.[82] But the normal Homeric rule is that a human is responsible for his or her actions, whether or not a god was involved (something which it is hard for the characters to establish). With rare exceptions, there is no suggestion that the presence of the gods eliminates human motivation or decision-making.[83]

The vindictiveness of Hera and Athena, and the frivolity of the gods in combat, astonish readers who assume that gods should be upholders of morality and should exemplify that morality in their own behaviour. Yet, although the links are sometimes tenuous, religion is not entirely dissociated from morality in Homer.[84] We have seen that the mortal characters expect that oath-breakers will receive punishment: the

---

[80] See esp. Lesky 1961; also Willcock 1970; Versnel 2011: 163–78.

[81] As 3.164, Priam to Helen; 19.86–138, Agamemnon's apology; more outrageously, Paris at 3.439 (see p. 106 below). See Dodds 1951: ch. 1; Hutchinson 1985 on Aesch. *Sept.* 4–9; Taplin 1990: 75–7; and M. W. Edwards 1991: 245–7 on 19.85–138.

[82] This was the starting point for Dodds's classic discussion, but for criticism of his analysis see already Barrett 1964 on Eur. *Hipp.* 241. On the interpretation of Ate ('harm' or 'Ruin'), see esp. Cairns 2012.

[83] For one particularly complex case, Aphrodite and Helen in *Iliad* 3, see pp. 104–6 below. Another in which psychic intervention is clearly involved, and which seems to involve some distortion of the mortal's 'natural' reactions, is Athena's prompting of Penelope to show herself to the suitors in *Odyssey* 18, a controversial scene (see R. B. Rutherford 1992: 29–33; D. Steiner 2010: 179–203).

[84] For an argument that divine justice is much more significant than I have allowed here, see Allan 2006.

invocations at solemn moments of ritual in Books 3 and 19 refer to
such punitive action as taking place in the underworld, and these
assumptions are not contradicted elsewhere in the poem. Zeus is also
concerned with oaths, and in certain passages seems to be regarded
as lord of hospitality.[85] A difficult passage in Book 1 seems to associate
the leading Greeks with Zeus in their function as overseers of the *the-
mistes* ('ordinances'; 1.238–9). In a famous simile, Zeus is described
as sending storms upon men who have perverted justice in the assembly
(16.384–93); the vocabulary and morality seem close to the *Odyssey* and
to Hesiod's *Works and Days*.[86] Most important of all is Book 24, where
the gods debate, if not the justice, at least the propriety of Achilles' continued revenge, and where Zeus declares that he must be brought to
rein or suffer the gods' anger. Hector's piety, stressed throughout
that book, deserves some recognition and reward. In a work which narrates an episode of destructive war, in which good men die on both
sides, the gods must often seem callous or malicious. In some episodes
they are depicted as anxious to save their favourites, but the opposition
from other gods is too great (a good example of the explanatory powers
of polytheism). In other cases it seems that the gods, including even
Zeus, must yield to the impersonal force of fate: thus Sarpedon must
die, and Zeus himself weeps tears of blood for his son.[87] This too is a poetic concept introduced for pathetic effect, and should not be pressed for
theology. There is more explicit reflection on the gods' role in relation to
human wrongdoing in the *Odyssey* (pp. 83–4 below), though even there
the poet does not achieve a totally coherent picture.[88]

4. Choices and consequences

As has already been implied, Homeric characters are clearly conceived
personalities who make deliberate decisions.[89] Often but not always

---

[85] Zeus invoked at oath-taking: 3.104, 274, 298–301, 320. See 3.351–4 and 13.625 (Menelaus)
for Zeus Xeinios. The oath-breaker Pandarus is indeed killed shortly after his offence, though it is
not clear whether this is to be seen as either divine or poetic justice: see A. Parry 1971: lvii n. 1;
Taplin 1992: 104–9.

[86] Cf. 18.507–8; Hes. *Theog.* 85–6 with West's note; Hes. *Op.* 35–6, 250–69.

[87] 16.458–61. In general, see Greene 1944; Dietrich 1965; Burkert 1985: 129–30; Janko 1992:
4–7.

[88] Dodds 1951: 32–4; Lloyd-Jones 1971: 28–32, Fenik 1974: 208–30; Kullmann 1985; Versnel
2011: ch. 2, esp. 156–7.

[89] Sharples 1983; Halliwell 1990; Gaskin 1990; M. Clarke 1999: 66–9.

these are based on rational considerations or moral assumptions: thus
Odysseus contemplates flight in Book 11, but concludes that this is
not a step that he, an *aristos*, one of the heroic elite, can legitimately
take (11.403–10).[90] In many cases, the character's choice is made in
the heat of the moment, sometimes in the grip of anger, grief, hatred,
anxiety, or some other highly emotional force. Aristotle compared
epic to drama: both genres present individuals in action, and it is
through their actions and choices that their character is illuminated.[91]
This could be shown in detail by following the presentation of many
of the characters, but the most important cases are Hector and
Achilles. A brief survey of the major choices of each of these two heroes
will assist comparison.

The chief scenes involving Hector in significant decisions are in
Book 6, where he resists the blandishments of his womenfolk, above
all the pleading of his wife, and resolves to return to the battle; in
Book 18, where he violently rejects the advice of Polydamas to return
to the city; and in Book 22, where he chooses to remain outside the
walls despite the pleas of his father and mother.[92] Later in the same
book his nerve cracks and he runs from Achilles, his former resolve sha-
ken; deceived by Athena, he stands and fights after running; finally, seeing his doom clearly, he makes a last heroic stand: 'let me at least not
die without effort and without glory, but only once I have achieved
some great deed, for posterity to be told of' (22.304–5). Each of
these scenes has been much discussed: in the first, we see what
Hector is fighting for, and what he means to his family, and we witness
the transition from bleak realism, as he acknowledges the inevitable fate
of Troy, to a tempered hope for the future founded on resolution.[93] In
the second, the key example of Hector's bad judgement, we see a more
violent and over-confident side of his character.[94] This enthusiasm for
battle and assurance of success has been steadily built up by the

---

[90] These and parallel speeches are discussed by Fenik 1978b and G. Petersmann 1974 .

[91] For bibliography on the relationship of Homer to tragedy, see Reichel 1994: 11; ancient texts
on the subject are gathered by Herington 1985: 213–15. Some of the connections are discussed in
R. B. Rutherford 1982, but I would now lay less emphasis on the Aristotelian concept of tragic
error (*hamartia*). Seaford 1994: 275–8, 338–44, stresses the differences between the genres.

[92] On Hector see esp. Redfield 1975: 109–27; also Erbse 1978; Schein 1984: 168–95; Reichel
1994: 156 n. 1 (bibliography).

[93] See further Lohmann 1988.

[94] The point is emphasized not only by the earlier series of exchanges with Polydamas, but also
by the carefully planned contrast between this scene and the corresponding Trojan assembly in
Book 8 (note esp. 8.542 = 18.310). Cf. R. B. Rutherford 1985: 135.

triumphs of Books 11 to 17, in a sense Hector's *aristeia*.[95] The energy of his attack can be seen as fuelling his own arrogance. The ancient scholiasts dealt harshly with Hector's proud declarations, and modern critics are sometimes tempted to speak of *hubris*,[96] but Hector's response is all too human. It is natural and even justifiable for him to be overjoyed by what the Trojans have achieved. His mistake is to forget the limitation set by Zeus and to think himself a match for Achilles. In Book 22 he is shown more sympathetically: in a moving soliloquy, he laments his folly in rejecting good advice, flinches at the thought of humiliation, considers and rejects the vain notion of throwing himself on Achilles' mercy, and finally braces himself – though only briefly – to confront his formidable opponent. His introspection, his moment of panic, and his deluded joy at the appearance of Athena/Deiphobus all show his humanity, as a foil to Achilles, who in this episode appears both more and less than human. In general, what emerges from a survey of this kind is that Hector's decisions are both more conventionally heroic and more constrained by external circumstance than the choices of Achilles.[97]

To illustrate this further requires some general comment on Achilles' situation.[98] Three points are highlighted from the beginning: Achilles is the supreme fighter, 'the best of the Achaeans',[99] far outshining his nominal overlord Agamemnon;[100] he is the son of a goddess, who has access even to the ear of Zeus; and he is to die young. The details of his fate are revealed gradually, and in Book 9 he apparently still has some freedom to choose another destiny, but the overwhelming impression is that Achilles is unlikely to accept that inglorious option. In his reply to the embassy he shows himself keenly aware of the progress of the war (esp. 9.348–55); he makes some concessions in the course of the episode; in Book 11 he is still observing the combat from a distance, and it is because he cannot turn his back on the war that he sends Patroclus on his fateful mission to gather news (11.599–617). Achilles' situation is more complex than

---

[95] There are of course setbacks, notably the episode in which Hector is wounded (14.402–522, 15.1–12, 220–70), but this does not affect the overall pattern.

[96] For the scholia, see N. J. Richardson 1980: 273–4. Moderns who use the term *hubris* (a word remarkably rare in the *Iliad*) are listed and criticized by Fisher 1992: 177–8 (now the standard work on this difficult term; but note the criticisms of Cairns 1996; also Chadwick 1996: 292–7).

[97] See also Schadewaldt 1965: 268–351 (translated as Schadewaldt 1997a).

[98] On Achilles generally, see the very full bibliography in Reichel 1994: 99 n. 1; also Zanker 1994; Muellner 1996; Burgess 2009.

[99] Much rhetorical play is made with this phrase: see 1.91, 244, 412; 2.82, 580, 761, etc.

[100] This formulation can stand, even if the case for informality of command structure pressed by Taplin 1990 is accepted in full.

Hector's, his personality still more passionate and impulsive. Each of his decisions is important and in its way extraordinary: his initial decision to withdraw from the war; his rejection of the embassy's overtures, contrary to precedent and to the original advice of Athena; his concession in Book 16 to send out Patroclus in his place; his determination to avenge Patroclus (this is the natural heroic response, but is made to seem momentous by the link with his own death: 'next after Hector is your death waiting', mourns Thetis); his resolve to pursue revenge even beyond Hector's death, by dragging and exposing his corpse; and finally, his willingness to respect Priam's supplication and release Hector's body for burial.

Achilles and Hector are contrasted throughout the poem,[101] not only as the crucial military figures on either side but in their confrontation of death. When Hector stands triumphant over the dead Patroclus, he rejects his victim's prophecy that Achilles will take revenge: 'who knows whether Achilles, son of Thetis of the lovely locks, may not lose his life, falling first beneath my spear?' (16.860-1). When Achilles stands in the same position above the dying Hector, his response to his enemy's warning is subject to no such delusions: 'Die. As for my own death, I shall accept it whenever Zeus and the other immortal gods desire to bring it about' (22.365-6). Hector, despite the brief moment of realism in Book 6, still believes he can win, and only at the very end recognizes that the gods have tricked him: death is inevitable. Achilles, who sought to impose his own will on the gods, finds that his prayers once fulfilled bring him only unhappiness, and accepts death with open eyes (18.98-9, 22.365-6 ~ 18.115-6), without fear though not without bitterness.[102]

Achilles is also a greater hero than Hector, and a more intriguing figure than any of the other heroes, because of his powers as a speaker.[103] This goes beyond formal oratory, of which Odysseus is a master, to a more eloquent style and a broader vision of the world. Recent work has established that Achilles, particularly in major speeches such as those in Books 9, 16, and 18, uses a highly individual style which transcends the usual vocabulary, idioms, and formulae of Homeric speakers.[104] His speeches are enriched by hyperbolic expressions, exotic place-names, violence which

---

[101] See further my remarks in R. B. Rutherford 1982: 157-8, and context.

[102] Schadewaldt 1965: 234-67 (translated as Schadewaldt 1997b); Griffin 1980: 163-4.

[103] On Homeric rhetoric, see Lohmann 1970; Latacz 1974; R. B. Rutherford 1992: 58-69.

[104] The essential discussion is by Griffin 1986, developed in 1995; some criticism in Kirk 1990: 28-35. See also Lohmann 1970, esp. 236-45 on Book 9; Martin 1989, important though vulnerable in some details.

can become tenderness; he also uses similes more abundantly than any other character. These observations reinforce the sense that Achilles is an exceptional hero, not only in his prowess as a warrior but in the extent of his demands, the intensity with which he pursues them, and the magnitude of his self-esteem. The depth of his emotional commitment to Patroclus also seems to go beyond the norms of heroic comradeship, illustrated in more conventional form by the alliance of Idomeneus and Meriones: notoriously, later Greek readers assumed that the two men were lovers.[105] That such a tradition was known to Homer is conceivable, but there is no suggestion of it in the poem. It is notable that in Book 9 Achilles and Patroclus retire to bed not together but each with a separate slave-girl (9.664–8).

The eloquence of the speech in Book 9 in which Achilles rejects Odysseus' overtures and expresses his own dilemma has led to a wide range of interpretations. In one view, Achilles is violating the 'heroic code'; in another, he questions its very foundations; or is it that the conventions and assumptions of his world cannot cope with a hero who goes as far as he does?[106] Certainly the embassy, and perhaps even Patroclus himself, find it hard to understand him. Without insisting on an over-rigid definition of 'normal' heroic behaviour, we can at least agree that Achilles sees more clearly and, more importantly, feels more intensely and expresses himself more powerfully than other characters in the poem. He proclaims his disillusionment with the war and with his destiny, without having an alternative to put in its place. In the superb speech in which he responds to Patroclus' appeal, we see him shift from annoyance to anger, resignation to concession, renewed vindictiveness to sympathetic concern, culminating in the impossible wish that all others should perish, leaving him and Patroclus to sack Troy together: throughout this speech there is the same passionate intensity, but he is no longer certain how he wishes to direct his energy. Once he learns of his friend's death in battle, there is no more room for restraint or indecision, and again his

---

[105] Aeschylus' *Myrmidons* seems to have been particularly important: see frr. 134–7 Radt, with Dover 1978: 196–201; Halperin 1990: 75–87; M. W. Edwards 1991 on 18.82. Even the favour shown by Zeus to Ganymede is treated in asexual terms in the *Iliad*, despite reference to the young man's beauty (5.266; 20.232–5). Davidson 2007: 255–60, insists that the Achilles–Patroclus relationship is erotic already in Homer, with much polemic but no new arguments.

[106] A. Parry 1956 was seminal in this discussion. For specific criticism see Reeve 1973; Lynn-George 1988: ch. 2 (esp. 93–101); and for development see e.g. Redfield 1975: 3–23, 103–6; M. W. Edwards 1987a: 231–6; Martin 1989: ch. 4.

determination to fight, to avenge, and to die is expressed in a series of powerful speeches (esp. 18.79–93, 98–126, 324–42; 19.315–57). As in the embassy book, so in the scene in which the hero is 'reconciled' with Agamemnon, it is clear that the other Greek leaders do not fully understand Achilles, who can hardly be restrained from entering battle immediately: they want everything to be as it was before, whereas he is impatient with their talk of gifts and food.[107] Once he has returned to the conflict, the certainty of his own death adds a further note of cruelty to his voice, as most unforgettably in the speech to the ill-fated Lycaon (21.99–113, cf. 122–35). Although Book 9 has been the focus of most discussion of Achilles since the landmark article of Adam Parry, my own inclination would be to attach still more importance to Book 24. There, and particularly in the dialogue with Priam, the motifs of impending death and exhaustion with the war recur (540–2), but passion and egotism give way to generosity and resignation, in a sublime expression of the human situation (522–40). The original quarrel had turned Achilles against Agamemnon and all his comrades. His new wrath following the death of Patroclus brought him back to fight against the enemy with far greater fury than before. In the last book of the *Iliad*, he comes to recognize that even an enemy may deserve compassion and respect. This is both heroism and humanity.[108]

---

[107] Edwards' commentary (M. W. Edwards 1991) is invaluable on Book 19, which earlier treatments often underrated; also helpful is Taplin 1992: 203–18. On the importance of feasting together, see Griffin 1980: 14–21, an excellent section; van Wees 1992b: 44–7.

[108] For a different approach see Seaford 1994: 159–80, who lays much emphasis on the importance of ritual in re-integrating Achilles into the community.

III THE *ODYSSEY*[1]

1. Must a sequel be inferior?[2]

Although it is theoretically possible (and has been asserted) that the *Iliad* followed the *Odyssey*, or that the two poems were composed quite independently, with no influence from one to the other,[3] majority opinion ancient and modern puts the *Odyssey* later, and assumes it to be in important respects a successor, even a sequel, to the *Iliad*. This position can be maintained in two main forms: those who believe in a single master-poet as the creator of both epics may assign the *Iliad* to Homer's youth, the *Odyssey* to his riper years (a position memorably expressed by Longinus); those who follow the ancient separatists can regard the *Odyssey* as a rival work, composed by a poet who immensely admired the *Iliad* but whose own poetic and moral concerns lay elsewhere. This view is now much more common. It may be difficult, however, in a tradition which involved so much use of conventional themes and formulaic material, to decide firmly in favour of common or separate authorship. Whichever view one prefers, the important point seems

---

[1] The standard commentary for scholars is now Heubeck et al. (originally published with a text, and in a more attractive format, in Italian (6 vols, 1981–6); now translated and published in 3 vols by Oxford University Press (Heubeck et al. 1988; Heubeck and Hoekstra 1990; Russo 1992). The first volume is the most valuable, with important introductory essays. See also Jones 1991, for Books 1 and 2; more advanced, Garvie 1994 on Books 6–8; D. Steiner 2010 on Books 17 and 18; R. B. Rutherford 1992 on Books 19 and 20. Jones 1988 is an unpretentious and informative guide to the poem aimed at readers of Lattimore's translations. For book-length studies see Clarke 1967; Thornton 1970; Eisenberger 1973; N. Austin 1975; Griffin 1987; Hölscher 1989; Tracy 1990 (rather elementary); Thalmann 1998; Louden 1999; and especially Saïd 2011. Dimock 1989 is a book-by-book reading, sometimes rather disappointing: see R. B. Rutherford 1991. Page 1973a is an enjoyable essay on the adventures of Books 9–12 (cf. Page 1955: ch. 1). Hölscher 1939 and especially Fenik 1974 are indispensable on the thematic structure. A good deal of the material in part 1 of M. L. Edwards 1987a concerns both epics.

[2] For a fuller treatment of the topics covered in this section see R. B. Rutherford 1991–3; also Heubeck 1954; Burkert 1960; Griffin 1987: 63–70; and (most fully) Usener 1990 (reviewed in Griffin 1991).

[3] Sen. *De brev. vit.* 13.2 refers to the argument over priority as one of the pointless debates of Greek scholarship. The narrator of Lucian's parodic *True History* meets Homer's ghost in Hades, and the bard denies having written the *Odyssey* before the *Iliad* (*Ver. hist.* 2.20); this at least implies a continuing controversy. Page 1955: 149–59 argued for complete independence, but has not generally been followed.

to be that the *Odyssey* is later, and that it is conceived as a poem on the same scale as the *Iliad*, but differing strikingly in content and ethos.

Some of the arguments for that conclusion are based on detailed allusion and apparent verbal reminiscences, which cannot be reviewed here, and which some scholars, doubtful of the possibility of allusion in an oral poetic tradition, would not accept. More substantial points include the following. (1) The scale of the epics seems to mark them out as unusual in the early period; the Cyclic poems, to judge by the figures that have come down to us, were much shorter. (2) The *Odyssey* adopts a similar technique to the *Iliad* in selecting a limited period from a much longer tale, while using digressions, recapitulation, and prophecy to bring more of that tale within its scope. Most obviously, Odysseus narrates his previous wanderings to the Phaeacians; Nestor, Menelaus, and Helen also recount some of the hero's earlier exploits. (3) The *Odyssey* looks like a sequel, in that many of the cast of characters of the *Iliad* reappear and act in character-istic fashion: Achilles is disillusioned and bitter, Nestor garrulous, Helen enchanting yet rather enigmatic. Moreover, a very efficient job is done of filling in the background, giving the audience at least in sum-mary form some account of the events since the close of the *Iliad* (Longinus 9.12 makes this point, describing the *Odyssey* as the 'epilo-gue' to the *Iliad*). (4) A number of parallels in theme and structure can be detected: in particular, the culmination in the hero's long-delayed but bloodthirsty revenge against his enemy (Hector, the sui-tors), followed by scenes involving gentler emotions and resolution of tensions (in the *Iliad*, the funeral games and the encounter with Priam; in the *Odyssey*, the reunion with Penelope, and perhaps the com-ing of peace in Ithaca).[4] Other parallels which have been suggested include: (a) the absence of the hero from his proper sphere, and the dif-ficulties this causes for his comrades or family; (b) the hero's rejection of an easier option, choosing instead a life which will fulfil his human potential (Achilles in the end rejects a long but inglorious life; Odysseus rejects immortality with Calypso); (c) the importance of family ties, and especially the father–son relationship, in both epics.

The relationship of the *Iliad* and the *Odyssey* can also be seen as an opposition. The former is a poem of warfare and death; the latter describes the aftermath of that war, and presents a society in peacetime,

---

[4] For the problems of the conclusion of the *Odyssey*, see pp. 97–102 below.

though disrupted by abnormal circumstances. The scene of the *Iliad* is deliberately restricted; the *Odyssey* is a poem of wide horizons (1.3, 'many were the cities of men that he saw, and he learned their minds'). The *Iliad* ends tragically, with the threat of death hanging over both Achilles and the people of Priam; in the *Odyssey*, the prospects are brighter, with the reunion of husband and wife and the restoration of order to the community of Ithaca. Above all, there is a strong contrast between the heroes of the two epics. On the one hand, the youthful, outspoken, quick-tempered, and glory-hungry Achilles, the supreme fighter; on the other, the older, cannier Odysseus, devious and subtle, skilled orator and cunning trickster. Many of the differences between the poems arise from the nature of the heroes. It is interesting that they are already seen in the *Iliad* as potential opposites, even antagonists (note esp. 9.312–3).[5]

There is a tendency, already evident in ancient criticism, to devalue the *Odyssey* in comparison with the *Iliad*.[6] Socrates in Plato refers to this kind of judgement: 'I have heard your father say that the *Iliad* is a finer poem than the *Odyssey* by as much as Achilles is a better man than Odysseus' (*Hp. mi.* 363b). Longinus notoriously thought it showed signs of an old man's weakening powers (9.13–15). But, given the differences already described, it should be clear that it is dangerous to judge the two poems by the same criteria. If the *Odyssey* follows on from the *Iliad* while also seeking to achieve something different, if indeed it represents a challenge or a transformation of Iliadic themes, then differences are what we would expect. We do not criticize a comedy because it does not live up to the criteria required of a tragedy. Happily, recent criticism has been much more sensitive to the special qualities of the *Odyssey* – its subtlety of characterization, the skill with which narrative situations are developed, the extensive use of irony and double meanings. The fascination of the travel books, full of magic, monsters, and mystery, has always captured the imagination. The *Odyssey* combines what we may call folk tales (not only scenes such as the adventures with a one-eyed giant, but the disguise of Odysseus and the test of the bow) with heroic mythology, and integrates both within a firm and explicit moral framework. The

---

[5] On Odysseus in the *Iliad*, see further Stanford 1963: chs. 2–5.

[6] The scholiastic tradition of commentary on the *Odyssey* is much thinner than that on the *Iliad*, and there are far fewer manuscripts and papyri. Nevertheless, F. Cairns 1990: ch. 8 attempts to argue that the *Odyssey* had a higher status in some periods of antiquity than the *Iliad*.

combination is more elaborate than that of the *Iliad*, where the fixed setting and wartime conditions impose a greater uniformity. Yet, in spite of the complex structure and diverse materials, the poem presents the reader with a vivid and coherent picture of an imagined world.

In some ways the *Odyssey* is a more self-consciously 'literary' poem than the *Iliad*.[7] Although the *Iliad* includes invocations of the Muse, Helen's weaving (a figure for the artist at work?), Achilles' solitary singing of the 'glorious deeds of men', and the magnificent description of the shield, the *Odyssey* goes further, including poets among the cast of characters (Phemius in Ithaca, Demodocus at Alcinous' court). In the final book, Agamemnon's ghost remarks that the virtue of Penelope will be acclaimed through the ages, while the treacherous Clytemnestra will be remembered with ignominy. This passage comes very close to self-reference (24.196–202). Moreover, there is storytelling elsewhere, as the heroes reminisce about the Trojan War or recount their experiences to the admiring Telemachus.[8] Odysseus himself is on several occasions compared to a bard (17.518–21; 21.404–9), and once a comparison of this kind includes a reference to the lying tales of strangers (11.364–9); although this is used as a contrast with Odysseus' narrative, it is a two-edged comment, since we see the hero spinning fictitious tales about himself with equal fluency.[9] Some ancient readers even seem to have taken the 'authentic' travel narrative, with which Odysseus entertains the Phaeacians, as another lying tale invented by the hero himself,[10] though Homer gives us no justification for this.[11]

More specifically, the songs of Demodocus described in Book 8 can be read as each contributing to an allusive commentary on the *Iliad*.[12] The first song refers to a quarrel between two Greek heroes, Achilles and Odysseus, at which Agamemnon rejoices (8.72–82). He reacts in this unexpected way, it seems, because he sees their quarrel as fulfilling a prophecy; but in fact the prophecy referred to his own much deadlier

---

[7] Cf. Goldhill 1991: 1–68; R. B. Rutherford 1991–3: 48–9; Segal 1995: chs. 6–8.

[8] See further Olson 1995.

[9] On Odysseus' lies, see Emlyn-Jones 1986; Most 1989; Goldhill 1991: 36–48; R. B. Rutherford 1992: 69–73; Kelly 2008c.

[10] Juv. 15.13–26; Luc. *Ver. hist.* 1. 3; Dio Chrys. 11.34; cf. Goldhill 1991: 47–8.

[11] Indeed, the narrative itself contradicts this interpretation as far as the Cyclops tale is concerned: see esp. 1.20–1 with 68–75; 5.282–90. That the hero may give us a slanted or self-glorifying view of these episodes remains a possibility: see pp. 122–3 below.

[12] See Marg 1956; Macleod 1982: 1–8, 1983; Danek 1998: 142–59; differently Nagy 1979: 42–58.

conflict with Achilles, still in the future. The motifs of Agamemnon's
error, delusive prophecy, and the will of Zeus all recall important
themes of the *Iliad*. The second song describes the love affair of Ares
and Aphrodite and Hephaestus' successful trapping of the adulterous
pair: Hephaestus pretends to go away on a journey but lays a snare
and returns to find Ares and Aphrodite naked and entrammelled
(8.266–366). The sensuous, immoral behaviour of the gods remind
us of the love scene of Zeus and Hera on Ida (*Il.* 14.292–353), and
more generally of the conduct of the gods in the *Iliad*. Moreover, looking beyond the song itself, we can see analogies between the plotting
Hephaestus, who deceives others and unexpectedly returns, and the
role of Odysseus later in the poem. Yet the contrast between divine
and human worlds is equally important: Aphrodite is no Penelope,
and the immortal Ares cannot be punished by death but only by ineffectual bargains over compensation.[13] The third song of Demodocus
(8.499–520) describes the sack of Troy, so often anticipated in the
last part of the *Iliad*. Here Odysseus breaks down and weeps over the
past: the simile which describes his reaction compares him to a wife
bereaved of her husband and dragged away by callous soldiers. This
passage reminds us of the sympathetic treatment in the *Iliad* of the
women of Troy, above all the widowed Andromache, and of the cruelty
that accompanies the sack of a city. All of these scenes play a part in the
overall movement of the Phaeacian episode, which helps restore the
storm-tossed hero to his full heroic stature;[14] but they also suggest
new perspectives from which to regard the world of the *Iliad*.[15]

All of this presupposes an audience alert to such ingenious allusiveness. Whatever sceptics may maintain for the *Iliad*, it is hard to deny
that the *Odyssey* is composed with an eye to its predecessors – including
the *Iliad* itself. Misdirection and deviation from predictable story-lines
are even more evident than in the earlier poem, and it seems likely that
the poet knew other versions of the main plot (perhaps even his own). A
tantalizing reference in some manuscripts to a prospective journey by
Telemachus to see Idomeneus in Crete is one such indication
(1.93a). More significant are the suggestions of versions in which
Penelope may have recognized her husband (as Amphimedon wrongly

---

[13] See further Burkert 1960; Braswell 1982; and the notes in Garvie 1994.
[14] Mattes 1958, esp. 129 ff.; reservations in Fenik 1974: 13–18. See also Garvie 1994: 26–30.
[15] Cf. G. Steiner 1967: 221: 'it reminds one of the performance of an air from "The Marriage of Figaro" in the last act of "Don Giovanni"'.

assumes in 24.127 and 147–9). Georg Danek has produced a lengthy and impressive book on this whole area, which through the detail and range of his examples demonstrates the sophistication of the poet and his audience.[16] It used to be maintained that *arte allusiva* was a phenomenon of the Hellenistic era, but more recently 'Alexandrian' allusiveness has been traced back as far as Euripides, even to Pindar; perhaps we shall find that Homer was the founding father here as in so much else.[17]

2. Themes, structure, ethos

The construction of the *Odyssey* illuminates the character and general interpretation of the poem. First, there is the delay in introducing the hero. Whereas Achilles was named in the first line of the *Iliad*, was described as summoning the assembly at line 54, and dominated much of the first book, in the proem to the *Odyssey* the hero is not named[18] but only periphrastically described; he does not appear until well into Book 5. Before that we are introduced to most of the other principal characters of the poem, and hear much about the hero's past prowess; the scenes in Ithaca also make clear the urgent need for his return.

Secondly, the poem falls easily into two halves, the first half ending at 13.92, where the Phaeacian ship speeds across the waves towards Ithaca, carrying the sleeping Odysseus: he is there described in lines which seem to echo the proem of Book 1. At this point we move from seagoing adventures to land; the wanderings are coming to an end, and the remainder of the poem will be principally concerned with the kingdom of Ithaca. The poet is consciously marking the half-way point of his tale. In particular, there are numerous points in which Odysseus' arrival and experiences in Phaeacia anticipate and prepare for the homecoming to Ithaca.[19]

---

[16] Danek 1998: see e.g. 106–111 on the tales of Helen and Menelaus in Book 4; 255–7 on the Argo reference at 12.55–72; 247–50 on Heracles in Hades; 293–6 on Theoclymenus' introduction at 15.223–56. See also the same author's shorter treatment in Danek 2002. More generally on the audience, see Scodel 2002 (more briefly in Scodel 2004).

[17] *Arte allusiva*: Pasquali 1942. Euripides: Dover 1971: lxvii. Pindar: N. J. Richardson 1985, and much subsequent work. Currie 2006 is a valuable survey of the issues.

[18] On the importance of naming and anonymity in the *Odyssey*, see N. Austin 1972; Fenik 1974: 5–60; Goldhill 1991: 24–36; de Jong 1993.

[19] Rüter 1969: 228–46; Rutherford 1985; Garvie 1994: introduction.

Thirdly, the poem's narrative technique is throughout more complex than that of the *Iliad*, especially as regards scene-changing.[20] The poet has constructed parallel narratives, supposedly beginning at the same point: Athena is sent to Ithaca to despatch Telemachus on his travels in search of his father, and Hermes is to be sent to Calypso's isle, to instruct the nymph to launch Odysseus on his journey home. In fact, the second part of the proposed plan seems to be delayed, and a further divine exchange is required in Book 5 before Hermes sets off. Later, there is a similar blurring of the time-scale when Odysseus is back in Ithaca and Athena needs to bring Telemachus home from Sparta.[21] The poet is attempting something more elaborate than we find in the *Iliad*,[22] involving the simultaneous development of events on two fronts; indeed, the return of the narrative to Ithaca during Telemachus' absence introduces a third (4.624–847). Here, as in the lengthy narratives of past events, a technique which can be found on a smaller scale in the earlier epic is extended so ambitiously as to alter its nature.

The first four books of the *Odyssey* are conventionally known as the 'Telemachy', a title which highlights the special role of Odysseus' son in the poem.[23] In essence, Athena stirs him from his inertia, forces him to confront the real danger of his situation, and sends him to Pylos and Sparta not because he will find his father there (though he does learn of his present situation), but to 'win glory' and learn from his father's peers. The ancient description of the Telemachy as the 'education' of Telemachus is suggestive, though not universally accepted by moderns.[24] By the time Odysseus is back in Ithaca, Telemachus is behaving as a king's son and heir should do, and will be a worthy ally in the final crisis; at the contest of the bow, he shows himself his father's true son by being *about* to bend the bow successfully, but then holding himself back (21.124–9). The Odyssean qualities of self-discipline and concealment are transferred to Telemachus.

From another viewpoint, the wanderings of Telemachus make it possible for the poet to introduce some of the heroes of the Trojan

---

[20] See further Hölscher 1939: 37–50; Heubeck 1954.

[21] Apthorp 1980b; Hoekstra in Heubeck and Hoesktra 1990 on 15.1–3.

[22] Scenes such as *Il.* 15.142–261 provide a partial precedent, but on a much shorter time-scale. See Zielinski 1901; Krischer 1971: 131 ff.; Whitman and Scodel 1981; Janko 1992 on *Il.*14.1–152.

[23] Odysseus' self-description on two occasions in the *Iliad* as 'the father of Telemachus' is abnormal procedure in that epic, and seems to imply that this relationship was already important in earlier poetry (*Il.* 2.260; 4.354). It is probably relevant that Telemachus is the only son of an only son (*Od.* 16.118–20).

[24] Schol. 1.93 and 284. For doubts, see S. West 1988: 54–5.

War, and to show their present situation: Nestor secure and prosperous, though still grieving for his son Antilochus, who died saving his father's life; Menelaus also settled in his kingdom, but still saddened by the loss of so many comrades in the war, and enjoying a somewhat ambiguous and puzzling relationship with the still-beautiful Helen. Although Odysseus is still missing, and his household increasingly fear that he must be dead, we anticipate that he will return at last, later than all the other heroes, and win a greater victory, a more successful homecoming, than any of the others. Here the comparison between Odysseus' household and that of Agamemnon is particularly important:[25] Agamemnon returned openly, and his rash confidence laid him open to the assassin Aegisthus; his queen was unfaithful, seduced by her lover during his long absence; his son Orestes has had to take revenge. The disastrous history of Agamemnon shows what might have happened in Ithaca, if Odysseus were less prudent and Penelope less faithful.[26]

The punishment of Aegisthus, mentioned in the first divine scene of the poem, sets the moral tone for the epic. In this poem the gods oversee human morality more consistently and austerely than in the *Iliad*. In general, the Olympians seem more remote from the activities of mankind: there are few scenes in which Zeus and the other gods hold counsel, and several deities prominent in the *Iliad* never appear (especially Hera, Apollo, and, less surprisingly, Thetis; Aphrodite appears only in Demodocus' song). The main plot really requires only Athena, Odysseus' constant supporter,[27] Poseidon, his persecutor, and Zeus, who arbitrates between them. Other deities such as Hermes occasionally figure, but the general effect is very different. The Trojan War was a major event which aroused the passionate partisanship of many divinities; Odysseus, a single hero though a pious man, is of little concern to the gods other than his patroness and his arch-enemy.

Nevertheless, the gods are of central importance in that the *Odyssey* shows us a world governed by an ethical code which the gods endorse. Wrongdoing will be punished; callous and impious deeds do not prosper. Zeus watches over beggars, suppliants, and others in distress; those who mistreat a guest under their roof can expect to suffer for it. These moral principles are commonly cited by the characters, and, in one of

---

[25] Note also the fate of the lesser Ajax, described at 4.499–511. See further Klingner 1944.
[26] S. West 1988: 56–7, 60; Olson 1990.
[27] Müller 1966.

the most striking speeches of the poem, Odysseus draws the moral from
his success over the suitors, though forbidding the nurse to cry aloud in
exultation over the dead:

It is not holy to crow over dead men. These men were destroyed by the gods' dispensa-
tion and by their own wicked deeds, for they honoured none of the men on the earth,
neither bad nor good, who came amongst them. So it is that they have met an ugly end
through their own rash folly.   (22. 412–15)[28]

Here Odysseus speaks as an instrument of divine retribution, rather
than as a vengeful hero reclaiming his own property from upstarts.
It has been claimed that passages like this show the *Odyssey* to be
the product of a more advanced ethical or religious outlook than
the *Iliad*, but these arguments must be viewed with caution.[29] The
poet of the *Iliad* knows about gods concerned with justice (see
p. 70), and the *Odyssey* shows a strongly Iliadic divinity in
Poseidon, fierce in anger and conscious of his own status.
Moreover, although Athena praises Odysseus before Zeus for his
piety, she herself loves him for his lies and his deviousness (1.60–2
vs. 13.291–9 and 330–8).[30] The different emphasis in the *Odyssey*'s
presentation of the gods may well result from the different type of
story that the later poem has to tell. Both poems use the gods selec-
tively and appropriately.

But the Olympian gods do not exhaust the supernatural elements
of the poem. The *Odyssey* includes cannibal monsters, the bag of
winds, the mysterious lotus-flower with its amnesiac effects, the
Cyclops, the cattle of the sun, and a visit to the underworld.[31] Most
of these magical or monstrous features occur in the narrative of
Odysseus, which we have already seen to be less realistic than the
other parts of the *Odyssey*. It is also important that they take place
far away, beyond the familiar geography of the Greek mainland and
Ionia: Odysseus leaves the known world behind as early as 9.80,

[28] For the novelty of the sentiments expressed see Finley 1979: 140–1. More generally on the
morality of the *Odyssey*, see Redfield 1983, esp. 239–44; R. B. Rutherford 1986: 156.

[29] Dodds 1951: 28–37; contrast Fenik 1974: 208–30. For other views, see bibliography in
S. West 1988 on 1.32 ff.; Kullmann 1985; Erbse 1986: 237–41; R. Friedrich 1987;
Winterbottom 1989; Hankey 1990; Segal 1992; Allan 2006.

[30] Clay 1983 perversely argues that Odysseus' misfortunes are the result of Athena's anger with
her protégé. This has not been generally accepted, but her book contains many good observations
on Homer's gods.

[31] On most of these episodes, see Radermacher 1915; Page 1973a; also the works cited in n. 39
below.

and attempts to trace his wanderings on the map are inevitably doomed to failure.[32]

Given that the Telemachy and the Ithacan narrative are rooted more deeply in heroic society, it is natural to ask how successfully the poet has integrated the more magical adventures with the rest of Odysseus' experience. Perhaps the most striking point is the way in which this very difference of tone is exploited: Odysseus is presented as a man who must gradually learn to cope with unfamiliar challenges, which conventional heroic behaviour cannot overcome.[33] The claim to be conqueror of Troy cuts little ice with the Cyclops, and to kill the monster while he lies slumbering would be fatal, since Odysseus and his men have not the strength to shift the stone blocking the cave's mouth. Later, open defiance is useless against the immortal Scylla: Odysseus arms himself in vain, and the loss of six of his comrades to the monstrous creature is described as the most pitiful sight he has witnessed in all his wanderings (12.244–59, see p. 123 below). Odysseus, the untypical hero, must use his wits and cunning; he has the adaptability to deal with these otherworldly horrors. Among other things, he learns to conceal his identity, to observe and wait before risking self-exposure. The trick with the pseudonym 'No-man' is the first instance, but this clever stroke is thrown away when Odysseus reveals his identity to the Cyclops once safely out of the cave. In the second half of the poem he will further cultivate anonymity and false identities.

The eleventh book illuminates Odysseus' character and the meaning of the poem through the encounter with Odysseus' past. Homer uses the supernatural setting of the underworld for other purposes beyond the ostensible motive of seeking directions from Tiresias. Besides the moving exchange between the hero and his dead mother, a memorable scene introduces the ghosts of three heroes who perished at Troy or after returning from the war – Agamemnon, Achilles, and Ajax.[34] In ways none the less important for being implicit, these three men are contrasted with the living Odysseus, the survivor, who will go on to find his way home and reclaim wife, family, and kingdom. Particularly effective in this episode is the dialogue with Achilles:

---

[32] As already remarked by Eratosthenes ap. Strabo 1.2.15–7. See further Walbank 1979 on Polyb. 34.2–4; Luce in Stanford and Luce 1974: 118–38; Wolf and Wolf 1968; and see Haller 2011.

[33] Reinhardt 1948.

[34] For the importance of Agamemnon see p. 83 above; for the silent departure of Ajax see p. 121 below.

nowhere else in Homer is the contrast between their characters clearer, and yet here Achilles has moved closer to the viewpoint of Odysseus, for whom heroic achievement is not the only precious thing in life. For all the disillusionment expressed in Book 24 of the *Iliad*, Achilles' bitterness at his present state sounds a note of realism unheard in the earlier poem.[35] Book 11 is also of great importance in that it makes clear, through Tiresias' prophecy, that Odysseus' wanderings will not be ended when he reaches Ithaca: he has 'immeasurable toil, long and hard' still to come (23.248–50; cf. 11.119–37). The end of the *Odyssey* does not leave the couple to live 'happily ever after'.[36]

Another aspect of the wanderings may be described in cultural or anthropological terms.[37] The different beings and communities among whom Odysseus finds himself are characterized by strange practices and behaviour in comparison with 'normal' human society. The Laestrygonians do not farm (10.98); Calypso's island is wooded, and has a vine, but is not cultivated (5.63–74). The lotus-eaters do not have to farm or work, and they do not cook or eat bread, only the lotus-flower; the food they offer Odysseus' companions deprives them of an essential aspect of their humanity, memory (9.84, 94–7). The Cyclopes, as Odysseus explicitly comments, have no assembly place or laws and do not combine as a community (9.112, with context). In Polyphemus' cave other divergences from human social and ethical codes become manifest. Instead of feeding his guests, he eats them, and his offer of a 'guest-gift' is a grotesque parody of the institution: he will eat Odysseus last. Odysseus' wanderings are not just a series of randomly combined adventures but are subordinate to an overall conception, whether fully articulated or not, of the nature of human life; through his encounters with superhuman and subhuman creatures and their *mores*, Odysseus defines the limits and nature of the human condition. On this argument it is appropriate that the Phaeacians should represent his final port of call before his homecoming. They are human, but not wholly of our world: isolated from humankind, they enjoy an existence close to the gods, and sail magical ships. But

---

[35] See e.g. Jacoby 1933; Rüter 1969: 251 ff.; Wender 1978: 41–4; Griffin 1980: 100–1; Clay 1983: 108 ff.; Goldhill 1991: 104–6. Some aspects of the differences of outlook between the *Odyssey* and the *Iliad* are discussed further in R. B. Rutherford 1991–3.

[36] On the question of Odysseus' death (violent or peaceful?), see Hartmann 1917; Stanford 1963: 86–9; Heubeck in Heubeck and Hoekstra 1990 on 11.134b–7. An ingenious solution is offered by M. L. West in his commentary on the Epic Cycle, 2013: 307–15.

[37] For what follows see esp. Vidal-Naquet 1981.

in other respects they seem less than fully human, for their society is protected from war and they enjoy a carefree, hedonistic existence.[38]

The folk-tale element is not confined to Books 9–12, however. The themes of the wanderer's return and the woman perpetually weaving are both found in folklore; the contest of the bow has been paralleled in Indian epic.[39] As for the supernatural aspect, Menelaus in Book 4 describes how, near Egypt, he was obliged to ambush and capture the shape-changing prophet, Proteus; again, the remote and exotic setting makes this kind of tale more acceptable. Even in Ithaca Odysseus is magically transformed by Athena ('I shall make you unrecognizable to all men', 13.397), though the nature and degree of his transformation remain ambiguous.[40] This seems to be an example of a general tendency in the *Odyssey*: comparison with parallel versions suggests that Homer has somewhat reduced or underplayed the magical aspects, in order to preserve the sense that this is above all a human drama. Thus in Book 10 the magical plant *moly*, introduced as a protective charm against Circe's enchantment, is forgotten after Odysseus has received it from Hermes, and it is Odysseus' own strength of will that frustrates Circe (10.327, 329).[41]

Some reference has already been made to the importance of disguise and concealment,[42] and many of the *Odyssey*'s most striking episodes depend on a contrast between appearance and actuality. This has two major aspects: the failure to recognize a stranger or new arrival, and the concealment or suppression of one's true feelings, whether out of caution or to delay a moment of emotional outpouring. The first book already introduces this type of effect: Athena comes to visit Telemachus in disguise as a mortal trader; only gradually does she reveal some (false) information about herself; and only on her miraculous departure does he realize that she must be a divinity. Thereafter he must conceal this insight and her advice, revealing nothing to the suitors about his plans and new hopes. The poet is fascinated by the notion of the unrecognized stranger, the disguised guest whose identity

---

[38] Cf. Segal 1962, 1967; Fenik 1974: 54–5; Garvie 1994: 22–5. For the hedonism see esp. 8.246–9; Dickie 1983.

[39] Crooke 1898, 1908; Calhoun 1939; Page 1955, 18 n. 1; S. Thompson 1955–8: N681, H331; Zhirmunsky 1966; Hansen 2002: 201–11; S. West 2012b. For different analogies, see Burkert 1973.

[40] See R. B. Rutherford 1992 on 19.380–1 on the question whether Odysseus is recognizable or not.

[41] See further Radermacher 1915; Page 1973a: 55, 69, etc.

[42] See Fenik 1974: 5–60; Stewart 1976; Murnaghan 1987.

is relevant, even crucial to the conversation going on around him. This typical Odyssean situation is used with Telemachus at Sparta, with Odysseus in Alcinous' court, in the hut of the swineherd, and above all in his own palace. Multiple ironies result: while Athena in disguise talks with Telemachus of his father's return, Phemius has been singing to the suitors of the homecoming of the Greeks from Troy, and of the part which Athena played in that voyage. In the palace of Menelaus, the subject of Odysseus comes up even before Telemachus has been identified as the hero's son, and the young man is overcome by emotion: recognition soon follows. While Odysseus sits unrecognized in the halls of the Phaeacians, the minstrel sings of the quarrel between Achilles and Odysseus. In Eumaeus' hut, he hears talk of himself and his estates. Delayed recognition and ironic double meanings are typical of the *Odyssey*, and especially of its second half, once Odysseus is back among his own people.

Other aspects of these scenes are of equal interest. We see a king in beggar's clothes, kindly treated by poorer folk but spurned and mocked by the aristocrats of the kingdom, who should respect him. The sympathetic treatment of humbler and less heroic characters is another point in which the *Odyssey* offers something new and different from the *Iliad* (though it is true that common people and their lives do figure in similes and on Achilles' shield). The poet of the *Odyssey* does not confine himself to the situation in the royal household; he clearly takes pleasure in portraying his hero spending time in a simple rural settlement, sharing the life of his own herdsmen.[43] He also hints at the unhappiness and resentment of the Ithacan population. Eumaeus complains of the reduction of his master's property (14.91–108); Philoetius is so discontented that he is considering emigrating (20.209–25). Most touching of all is the little episode in which Odysseus, lying awake in the palace just before dawn, hears one of the women of the house, 'the weakest of them', struggling to finish her stint of grinding corn and cursing the suitors ('may this very day be the last and final time that the suitors eat their sumptuous meal in Odysseus' halls, those men who have worn my knees away with the wretched drudgery of this grinding!'). Odysseus rejoices at the prayer as a good omen; the passage makes clear that his victory will be a victory for the Ithacan people as well (20.110–21).

---

[43] Steiner's commentary (2010) on Books 17 and 18 includes much useful comment on this aspect of the poem.

The disguised Odysseus is in a position of unsuspected superiority over those around him: he can question and test them, sounding them out about their feelings towards himself and the prospect of his return. This testing procedure is applied not only to Eumaeus and the suitors, but to Penelope herself. It is in the scenes with her (as earlier, before he reveals himself to Telemachus) that he must work hardest to govern his own feelings.

With these words he kissed his son, and shed a tear that fell down his cheeks and to the ground; until that moment he had held the tear back always.   (16.190–1)

As for Odysseus, his heart went out to his weeping wife, but beneath his eyelids his eyes kept as firm as horn or iron; he still dissembled, and showed no tears.   (19.209–12)

Once Odysseus has identified himself to Telemachus, the young man must show the same self-control and avoid any outbursts of rage at the way the suitors treat his father. The fidelity and caution of Penelope, who will hardly believe that her husband is really home even after the slaughter, show that she too has the self-discipline appropriate to the wife of Odysseus.

In the *Iliad*, 'recognition scenes' are not needed: the heroes generally seem to have no difficulty identifying one another, and, if uncertainty exists, an enquiry swiftly yields a frank answer (as with Glaucus and Diomedes). Men in the *Iliad* deal with one another openly and in full awareness of each other's status and strength: even in the dubious *Doloneia*, Odysseus and Diomedes have no need to ask the spy who he is, but know him already (*Il.* 10.447). It is the gods who deceive, as when Athena tempts Pandarus to break the truce, or Zeus sends a lying dream to Agamemnon. In the *Odyssey*, where the mortals do not deal so honestly with one another, the characters dwell in a state of uncertainty. The suitors speak hypocritically to Penelope and Telemachus, and plan an ambush against the latter; Telemachus deceives his mother and steals away by night; Eumaeus was abducted by his nurse and sold into slavery; Troy was taken by a treacherous device, the Wooden Horse, to which the *Iliad* never refers. So too with the gods: even Athena normally disguises herself when visiting Telemachus or Odysseus, and in Book 13 she tests the hero's prowess before revealing herself. The world of the *Odyssey* has a devious and deceptive atmosphere which matches the wily personality of the hero, and with which he is uniquely suited to cope. We come to relish his deceptions and his fluent lying, to delight in the irony as he extracts praise of himself from the wretched Eumaeus or provokes the hubristic suitors on to further crimes.

After deception, recognition.[44] Telemachus is recognized by Helen in Book 4; she also recalls how she once identified Odysseus when he entered Troy in disguise during the siege (4.240–56), an episode that seems to anticipate the scene in Book 19 with Eurycleia and the scar. In Phaeacia Odysseus finally reveals his identity at the opening of Book 9. But it is in the second half that the motif becomes more frequent: after the encounter with Athena in Book 13, there are recognition scenes with Telemachus, the dog Argus, Eurycleia, Eumaeus and Philoetius together, the revelation scene with the suitors, and the climactic scene in which Odysseus and Penelope are re-united, followed by a final pendant in Book 24, the encounter with his father. These episodes are not randomly distributed. There is a clear contrast between the scenes in which the hero deliberately reveals his identity (e.g. to Telemachus), and those in which he is accidentally exposed (especially with Eurycleia). On the one hand we see and share the hero's superior knowledge; on the other we feel that he is not infallible, but can make mistakes.

There is also a significant relationship between the scene in Book 13, in which Athena tries to make Odysseus give himself away, but unsuccessfully, and the later scene in which Penelope succeeds in upsetting and exposing her husband. Athena, though she deceived Odysseus, was unable to make him lower his guard. Only in Book 23, in the second encounter with his wife, is the hero finally and incontrovertibly out-tested and outwitted. Here it is Penelope, in her uncertainty and doubt, who conceives a test to see whether Odysseus is truly her husband (23.108–110, 113–14). Once before, in Book 19, she had attempted to do so (19.215), but Odysseus had side-stepped. In Book 23 we see the tables turned, the biter bit, when Penelope asks the old nurse to bring out their marital bed for Odysseus to sleep in that night. 'Thus she spoke, testing her husband' (23.181). At the thought of anyone having tampered with the immovable bed, around which he had built the palace, Odysseus bursts out with open indignation: his famous caution and self-control vanish. The scene thus trumps all Odysseus' previous testing and reverses Penelope's earlier failure. Her success surpasses even the wiles of Athena, the only other female who matches the hero in cleverness and guile.

---

[44] N. J. Richardson 1983; Cave 1988 (a superb survey); Gainsford 2003; Kelly 2012a.

Finally, the medium of recognition is appropriate in most cases. The scar is apt for Eurycleia and the other servants, since they were present when Odysseus came home with that wound; it represents their ties with Odysseus' youth. With Laertes, Odysseus appeals not only to the evidence of the scar but also to his patrimony, the trees in the orchard where they stand (24.336–44). With Penelope, it is fitting and symbolic that the crucial sign, the proof of Odysseus' return, should be his knowledge of their bed, a shared secret: like their marriage, it is deep-rooted, immovably set, unchanged by time.[45]

Although the *Odyssey* also has a public dimension, in its presentation of Odysseus as the ideal king and of Ithaca as a society disrupted because of his absence,[46] it is arguable that the central family relationships are more important, and that the sensitive presentation of human feelings, both masculine and feminine, goes beyond anything we find in the *Iliad*. This is one reason why many readers have found it an astonishingly modern work, a distant ancestor of the novel.[47]

3. Men, women, and goddesses[48]

One of the most notorious pronouncements in Homeric studies was the suggestion by Samuel Butler that the *Odyssey* was composed by a woman.[49] Whatever one thinks of the theory itself, it is certainly obvious that female characters are more prominent in the *Odyssey* than in the *Iliad*, where they figure principally as victims of the war, often passive and unspeaking. Chryseis has no opportunity to speak for herself, and Briseis speaks only once, and among her fellow captives, when she mourns the dead Patroclus, unheeded by Achilles

---

[45] See further Whitman 1958: 300–5; Wender 1978: 60–2. For a semiotic reading of Odysseus' bed, see Zeitlin 1995.

[46] Thornton 1970: ch. 6; N. Austin 1975: 162–71. This aspect seems to me understated by S. West 1988: 59–60; contrast R. B. Rutherford 1992: 13–15.

[47] Cf. Stanford 1963: note especially the well-known claim by Joyce that Odysseus was a truly rounded character, more so even than Hamlet or Faust (quoted in Ellmann 1982: 435–6; see also Ellmann 1974; Kenner 1980).

[48] The fertile field of classical scholarship on women cannot be sifted here: see e.g. G. Clark 1989; Peradotto and Sullivan 1984; and Helen King in *OCD* s.v. 'women'. On the Odyssean women, see Doherty 1995; also n. 59 below on Penelope.

[49] Butler 1897; see also Graves 1955. Butler's outlook is discussed satirically from a modern standpoint by Winkler 1990: 129 ff. Another enjoyable essay is Whitmarsh 2002.

(*Il.* 19.282–300).[50] It is of course true that the goddesses of the poem play a more active part: it would seem that the gulf between mortal and immortal is more important than that between man and woman – though we may ask whether this is equally the case in both epics. But in the *Odyssey* female characters are numerous among both mortals and immortals, and are important in both worlds. In some cases, indeed, the women are cleverer and more effective agents than the men: Helen is shrewder than Menelaus and quicker at recognizing Telemachus; Arete is in some ways more influential in Scheria than Alcinous (6.303–15; 7.53–77). Even on the divine level, Athena's quick-witted appeal to Zeus frustrates her absent uncle Poseidon.[51]

Special interest attaches to Odysseus' dealings and relationships with women. Two of these are divine, Circe and Calypso.[52] It seems that the poet has done his best to differentiate these. Circe, probably the older figure, is a sorceress and a mysterious being, who cannot be fully trusted and with whom the hero forms no real attachment in a year's sojourn. She turns swiftly from threatening witch to generous hostess, but when Odysseus declares that he must leave she raises no objection. Calypso is a more sympathetic and affectionate figure, devoted to Odysseus and anxious to keep him with her. Her emotions are more human: outrage at the import of Hermes' message, pique at Odysseus' preference for a mortal woman. The scene in which she tries for the last time to prevail on him to stay and accept a life of immortal ease is important in establishing Odysseus' heroic status, but is also a touching and delicate interchange, rich in understated pathos.[53] The gulf between humanity and divinity, tragically exploited in the *Iliad* (especially in the relationship of Achilles and Thetis), here becomes a source of personal sadness, as Calypso accepts abandonment with reluctance but nevertheless gives Odysseus the help he must have to depart. It is a pleasing touch that she does not reveal to him the command of Zeus, but leaves him to suppose that she has decided to let him go of her own accord. The theme of dissimulation, ubiquitous in the *Odyssey*, here enables Calypso to preserve her dignity.

---

[50] The admiration of Taplin (which in most respects I endorse) for the *Iliad* goes much too far when he claims that the sympathetic treatment of women in that poem make it *more* likely than the *Odyssey* to be a woman's work (1992: 32).

[51] See further Detienne and Vernant 1974.

[52] See especially Crane 1988, with ample references to older discussions.

[53] See also Griffin 1980: 59–61, esp. 59 n. 17.

There remains Nausicaa, the only human female with whom Odysseus has the opportunity for dalliance (in fact he behaves with perfect propriety).[54] Here again the proximity of the *Odyssey* to 'folk tale' is evident: a wanderer appears in a strange land, excels in contests, impresses the people of the country, and wins the king's daughter.[55] Of course, Odysseus tactfully evades the offer of Nausicaa's hand, though the reader is left in no doubt that she is attracted to him (6.244–6; 7.311–16). Some critics regret that the poet has denied us so charming a romance, but an erotic encounter with Nausicaa would have been a shocking and culpable misdemeanour on Odysseus' part,[56] on quite a different plane from the infidelities with Circe and Calypso: it is rash to deny a deity who offers such favours. The *Odyssey* poet is prepared to hint that Calypso was not an altogether uncongenial companion in the early years, and we must grant that the epic, like later Greek society, accepts a double standard for the sexual behaviour of men and women, but the importance of fidelity and family ties in this poem have their effect on the hero's character. There is some evidence that Odysseus' *amours* were more numerous in other sources.[57]

The character of Penelope is essential to the plot of the *Odyssey*, and she is clearly the most intriguing female figure in the poem: older descriptions of her as 'a healthy well-nourished lady…without any gift of intellect or strength of character' now arouse incredulity and outrage.[58] More recent discussions have laid much more stress on her devotion to her husband, her intelligence, the intensity of her grief, pathetically described in many passages, her attempts to assert her authority, and particularly her satisfying success in outwitting her husband.[59] Recognizing the constraints on her behaviour, as a woman in a

---

[54] See Garvie 1994: 29–30.
[55] Woodhouse 1930, H. Petersmann 1981.
[56] See esp. Stanford 1963: 51–5, against the sentimentality of Woodhouse 1930: 64.
[57] E.g. with the queen of the Thesprotians in the Cyclic *Telegony*.
[58] Woodhouse 1930: 201.
[59] The secondary literature is enormous (see n. 48). In general on the mythical figure of Penelope, see Mactoux 1975. On her presentation in Homer, see Büchner 1940; Harsh 1950 (an enjoyable but misguided attempt to prove that Penelope did indeed recognize her husband on his return); Amory 1963 (important for moving the debate on to a more subtle psychological level); Vester 1968; N. Austin 1975: ch. 4; Emlyn-Jones 1984; Russo's introduction to the English edition of his commentary on *Odyssey* 17–20 (Russo 1992: 3–16); Winkler 1990; Katz 1991 (deconstructive reading); Felson-Rubin 1987, 1993 (combining psychology and narratology); Doherty 1995; Murnaghan 1995; Zeitlin 1995; Felson and Slatkin 2004. I had my say in R. B. Rutherford 1992: 27–38.

male-dominated society, some critics see her as manipulating the men she encounters, using what tools she has and exploiting her very limited range of choices.[60] She can even be seen as enduring in her own sphere sufferings such as heroes undergo: in a simile at 4.791–3, she is compared to a lion, a comparison normally confined to male characters.[61] Whereas the analysts complained that Penelope's behaviour was inconsistent or inexplicable, readers now admit greater subtleties and see some of the more puzzling scenes as 'provocatively enigmatic'.[62] A more sophisticated model of the poet's allusive technique also helps the interpreter: traditional analysis detected an unhappy conflation of a version in which Penelope did recognize her husband with one in which she did not, but it is perfectly possible that the poet is consistently following one version while playing on his audience's awareness of another. This seems plausible in Book 19, where the poet, having brought husband and wife together in a secluded spot at night, seems to be leading us to expect a recognition (as in previous versions of the tale?); but, although a recognition does take place in this scene, it is inadvertent, and involves not the queen but the old nurse Eurycleia.

Problematic scenes remain, which cannot be discussed in detail here. Particularly prominent in discussion are the scene in which Penelope extorts gifts from the suitors, the episode in which she converses with the beggar Odysseus but (as is now rightly accepted) fails to recognize her husband (Book 19), the passage in which she narrates a dream that foreshadows the doom of the suitors (19.535–58), the proposal to hold the contest of the bow, initiated by Penelope with Odysseus' encouragement (572–81), and the final sequence in which she is awakened by the nurse and after initial disbelief eventually accepts that Odysseus has indeed returned (Book 23). Other puzzling passages include the lines in which one suitor is said to be 'the one who appealed most to Penelope' (16.397–8) and the speech in which she compares herself, in opaque and elliptical terms, to Helen.[63] All of these shed light on Penelope's personality and emotions: although in some passages we may be surprised or forced to modify our earlier impressions, the fundamental premises of the story – that Penelope is a faithful wife

---

[60] Winkler 1990.

[61] See further H. Foley 1978 on 'reverse-sex similes'.

[62] Felson-Rubin 1987: 82.

[63] 23.218–24, defended by Heubeck in Russo 1992 ad loc. but by few others. See Fredericksmeyer 1997.

and will re-marry only with deep reluctance, in order to protect Telemachus and his patrimony – should not be questioned.[64] The homecoming of Odysseus would be hollow if that were not so: he has sacrificed even immortality in order to come home to his wife, one who is 'like-minded'. Odysseus himself describes the ideal, in a much earlier passage which sums up several of the poem's fundamental assumptions: 'there is nothing nobler, nothing better, than when man and wife dwell together with their thoughts in common: that brings much grief to their enemies, joy to their friends; and they themselves know it best of all' (6.182–5). Their eventual embrace is marked by a simile which is applied to both parties: it starts from Odysseus and finishes with Penelope, and describes their joy in terms of the experiences of a shipwrecked sailor finding his way at last to shore:

These were her words, and she roused still more in him the desire to weep. He cried as he held his beloved wife close to him, that clever woman. As land is welcome when spotted by swimmers whose sturdy vessel Poseidon has wrecked at sea, driven by storm and solid waves – few of them have escaped the grey sea on to land by swimming, and much brine is encrusted on their skin; but gladly they climb on to the shore, escaping from suffering – so glad was the sight of her husband to Penelope, and she still would not release his neck from her white arms' embrace.   (23.231–40)[65]

The linking of Penelope with Odysseus' sufferings stresses not only their reunion but also the parallels between their different ordeals and achievements – both alone, both enduring, planning, and hoping. Penelope's exceptional qualities are further shown by the calmness with which she accepts that Odysseus must undertake a further journey to placate Poseidon. Past suffering and future parting serve to set their present joy in sharper relief.

The other important female in Odysseus' life is of course the goddess Athena. Theirs was already regarded as a special relationship in the *Iliad* (see especially 23.782–3), but in that epic she also befriends other heroes (Achilles and Diomedes). In the *Odyssey* her attention is focused on a single favourite, and the poet expands this conception to create something almost unique: a close friendship between man and deity. Sometimes she aids him without his knowledge, sometimes more openly; on the whole her interventions become more frequent in

---

[64] The cynical view that Penelope was not faithful to Odysseus was already current in antiquity: see e.g. Hor. *Sat.* 2.5.78–83; Sen. *Ep.* 88.8 (the latter passage also refers to the debate about whether she recognized her husband or not).
[65] For other parallels between husband and wife, see R. B. Rutherford 1986: 160 n. 77.

the second half. Her interaction with others, even with Telemachus, is more distant, often deceptive: thus in Book 15 she misleads Telemachus with tales of his mother's eagerness to marry, playing on the young man's fears. In Book 18 she puts an impulse in Penelope's mind, and the queen responds without really understanding what she is doing and why. But with Odysseus she is affectionate and reassuring, even teasing, as shown above all in Book 13, where the basis of their relationship is most explicitly defined. She cares for him because they are alike:

'But come, let us talk thus no longer; the two of us both know our tricks – you excel all mankind in stratagem and well-chosen words, while I am renowned among the gods for my wiles and wisdom. Nor did you yourself discern in me Pallas Athene, the daughter of Zeus, I who am always beside you and guard you in all your trials. It was I who endeared you to the Phaeacians; it is I again who am here now to weave a plan together with you...'   (13.296–303)

Although there is doubtless an extra frisson to their relationship because they are male and female, the respect with which Odysseus always speaks to her and the traditional chastity of Athena reduce the significance of this factor: this is a partnership based on intellectual equality. We may contrast both the relationship between Aphrodite and Paris in the *Iliad*, where there is no common ground other than their sensual natures, and the moving portrayal of Hippolytus' devotion to Artemis in the *Hippolytus*, where there is no physical or even visual contact, and indeed no equality: favoured for a time, Hippolytus is left behind to die.[66]

It has sometimes been felt that the constant support and advice of Athena, especially in the second half of the poem, diminishes the triumph of the hero.[67] Even with her encouragement, however, he has still to execute his intentions, and it is notable that, although she promises her support against the suitors, she gives him no guidance as to how he should win a position of advantage over them. His fluent lying and clever coaxing of help or comforts out of Eumaeus and others need no divine backing. Moreover, in the actual slaughter she abstains from intervention until it is no longer needed: withdrawing from the battle, she observes it from the roof of the hall (22.236–8). In the end she

[66] See esp. Eur. *Hipp.* 85–6, 1389–1401, 1437–41 (Vernant 1965: ch. 14). Even the Odysseus–Athena relationship is given something of this chilly remoteness in the prologue to Sophocles' *Ajax*.

[67] See e.g. Kirk 1962: 365, 378–9.

holds up the aegis and sends the suitors running in panic, but by that point the hero and his allies have already gained the upper hand. This is consistent with the practice of the *Iliad* and with later Greek attitudes: the gods help those who are prepared to help themselves.[68]

In one notable respect Athena has the advantage over Penelope: as a goddess, she can take any form she wishes, and in masculine disguise as Mentes or Mentor can play a part in the affairs of Ithaca, organizing a ship for Telemachus and performing other tasks where a woman would be ignored or sent back to her home.[69] As in Aeschylus' *Oresteia*, the goddess who favours the male in all things restores order to a patriarchal society: 'the king's in his palace, all's right with the world'. The masculine personality of the warrior-goddess means that she is even at home in war. Although such qualities were attributed to the Amazons, who figured in the epic *Aethiopis*, the conventions of Greek family life make it impossible for Penelope to participate in the governing of Ithaca or in state affairs: the most that is possible is for her husband to *compare* her 'renown'[70] with that of a virtuous king whose land is prosperous and governed justly (19.108–14).[71] It is striking that the word *kleos*, so closely associated with heroic prowess, should be used to describe the passive and domestic virtue of Penelope; but her virtue is still assimilated to, and subordinate to, that of a man, ultimately her husband. Hence for Penelope to have her husband home and her long years of fidelity rewarded means the end of the story. Whether the passage in which husband and wife retire to bed together also marks the end of the epic will be discussed in the next section.

4. Endings

For the most part it has been assumed above that we are considering a poem which draws upon older sources and traditional material but which is itself shaped by a single mind, a 'monumental poet' who

---

[68] Cf. Fraenkel 1950, note on Aesch. *Agam.* 811; Mikalson 1983: ch. 2.

[69] For comparison between Athena and Penelope, see also Murnaghan 1995.

[70] 19.108, *kleos*; and cf. 19.128 = 18.255. See further H. Foley 1978; Segal 1983; A. T. Edwards 1985: 78–82; Goldhill 1991: 93–108, arguing for 'revisionist' use of the vocabulary of fame.

[71] That Arete does have some say in these matters is another oddity about the Phaeacian community; but it is notable that in fact she does little to justify her reputation, and that when she does initiate a proposal she is told firmly by Echeneus that 'On Alcinous here depends deed and word' (11.346; see also Finley 1979: 89; Garvie 1994 on 6.310–15).

may or may not also be the composer of the *Iliad*. Minor interpolations, sometimes identified by awkwardness or by poor manuscript attestation, do certainly occur, but these are normally a matter of a few lines at most. Far more significant and disquieting are the doubts which have overshadowed the conclusion of the *Odyssey*, from 23.297 to the end of Book 24, ever since antiquity.[72] This section embraces the conversation which husband and wife hold in bed together (including an account of his travels); the descent of the suitors to the underworld, where they find Agamemnon and Achilles in conversation, and where the scene ends with Agamemnon congratulating the absent Odysseus on his good fortune, and praising Penelope; the episode in which Odysseus visits his aged father Laertes, tests him in the by now familiar manner, and eventually reveals himself once Laertes is helpless with grief; and, finally, the brief and abortive attempt of the suitors' kinsmen to retaliate against Odysseus and his followers. In the last episode of the poem, in a strangely accelerated narrative, Athena and Zeus impose peace on Ithaca. A full review of the problems cannot be given here, but the main issues and their implications should be aired.

The Alexandrian scholars Aristophanes and Aristarchus judged 23.296 to be the 'end' (*telos*) or 'limit' (*peras*) of the *Odyssey*.[73] Arguments that they meant by this not the textual conclusion but the climax or 'goal' of the action are more persuasive with *telos* than with *peras*, and should probably be abandoned.[74] It is much less clear whether they judged the remainder of the poem spurious on textual or internal grounds.[75] Internal difficulties certainly exist, though one does sometimes wonder if modern scholarship would have pursued these with the same ruthlessness if the ancient testimonies had not given them this lead. Further complexities are introduced by modern critical studies of closure, the ways in which literary works reach their

---

[72] See Heubeck in Russo 1992 on 23.296 for basic arguments and bibliography. The modern assailants are best represented by Page 1955: ch. 5 (overstating his case, and with many purely rhetorical arguments); S. West 1989; Oswald 1993. Defenders include especially Heubeck in his commentary in Russo 1992; Erbse 1972: 97–109, 166–244; Moulton 1974; Stössel 1975; Wender 1978.

[73] Their views are quoted by the scholia and Eustathius; see e.g. S. West 1989: 118 for the relevant passages.

[74] So Pfeiffer 1968: 175; see now S. West 1989: 118–19.

[75] S. West 1989 argues that they did not even think it spurious, but saw it as a separate lay by the poet. This does not, however, much affect the modern debate.

conclusion.[76] Comparative study strongly suggests differences between ancient and modern taste in these matters; and we must also ask whether the same criteria should be applied to works intended for oral performance.[77]

The arguments for condemning the section are of different kinds. First there is linguistic usage: the last part of the poem contains many odd forms or unique and difficult expressions which cast doubt on its being authentic work of the main *Odyssey* poet. Page's exposition of these was severely criticized by Erbse, but Stephanie West, in an important study, has shown that some recalcitrant cases still lack justification and that certain phrases are hard even to understand. Secondly, there are arguments from religious belief, especially about the underworld and the afterlife. The debate here is closely related to discussion of Book 11, Odysseus' own visit to the land of the dead, which has itself been found controversial.[78] Are the dead conscious or not? Can they converse with one another? Can a dead man enter the underworld before being buried, as the suitors seem to? How coherent is Homer's picture of the afterlife? How consistent should we expect it to be, given that this is imaginative literature and that we find inconsistencies elsewhere in the religious 'system' of the epics? After over-rigid analyses in the past, the recent tendency has been to allow for much more variety and flexibility in Homer's conception of Hades,[79] but Sourvinou-Inwood has thoroughly re-examined the question and insists that the picture in Book 24 must derive from a later period than that of Book 11 and the rest of the *Odyssey*.[80] This conclusion may be contested, but her argument needs to be confronted. Some would no doubt wish to reply that inconsistency and vagueness of

---

[76] B. H. Smith 1968 is a classic treatment in English literature; for classicists, D. P. Fowler 1989 is seminal; see also D. P. Fowler 1997 and the other essays in Roberts et al. 1997, and S. West 2007.

[77] See Kelly 2007a, esp. 384–7 on the *Odyssey*. He argues that early epic characteristically concludes with a kind of diminuendo. One may still feel that the poet of the *Odyssey* might have achieved this effect more skilfully.

[78] See further Petzl 1969; Sourvinou-Inwood 1986; S. West 2012a.

[79] Older views e.g. in Rohde 1925: ch. 1; Page 1955: 21–7. More flexibility: e.g. Vermeule 1979: 29, 34–5, 218 n. 49 (cf. S. West 1989: 138 n. 51); see also M. Clarke 1999, esp. chs. 5 and 6.

[80] Sourvinou-Inwood 1995: ch. 2, esp. 94–107. In the first edition of this survey, fresh from a reading of her work, I endorsed this conclusion, but I am now inclined to treat it with more reserve. For more recent discussions, see M. Clarke 1999: 225–8; Albinus 2000: 67–86; Tsagarakis 2000: 110–19.

conception are what we would expect when the poet is dealing with the mysteries of life after death.

Thirdly, and perhaps most important for non-specialists, there is the question of poetic quality. Here of course there is much scope for disagreement. Most people would agree that the scene in the underworld (leaving aside the eschatological difficulties) is a valuable episode: it shows us Odysseus' fellow-heroes once more, and emphasizes their miserable state, whether their deaths were glorious (Achilles) or humiliating (Agamemnon): death is the same for all. Their misfortune is contrasted with Odysseus' triumph, now reunited with wife and son and victorious over his foes. The episode also enables Penelope to be given her due. As for the scene with Laertes, frequent references earlier in the poem have led us to expect an appearance of Odysseus' father,[81] and this is reinforced both by the importance of the father–son theme in the poem and by the potential contrast with the *Iliad*, in which Achilles will never again see his old father and must be content with the momentary union with Priam, an enemy but a mirror image of Peleus.[82] The way in which Odysseus tests and plays games with his wretched father has outraged many critics, but it should not surprise those who recognize that the hero is not simply a paragon of gentlemanly virtues.[83] By now deception has become second nature to him; nevertheless, as he observes Laertes from a distance he does hesitate, as he never has before, and considers a more open approach. It is consistent with both his character and the thematic tendencies of the poem that he should choose the more devious and potentially more painful option.[84]

The first and last of the four sections are the least satisfactory. Of these the first, in which Odysseus and Penelope recount their stories to one another, is a natural and fitting consequence of their reunion (and storytelling is, of course, one of the recurring activities of the poem), but the way in which it is narrated is somewhat banal.[85] Far

---

[81] S. West 1989 argues that these are all interpolated by the author of this section, but this is not the most persuasive part of her article.

[82] See Rutherford 1986: 162 n. 87.

[83] See Walcot 1977.

[84] Hence I do not agree with S. West 1989: 125, who writes that 'We should of course all like to avoid this conclusion' (i.e. that Odysseus is now habitually a deceiver).

[85] Wender 1978: 15–8 attempts to defend it, but succeeds only in some small details. S. West 1989: 121 points out that Odysseus' narrative here (24.310–43) is the longest piece of indirect speech in all of Homer (though see Dover 1968: 96 for the limited value of such arguments). In view of the almost universal modern dissatisfaction with this passage, it is amusing that Aristotle appears to have considered it a model of concise narration (*Rh.* 3.16.7).

more serious are the charges brought against the conclusion, in which the suitors' relatives summon an assembly, seeking to arouse the community to outrage over the slaughter. Medon and Halitherses warn them not to challenge Odysseus, and they proceed to battle despite this warning. A brief moment of tension is followed by the miraculous charge of Laertes, momentarily restored to youthful strength; in a few more lines the conflict comes to an end, much to Odysseus' satisfaction, and Athena brings harmony to the community. What is peculiar here is that all of the elements seem appropriate and potentially interesting: it is the cursory and over-hasty execution that fails to satisfy, particularly after so leisurely an episode at Laertes' farm. It is almost as though this last section, and in particular the last sixty lines, were a rough sketch which was awaiting further elaboration. Neither the supporters nor the opponents of the Continuation have adequately explained this strange unevenness of style.

Two passages earlier in the *Odyssey* seem to prepare for the events of Book 24, making reference to the danger from the suitors' kinsmen and the prospect of Odysseus visiting his father (20.41–3: 23.137–8). Those who see the Continuation as a later composition must argue that these lines too are interpolated, or that they refer to an earlier version which also contained these events. Defenders of the Continuation often claim that it picks up ideas or develops themes present in the earlier part of the epic, but analysts can dispose of this argument with ease, by maintaining that this is obviously what an imitator would do. Thus the scene in the Ithacan assembly clearly builds on Book 2 (where Halitherses also appeared), but that does not guarantee the authenticity of Book 24. Similarly, the second underworld scene develops themes of Book 11 (especially the superiority of Odysseus' career to that of Achilles), but that need not mean they are by the same hand.[86]

Perhaps the most substantial question arising from this debate is whether the *Odyssey* originally ended with Odysseus and Penelope in bed together, in which case the poet is treating the continuity of their marriage as all-important, or with the aftermath of the slaughter, with potential civil war in Ithaca averted – clearly a more public and political finale. The answer will be different depending on which passages the critic selects and emphasizes from the earlier stages of the poem. But it is hard to believe that nothing was said about the reclaiming of the

---

[86] Thus Sourvinou-Inwood 1995: 101.

kingdom, though some have maintained that epic values would not necessarily require an avenging hero to give any justification for his actions, and that it was only in the later stages of the tradition, when kingship was giving way to aristocratic government, that the need was felt to provide some statement of how the community of Ithaca reacted to the extermination of 110 suitors. In the past I have generally felt that the good parts of the Continuation outweighed the bad, but some of the recent discussions have made me feel that it is more likely to be the work of a later poet. Nevertheless, I continue to think that the tale is unlikely to have ended as Aristarchus and Aristophanes maintained, and that, since it is necessary to take their statement seriously, we should allow that something has gone wrong in the tradition and that an older conclusion has been either lost or reworked, perhaps abbreviated in its final stages. The exact process involved is of course beyond us, but there has clearly been some thought given to the integration of the ending, in view of the anticipatory passages already cited. Hence the tenth book of the *Iliad* is not truly parallel,[87] for the most striking fact about that book is that it can be removed with no adjustment to the surrounding text.

If the Continuation is rejected, then the 'authentic' *Odyssey* reaches its climax with the violent revenge of the hero, at his most Iliadic, upon his enemies and on those who have betrayed him;[88] it then proceeds to a conclusion in a gentler and more subtle style, with dialogue more significant than action, in the recognition and reunion of husband and wife. It thus shows Odysseus supreme in battle but also successful in peace. Although Penelope would be denied the words of commendation which she receives from Agamemnon in Book 24, the sequence of recognitions would end with hers, in which she emerges as the 'victor', and the poem would end with celebration of their marital union. Debate over the merits and status of the existing conclusion will no doubt continue, but 23.296 is an ending we may be able to learn to live with.

---

[87] See S. West 1989: 120. On the *Doloneia*, see p. 35 above.

[88] Modern readers are repelled by the mutilation of the disloyal Melanthius (on which see Davies 1994) and by the hanging of the maids. By contrast with the momentous significance which the *Iliad* attaches to the issue of mutilation (Segal 1971b), the *Odyssey* seems remarkably casual (cf. G. Murray 1934: 126–8, who surely misinterprets the tone of 22.473). Perhaps one simply has to accept that Homer's audience would have thought any punishment justifiable for such treachery within the household.

IV SOME MEMORABLE SCENES

In the remaining pages I offer some more detailed comments on a number of passages from both epics. Besides allowing slightly more attention to stylistic matters than was possible in the earlier chapters, this procedure also gives an opportunity to comment on some specific problems, and on a number of other approaches which have not been discussed so far.

1. Paris' bedchamber (*Iliad* 3.424–47)

And Aphrodite, smiling goddess, herself took up a chair for Helen, and brought it and placed it in front of Alexandros [Paris]. There Helen, daughter of Zeus who wields the aegis, took her seat, turning her eyes aside, and spoke slightingly to her husband: 'You came back from the fighting, then. I wish you had died there, brought down by a man of strength, who was once my husband. Oh, before now you used to boast that you were superior to the warrior Menelaus in strength and power of hand and spear. Well, go now, challenge the warrior Menelaus to fight you again face to face. But no, I would advise you to stop now, and not pit yourself against fair-haired Menelaus in warfare or combat without thinking – you might well be brought down by his spear.'
Paris then answered her: 'Wife, do not deride my courage with these hard taunts. This time Menelaus has beaten me with Athena's aid, but another time I shall beat him: there are gods on our side too. No, come, let us enjoy the bed of love. Never before has desire so enveloped my heart, not even on that first time when I stole you away from lovely Lacedaimon and sailed off with you in my seafaring ships, and lay with you in love's union in the island of Kranae – even that was less than the love and sweet desire for you that comes over me now.'
So he spoke, and led the way to their bed: and his wife followed.[1]

Later readers thought it implausible that a ten-year war should be undertaken to recover a faithless wife, and in Greek lyric and tragedy Helen generally receives unfriendly treatment.[2] The Trojan elders gaze admiringly at her as she appears on the walls, but their attitude is divided: it is no cause for reproach that Greeks and Trojans should fight over such a woman, and yet it would be better if she left and returned home. Helen herself comments that the women of Troy, not surprisingly, regard her with deep hostility (3.411–2; 24.768–70,

---

[1] Translation from Hammond 1987.
[2] Cf. Hdt. 2.113–20, esp. 120.1–2, for scepticism; for disapproval, see Alcaeus 42, 283 Lobel and Page; Aesch. *Agam.* 62, 225, 448, 681–716; Eur. *Andr.* 590–69; *IT* 356, 438–55; *Cyc.* 179–87 (!), etc.

774–5). But Helen's own attitude has been found ambiguous by many. Uncertainty surrounds the original flight with Paris: was she abducted against her will, or did she come with him voluntarily? The repeated line in which Greeks speak of 'avenging the struggles and moaning of Helen' (2.356 = 590), though it can be twisted to mean their own struggles over her, is more naturally read as implying that she left Sparta reluctantly; but it is possible that this is a misguided opinion, even a kind of wishful thinking, on the part of the speakers. That Paris was also able to carry off much treasure (e.g. 7.363–4) suggests that the 'abduction' was not a violent or rapid process but involved cooperation on Helen's part. Most important of all are Helen's own comments on her actions. In each of the three episodes in which she appears, she blames herself and wishes that she had died before she came to Troy; although she speaks with respect and affection to Priam and Hector (and values their gentle treatment of her), she is bitter and contemptuous towards Paris. All of this suggests that she feels considerable responsibility and guilt over her original departure – that, in short, she was sufficiently infatuated with Paris to make what has proved to be a disastrous choice, abandoning her husband and child for a lesser man.[3]

The extract above follows on Aphrodite's rescue of Paris from seemingly certain death at Menelaus' hands. His efforts on the field were inglorious, his 'withdrawal' seems to ensure a Greek victory, given the terms laid down for the duel. Helen comes to him reluctantly: Aphrodite has first cajoled and then, meeting a defiant reply, has threatened her, effectively forcing her to come to Paris' bedchamber. Aphrodite is in control of the situation, acting to bring pleasure to Paris, her favourite. Helen's distaste is indicated by her turning her eyes away, and by the sharpness of her opening line; her repeated references to her former husband make clear that she is still, as earlier in the episode, full of longing for the past that she has left behind in Greece (cf. 3.139–40, 173–80, 232–3, 236–44).

In view of this, it is surprising that some readers have detected a change of tone at 433 ('But no, I would advise you…'), assuming that this represents a softening on Helen's part: yes, Menelaus is the better man, and yet her love is still for Paris.[4] Is her conclusion a sign

[3] On Helen, see also Reckford 1964; J. T. Kakridis 1971: 25–53; Reichel 1994: 264–71 (with bibliography). On this episode, see Lendle 1968.

[4] See e.g. the notes in Hooker's (1980) and Willcock's (1978) commentaries on the scene; also the older edition, Leaf 1900–2. Kirk 1985: 327 sits on the fence.

of resurgent affection and concern, or a sarcastic and sceptical comment ('no, I don't think you would be wise to do that')? We should note the disparaging adverb 'foolishly' in 436 (Hammond's 'without thinking' is probably too mild); this, and the fact that Paris himself refers to her speech as 'hard taunts' (438), seem to support the latter interpretation. It is Paris who is passionate in this scene; Helen in his chamber remains as reluctant as when she spoke out against Aphrodite. Paris is the comical, lustful figure, in contrast with Helen, a tragic victim.

The other reading, which sees Helen as overwhelmed by passion and returning willingly to Paris' arms, is undoubtedly influenced by the presence of Aphrodite throughout the episode. The goddess of love, it is argued, must have the power to alter a mortal woman's feelings; is this not what Aphrodite does here with Helen? Important for this argument is the line which follows Aphrodite's approach to Helen on the walls: 'thus she spoke, and stirred *thumon* [emotion? enthusiasm?] in her [Helen's] breast' (3.395). What emotion is kindled here – desire or anger? Parallel passages give limited help here: elsewhere, it is true, this expression seems to indicate that the listener is convinced or stimulated to do what the speaker has advised,[5] but it is not certain that this must be the case wherever the line is used: moreover, this is a less straightforward situation, as in the other cases the speaker is a mortal addressing a mortal, and there is normally no reason to doubt that the other will respond (11.803 is perhaps the closest analogy to the present passage). Perhaps it is a mistake to try to identify the emotion precisely: does the line mean more than 'Thus Aphrodite spoke, and Helen was moved by what she said'?

A subtle and ingenious interpretation, which owes something to the school of 'neo-analysis' discussed below (p. 118), sees this scene as a re-enactment of Helen's original crime.[6] As Aphrodite prompted her to leave with Paris in the first place (or, in human terms, in the same way that she fell in love with her glamorous foreign guest), so now, though years afterwards, despite Helen's longing for Menelaus, Aphrodite brings her back to Paris' bed. This theory gains some support from the fact that Aphrodite at first takes the form of an old woman, a wool-worker, who served Helen in Sparta: perhaps she

[5] A point stressed by Kirk 1985 ad loc. Almost identical lines are found at 4.208; 11.803; 13. 468. Compare also 2.142; 3.395; 14.459; 17.123.

[6] Kullmann 1960: 250–1, who regards the scene as indebted to the Cyclic poem the *Cypria*; cf. e.g. M. W. Edwards 1987a: 196.

played the part of a go-between at the time of the original seduction? The parallelism would be a further example of the way in which episodes of the early years of the war are recalled or remoulded in the early books of the *Iliad* (see p. 44 above). But in the absence of a narration by the *Iliad* poet of the seduction, the theory must remain speculation. Even if the parallel is allowed, the differences between the scenes are at least as important. If line 395 does imply some renewal of Helen's desire for Paris, it is swiftly dispelled; Aphrodite's influence upon her emotions is ineffectual, and the goddess must resort to threats. If Helen does soften and go willingly to bed with Paris, the poet gives us no clear indication of this: the final line of the scene is carefully neutral (447). When we next see Helen with Paris, he is cheerfully playing with his armour rather than putting it on, and she is again bitter in reproach of herself and her lover (6.321-2, 343-58). While it may be wrong to deny any hint whatsoever of erotic attraction on Helen's side, any such passion on her part is short-lived and joyless.

This scene, then, is a particularly complex test case for discussion of the interplay between human psychology and divine intervention, a topic treated in Chapter 2. I have argued that Helen's emotions are her own, and that she no longer feels any emotional involvement with Paris. Other positions are possible, and this may be a case where the poet has deliberately allowed some ambiguity. It remains important that Helen tries to reject Aphrodite's overtures, and is critical of Paris. If this were not so, she would be a much less sympathetic character.

Lighter aspects of the scene may be found in the reaction of Paris to Helen's rebuke. His declaration that Menelaus has won 'with Athena's aid', while he will have his chance another day, is particularly shameless from one who only escaped death through Aphrodite's aid; nor did the poet give us any hint of Athena's involvement in Menelaus' onslaught. The reference to Paris' passionate desire for Helen, which led him to make love to her at the first opportunity 'on a rocky island',[7] humorously enhances our sense of his frivolous sensuality. The scene is a close relation of the amorous encounter between the lustful Zeus and the less enthusiastic Hera in Book 14 (cf. esp. 3.442-6 with 14.315-28); but there the goddess is deliberately setting out to deceive her husband, whereas here the woman has no power to resist.[8] Moreover, the whole scene is a witty

---

[7] In 445 it is unclear whether Kranae is a proper name (as we might speak of the island of Rockall) or an adjective. Even if the former is right, the name suggests the discomfort of the lovers.
[8] Cf. Macleod 1983: 10.

inversion of a 'typical' situation in Homeric epic. It is common for a woman to restrain a man, trying to prevent him from going out to battle or into danger.[9] Thus Andromache does her best to induce Hector to remain in Troy, and Hecuba begs Priam not to go to confront Achilles; in the *Odyssey*, Eurycleia tries to persuade Telemachus not to set out in search of his father. In all these cases the man resists these overtures and shows himself a hero. But in Book 3 the motif is reversed, for Helen, disgusted at Paris' poor showing in battle, tells him to go out and fight like a man, whereupon he replies that he will not go, and urges her to come to bed (see also 6.337–8). Comic and enjoyable in itself, the scene gains in sophistication if we see it as a clever adaptation of familiar material.

2. Phoenix's memories (*Iliad* 9.478–97)

And away I fled through the whole expanse of Hellas
and gaining the good dark soil of Phthia, mother of flocks,
I reached the king, and Peleus gave me a royal welcome.
Peleus loved me as a father loves a son, I tell you,
his only child, the heir to his boundless wealth,
he made me a rich man, he gave me throngs of subjects,
I ruled the Dolopes, settling down on Phthia's west frontier.
And I made you what you are – strong as the gods, Achilles –
I loved you from the heart. You'd never go with another
to banquet on the town or feast in your own halls.
Never, until I'd sat you down on my knees
and cut you the first bits of meat, remember?
You'd eat your fill, I'd hold the cup to your lips
and all too often you soaked the shirt on my chest,
spitting up some wine, a baby's way...a misery.
Oh I had my share of troubles for you, Achilles,
did my share of labour. Brooding, never forgetting
the gods would bring no son of mine to birth,
not from my own loins. So you, Achilles –
great, godlike Achilles – I made you my son, I tried,
so someday *you* might fight disaster off my back.
But now, Achilles, beat down your mounting fury!
It's wrong to have such an iron, ruthless heart...[10]

---

[9] See especially J. T. Kakridis 1971: 68–75; also Griffin 1980: 6–8.
[10] Translation from Fagles 1990.

The long speech of Phoenix, Achilles' mentor, has already been mentioned in Chapter 1 (p. 8 above). He is the second of the embassy to make an appeal to Achilles, coming between Odysseus and Ajax. His is the longest speech: like Nestor, he tends to garrulousness. Whereas Odysseus had used arguments based on profit and prestige, Phoenix addresses his former protégé in emotional and personal terms, narrating his own life history, recalling the bonds between him and Achilles, producing moral arguments backed up by quaint allegory, and telling the story of Meleager as a warning to Achilles: his example shows the dangers of intransigent anger.[11] The rather sentimental tone evident in this extract annoys Achilles ('do not try to disturb me by weeping and complaining'; 612), and he resents the fact that Phoenix of all people should be siding with his enemy (613–14); but he does make a concession in replying to Phoenix. Whereas in his answer to Odysseus he had declared that he would set off home next day, he now says that in the morning 'we shall consider whether to go back to our own lands or to remain' (618–19). In reaction to Ajax's short and contemptuous speech he goes still further. Phoenix, therefore, has an important part to play in Book 9. Particularly important is the prominence of the father–son theme in his speech: he treats Achilles as the son he never had (note especially 'dear child'; 437), and Achilles responds with the pet name *atta* ('dadda'; 607). The failure of Phoenix, an old man who has been like a father to Achilles, is countered in Book 24 by the success of Priam, a still more pitiful old man who wins over Achilles by comparing himself with Peleus, the hero's father (24.486–506).[12]

There is, however, a problem surrounding the membership of the embassy, and this is a case where the difficulties felt by the analysts cannot be waved away by either unitarian or oralist critics. It is not simply that Phoenix is a character unmentioned before Book 9: new characters are often introduced according to the poet's needs. Nestor refers to the embassy as consisting of Phoenix, who is to be the leader, Ajax, and Odysseus (they are to be accompanied by two heralds). But when they are proceeding along the shore, and when they arrive in Achilles' encampment, the ambassadors are repeatedly referred to in the dual form ('the two of them') – nine times in less than twenty

---

[11] On Phoenix's speech, see further Lohmann 1970: 245–76; Rosner 1976; Scodel 1982; Brenk 1986. On the Meleager paradigm, see above pp. 8–9.

[12] Macleod 1982: 34.

lines (182–99).[13] Soon afterwards the poet mentions Odysseus (218); and in line 223 all three names appear ('Ajax nodded to Phoenix; but godlike Odysseus noticed...'). From that point on the episode unfolds without difficulty; but we remain baffled by the shift between an embassy of three and one of two (most interpreters agree that the heralds can be ignored).[14] The conclusion seems inescapable that a version once existed which involved only two ambassadors, and the majority of critics think of Phoenix as the interloper. The analysts simply assumed that a later hand had added Phoenix; the elaborate theory of Page, in fact, identifies at least four layers: an *Iliad* without any embassy, then an embassy of two, then the version with Phoenix, then the addition of Book 19 (there are further subtleties). But Phoenix is more important and less easily dispensable than Page maintained: even without looking outside Book 9, if we omit the speech of Phoenix and Achilles' reply, the latter's concession to Ajax becomes inexplicably sudden. A different approach, starting from the assumption that a master-poet lies behind the work as a whole, is to see the *Iliad* as gradually developing in Homer's hands: the embassy book evolved, and Phoenix, while a later addition, was still added by the monumental poet, and integrated in the poem.[15] On this argument, the duals offer us a glimpse into 'Homer's workshop'.[16] That argument gains some support from the fact that Achilles' instructor is elsewhere said to have been Chiron the centaur, a supernatural figure (11.832; cf. 16.143 = 19.390), whereas here he is given a human teacher. As we have seen elsewhere, it seems to be characteristic of Homer, and especially the *Iliad*, to play down the more exotic features of heroic mythology.

While it may be correct to see the *Iliad* as developing throughout the poet's career, and it is certain that many of the objections to Phoenix's presence are outweighed by the positive contribution his speech makes, it remains peculiar that the poet should have overlooked the cluster of duals in a short section of text. Nowhere else does Homer nod in quite

---

[13] For obvious reasons, translations often gloss over this, translating the duals as plurals: e.g. Hammond 1987. Fitzgerald 1974 even inserts at 182 '*Following Phoenix,* Aias and Odysseus walked together...'! Exceptions include Lattimore 1951 and Fagles 1990.

[14] For a fuller account of the difficulties, see Hainsworth 1993: 57, 85–7; Griffin 1995: 51–3. In English the major analytic discussion is Page 1959: 297–315 (older treatments are listed by Motzkus 1964: 97). For subsequent argument see e.g. Segal 1968 (unpersuasive); Wyatt 1985; M. W. Edwards 1987a: 218–19, 228–30.

[15] Reinhardt 1961: 212–42, endorsed by Hainsworth 1993: 57.

[16] A phrase used by Willcock 1976: 99 and by Hainsworth 1993: 57; see also M. L. West 2011c: 13.

so marked and localized a fashion: there is nothing quite so strange as the problem of the duals elsewhere in the epic. Perhaps this is one case in which 'analytic' arguments may still have some validity, but not when directed at the existence of Phoenix. Rather, we might turn the problem on its head and consider the possibility that the passage in which the embassy is despatched has been interfered with by some post-Homeric rhapsode. A possible motive might be the oddity of Phoenix being present in Agamemnon's camp: this was, perhaps, accepted casually by the main poet, but seemed anomalous to a successor, for is not Phoenix part of the entourage of Achilles? Like Patroclus, he should be attendant upon the hero, listening to the embassy, eventually goaded into utterance when he hears Achilles speaking so rashly and with such hostility. (His protests can in fact be seen as a less successful anticipation of Patroclus' appeal in Book 16.[17]) If this hypothesis is correct, then the later poet would not be an interpolator but an imperfect editor, who, having decided that Phoenix ought to be in Achilles' camp already, changed Homer's plurals into duals accordingly, but overlooked the line in which Nestor appoints Phoenix as a member of the embassy (168) – the only line which makes it obvious that Phoenix is in Agamemnon's camp. It is easier still to suppose that he missed the later references to making up a bed for Phoenix (617–18, 620–2, 688). Problems, of course, remain, as with all discussion of this puzzling crux; but the false note is more plausibly ascribed to a later bard than to Homer himself.[18]

3. Patroclus brought low (*Iliad* 16. 777–800)

So long as the sun was climbing still to the middle heaven,
so long the thrown weapons of both took hold, and men dropped under them;
but when the sun had gone to the time for unyoking of cattle,
then beyond their very destiny the Achaeans were stronger   780
and dragged the hero Cebriones from under the weapons
and the clamour of the Trojans, and stripped the armour from his shoulders.
And Patroclus charged with evil intention in on the Trojans.
Three times he charged in with the force of the running war god,

---

[17] E.g. M. W. Edwards 1987a: 228, on whose discussion I am building here.
[18] See now S. West 2001, whose solution is similar to mine, but supported with new arguments involving the original form of Phoenix's autobiographical tale. For a different approach, see Scodel 2002: 160–71.

screaming a terrible cry, and three times he cut down nine men;   785
but as for the fourth time he swept in, like something greater
than human, there, Patroclus, the end of your life was shown forth,
since Phoebus came against you there in the strong encounter
dangerously, nor did Patroclus see him as he moved through
the battle, and shrouded in a deep mist came in against him   790
and stood behind him, and struck his back and his broad shoulders
with a flat stroke of the hand so that his eyes spun. Phoebus
Apollo now struck away from his head the helmet
four-horned and hollow-eyed, and under the feet of the horses
it rolled clattering, and the plumes above it were defiled   795
by blood and dust. Before this time it had not been permitted
to defile in the dust this great helmet crested in horse-hair;
rather it guarded the head and the gracious brow of a godlike
man, Achilles; but now Zeus gave it over to Hector
to wear on his head, Hector whose own death was close to him.[19]

The description of the coming of evening not only marks the passage of
long hours of fighting but also anticipates the downfall of Patroclus: the
setting sun symbolizes the hero's decline in fortune.[20] More generally,
we recall that this will mark the end of Hector's day of success
(11.191–4; see p. 66 above). In this final moment of his *aristeia*
Patroclus' prowess reaches supreme heights: his onslaught slays twenty-
seven men. Similarly the Achaeans are on the verge of achieving the
impossible, contrary to what is destined (780). Their champion is
described in godlike terms: 'with the force of the running war god'
(784), 'like something greater than human' (786); but as always with
such comparisons there is the implication that he remains less than a
god.[21] The sequence 'thrice. . .and then the third time' is ominous, regularly anticipating a change or reversal of fortune.

    The way in which the poet addresses Patroclus (the device called
'apostrophe') has aroused much comment. The technique has already
been used at earlier points in the book (lines 20, 584, and esp. 692–3:
'whom first, whom last did you slay, Patroclus, when the gods sum-
moned you to your death?'). In passages such as these the emotional
involvement of the poet is exceptionally prominent. The use of the
vocative may have originated as a metrical convenience, and in some
cases elsewhere seems relatively colourless (esp. 15.582), but the
ancient commentators regarded it as a deliberately pathetic device,

[19] Translation from Lattimore 1951.
[20] See further Fenik 1968: 216; Willcock 1976: 126, 189; Taplin 1992: 156.
[21] See Griffin 1980: ch. 3.

and most recent discussions agree.[22] The fact that Homer uses it most with sympathetic characters, especially Menelaus and Patroclus, supports this view.[23] It is poignant that the poet anticipates Patroclus' demise while speaking to his own character; the effect resembles the scenes in which Zeus, with similar detachment and compassion, speaks pityingly to mortals who cannot hear his words (esp. 17.201–8, addressing Hector).

The intervention of Apollo is momentous but invisible to Patroclus: he comes upon his victim suddenly and violently, 'dangerously' (789; more literally, 'terrible'). Here, again, a stylistic device which often has little or no significance is deployed powerfully, with the adjective *deinos* held back to the beginning of line 789.[24] The actions of Apollo are described in a lengthy passage, extending beyond the section quoted: the effect is almost that of seeing a sequence of events in slow motion. Both the direct action of a god and the prolonged narration of the attack enhance Patroclus' status. The whole episode is unusual in that three agents are involved in Patroclus' death: Apollo stuns the victim and strips off Achilles' armour, Euphorbus wounds him, Hector finishes him off.[25] The whole process from the beginning of this passage to the bold response of Hector to the dying man's words occupies nearly 100 lines. As elsewhere, the poet emphasizes important scenes by amplification and elaboration of detail.

The inner eye of the audience is directed not so much toward the bewildered Patroclus as to the armour falling from his body. This is the armour of Achilles, in which he had come forth to battle in the hope that the Trojans would be deceived. But Patroclus is an inadequate substitute for his friend, and the original arming scene in which he donned the greater man's armour is perhaps mirrored by the 'disarming' scene here, in which Patroclus is stripped of his defences. (It has also been suggested that the armour of Achilles may have been traditionally invulnerable, so that it had to be removed before the wearer could be slain; if so, this is another case of Homer's

---

[22] For the scholia, see N. J. Richardson 1980: 272. For modern discussion see e.g. A. Parry 1972: 8–22; Janko 1992 on 13.602–3.

[23] In the *Odyssey* the situation is less clear: there the device is exclusively reserved for the swineherd Eumaeus.

[24] For scepticism about the significance of this kind of placing of words, see Bassett 1926; M. W. Edwards 1966: 139–40; contrast Tsagarakis 1982: 10–31. There is a thorough investigation of this question in Higbie 1990.

[25] Janko 1992: 408–10 explains this in neo-analytical terms, according to which the episode is modelled on the death of Achilles.

preference for a less magical style of narrative.[26]) Divine armour befits a godlike hero: hence as long as Achilles wore this armour it was not fitting for it to be sullied by dirt and blood. The contrast between Patroclus and Achilles is emphasized again through the change in the condition of the helmet, now stained or 'defiled': the verb is tellingly repeated (795, 797). Glorious past is contrasted with ignominious present ('before this time...but now'); beauty and distinction are brought low, in both man and armour. Soon it will be Patroclus who is defiled in the dust. The final lines of the extract look to the future: Hector, favoured by Zeus, may now wear this helmet, but for a brief time only: his own death is near. The last line quoted above falls into two halves: the first completes the summing up of Hector's triumph; the second shows us a glimpse of his future defeat, implicit in his victory.[27]

This last point is reinforced by Patroclus' dying words, close to the end of book 16 (852–4):

> 'You yourself are not one who will live long, but now already
> death and powerful destiny are standing beside you,
> to go down under the hands of Aiakos' great son, Achilles.'[28]

When Homer comes to narrate the death of Hector and the dragging of his corpse, he is concerned to recall many aspects of Patroclus' death, and some of the same motifs of dust and defilement reappear. Especially close are 22.401–4:

> A cloud of dust rose where Hector was dragged, his dark hair was falling
> about him, and all that head that was once so handsome was tumbled
> in the dust; but at this time Zeus gave him over
> to his enemies, to be defiled in the land of his fathers.[29]

In both cases, a hero who was once triumphant and magnificent is laid low; in both, beauty is marred by dust and dirt; in both, the all-embracing power of Zeus is at work. The verbal techniques through which Homer arouses pity for his characters are as vital as his

---

[26] P. J. Kakridis 1961. The situation in the *Iliad* is complicated by the fact that Achilles at different stages has two separate sets of divine armour, the first being seized by Hector. See further Janko 1992 on 16.130–54.

[27] Compare the comment by J. Griffin, in his contribution to the joint article by Griffin and Hammond 1982, at 142 n. 17: '"Half-lines in Homer" is a less obvious title than "Half-lines in Virgil", but it might make an interesting study.'

[28] Translation from Lattimore 1951.

[29] Translation from ibid., modified. Also relevant are 16.638–40; 17.51–2, 439–40. See also Fenik 1968: 163; Segal 1971b: 41–2; Griffin 1980: 134–8.

unobtrusive but far-reaching control over the plot and thematic structure of his narrative.

4. The horses of Achilles, gifts of the gods (*Iliad* 17.426–53)

But the horses of Achilles Aeacides were still far from the combat weeping, ever since they had first learned that their rider lay in the dust, fallen thanks to Hector slayer of men. Indeed, Automedon brave son of Diores kept whipping and lashing them over and over with his swift whip, and many times he pleaded softly with them, and many times uttered threats. But still the two of them refused to move either towards the ships and the broad Hellespont or back into the conflict to join the Achaeans. Instead they stood there, as a pillar stands firm, one that is fixed on the burial mound of a man or a woman who has perished – so they stood firm, still fastened to the beautiful chariot, and their heads drooped down to the soil; hot tears welled forth from their eyes and dropped to the earth as they grieved, out of longing for their charioteer, and their rich manes were defiled falling forth on either side of the yoke.

And as they mourned there, Zeus son of Cronos saw and pitied them both, and shaking his head he reflected aloud: 'Poor creatures, why did we give the two of you to king Peleus, a mortal man, while you are both ageless and deathless? Was it so that you might suffer misery along with wretched mankind? For there is nothing at all more woeful than man, of all creatures that breathe and creep upon the earth. But even so, Hector Priam's son is not going to ride with you and your ornate chariot. For that I shall not allow. Is it not enough that he has the armour and exults in it as he does? No, I shall put strength in your limbs and your hearts, that you may carry Automedon to safety, out of the war and back to the hollow ships...'[30]

The faithful dog Argos is not the only animal in Homer with almost human emotions. Horses are prominent in the *Iliad*, and some are given names by their masters (e.g. Hector: see 8.184–97). The horses of Achilles, of immortal birth, are not unique (Zeus gave immortal horses to Tros in recompense for Ganymede), but they are more conspicuous in the narrative than any other steeds. In this passage, the noble beasts weep for their former charioteer, the dead Patroclus (whose special care for them is mentioned elsewhere, 23.281–2), paying no attention to Automedon's efforts to guide them back to the Greek camp. Ordinary horses are subordinate to their human owners, but these deathless horses are superior to mortals, although they feel distress at the loss of a good master. The inclusion of Zeus as compassionate observer enriches the scene still further: he pities not Patroclus,

[30] My translation.

who is dead, but the horses, who cannot die but must live among mortal kind. The tableau brings out in a novel way that central Iliadic theme, the gulf between the divine and the human world.[31]

This scene provides a starting point for an exploration of one strand of the mythological tradition. In line 443 Zeus asks why the gods gave these horses to Peleus, a mortal. This is one of several references to the gifts which Peleus received from the gods, some of which are explicitly said to have been given on the day of his wedding to Thetis;[32] in particular, the divine armour which Hector has just stripped from Patroclus (see 17.194–7, and esp. 18.84–5, where the wedding is mentioned). Another such gift is the great spear which only Achilles can now wield (16.140–4). In Book 24 (61–3) it is said that all the gods attended Peleus' wedding, a sign of exceptional favour. The occasion was popular in art from the early sixth century.[33]

M. L. West in a recent book comments that 'It looks as if P [his name for the *Iliad* poet] knows a poetic account of the wedding of Peleus and Thetis.'[34] Perhaps so, but the point deserves fuller consideration. Both the poet's and the audience's knowledge of and ability to draw on mythological data are in question. The wedding was a focal point of the myths relating to the Trojan War. At least as early as the *Cypria*, it was the occasion when a contest of beauty arose among Athena, Hera and Aphrodite, which had to be settled by the Judgement of Paris. We do not know whether Homer associated this dispute with the wedding; the judgement is mentioned only once, and elliptically.[35] If he did, the wedding would already have the potent ambiguity that it possesses in many later texts from Pindar onwards[36] – on the one hand, a moment of supreme felicity, when a man is privileged to wed a goddess who will give birth to the greatest of heroes, but, on the other, an occasion at which the seeds of sorrow are sown, with conflict among the gods leading to war and death among mortals, including the death of that unborn son. It is at any rate clear that the marriage of Thetis to Peleus was doomed to end badly;[37] by the time

---

[31] For more detailed discussion of this scene, see Schein 2002.

[32] In Book 23 Poseidon is said to have been the one who gave the horses (276–8); he is of course traditionally associated with horses.

[33] E.g. the Sophilos *dinos* and the François vase (T. H. Carpenter 1991: plates 38 and 1), *c.*580 and 570 respectively.

[34] M. L. West 2011c: 413, on 24.60–3.

[35] See above p. 44, n. 3.

[36] [Hes.] *Cat.* fr. 211; Pind. *Pyth.* 3.92–103; Eur. *IA* 1036–79; and of course the much-discussed ambiguities of Catullus 64.

of the *Iliad* they are living apart and, whereas Peleus is described as bowed down by grief and age, Thetis remembers with resentment how she was forced by Zeus into marriage to a mortal, against her own wishes (18.429–35). Homer may or may not have known a poem that recounted the wedding of Peleus (as opposed to its being an element in the mythical tradition), but he certainly found it a convenient symbol for the way in which human hopes can be disappointed even when the gods seem most favourable.

All of this makes good mythological sense in itself, but there are further ramifications. Why did Zeus make Thetis marry Peleus in the first place? According to later accounts, Zeus and Poseidon were both attracted by the notion of taking Thetis as their bride (in Zeus's case, one of many consorts), but changed their minds on learning of a prophecy that the son of Thetis would be more powerful than his father.[38] She was therefore married off to a deserving mortal. But the motive of the prophecy is first attested in Pindar and the *Prometheus Bound*; it cannot be established for early epic.[39] Indeed, there is an early testimony that Thetis declined Zeus's overtures to avoid giving offence to Hera ('Hes.' fr. 210; the source also refers to the *Cypria*, fr. 2).

There are still further complications. It seems that Thetis' marriage also served Zeus's purposes in other ways: his intention in starting the Trojan War was to bring the age of heroes to an end and to reduce the overpopulation of the earth (these motives are brought in by the Iliadic scholia, again referring to the *Cypria*, fr. 1). According to some critics, we should see all the early poets as working within this framework (most explicitly presented in the Hesiodic *Catalogue of Women*): the Trojan War brings the heroic age to an end, and already in the *Odyssey* that age is fading into memory. After this time, there will no longer be interaction between man and god, and no more heroes or 'demi-gods' will be born of divine parentage.[40] Here caution is in order: we cannot be certain that the developed chronological conception found in the *Catalogue* is to be read back into Homer, and in

---

[37] Cf. Gantz 1993: 230–1, citing schol. A *Il.* 16.22, 18.57, 60; Ap. Rhod. *Argon.* 4.869–79.

[38] There are analogies here with the succession to Cronos, where another female (Rhea) gives birth to the usurper. Compare the danger from Metis in Hes. *Theog.* 886–900, with West's note (M. L. West 1966).

[39] Pind. *Isthm.* 8.26–47 (cf. and contrast *Nem.* 5.34–7); later see esp. *PV* 755–68.

[40] [Hes.] *Cat.* F 1 and 204.95–104 (many uncertainties of text); M. L. West 1997a: 480–2. Clay's work has been influential here (e.g. 1983, 1989, and 2011); see also Graziosi and Haubold 2005: 35–45 on 'cosmic history'.

general we should not assume that each poet worked with the same mythical palette, still less that there was an orthodox chronology from which they could not deviate.

A minimalist reading, then, will take the marriage of Peleus and Thetis as a mythical datum which does not require justification and background, but which in later poetry generated further elaborations and explanations. A bolder approach, not necessarily well founded, sees Thetis as a more important figure in mythology than she seems to be in the *Iliad*, and assumes that these other accounts were known to Homer, so that we can detect undercurrents or resonances that are not made explicit in the text.[41] The attraction of this approach is that it helps explain why Thetis seems to have so close a bond with Zeus: there does seem to be a history there. (Achilles refers to her having assisted Zeus during conflicts among the gods, though Thetis does not in fact use this argument in her appeal; and Hera is clearly resentful and suspicious of Thetis's intimacy with her husband.) Little is certain here, but it does look as if Homer knew more about Thetis than is recounted in the *Iliad*.

5. News comes to Achilles (*Iliad* 18.15–37, 50–1)

While he was pondering this in his mind and his heart, the son of proud Nestor came up close to him with his warm tears falling, and gave his painful message: 'Alas, son of warrior Peleus, there is terrible news for you to hear, which I wish had never happened. Patroclus lies dead, and they are fighting over his body. It is naked now – Hector of the glinting helmet has his armour.'

So he spoke, and the black cloud of sorrow enveloped Achilles. He took up the sooty dust in both his hands and poured it down over his head, spoiling his handsome face: and the black ashes settled all over his sweet-smelling tunic. And he lay there with his whole body sprawling in the dust, huge and hugely fallen, tearing at his hair and defiling it with his own hands. And the serving-women that Achilles and Patroclus had won in war shrieked aloud in their hearts' grief, and ran out to flock round the warrior Achilles: all of them beat their breasts with their hands, and the strength collapsed from their bodies. And to one side Antilochus mourned with his tears falling, and he held the hands of Achilles as his glorious heart groaned: he was afraid that Achilles might take a knife and cut his own throat. Achilles gave out a terrible cry, and his honoured mother heard him, where she sat by the side of her old father in the depths of the sea, and she wailed loud in response. And the goddesses gathered round her, all the

---

[41] Slatkin 1991 (discussed by D. Cairns in his introduction to Cairns 2001: 45–8). An interesting development of this approach for Hera and Athena can be found in Kelly 2007b: 422–5.

daughters of Nereus... The silvery cave filled with them; and they all beat their breasts together...[42]

This is the most painful moment for Achilles in the entire poem – the moment in which he discovers that by persevering in his wrath and sending Patroclus out in his place he has doomed his beloved friend. The fact that Patroclus himself bears some responsibility, stressed in Book 16 by the poet and briefly implied in Achilles' earlier speech of misgiving (12–14), is ignored in the flood of emotion which overwhelms the hero. From Antilochus' tears and from the opening words of his speech it is clear that he brings bad news, and he makes no effort to delay or conceal it. Achilles' failure to reply indicates the enormity of his grief: Homer here anticipates one of the dramatic devices of Greek tragedy, the momentous silence.[43]

This passage, and the scene which follows, forms one of the chief examples put forward by critics practising what has been rather unsatisfactorily called 'neo-analysis'. The label associates this approach with the older methods of the analysts, but the similarity is not very great. Both schools have attempted to discern different layers or stages in the compositional processes, but, whereas the analysts normally tried to divide the poem into strata, the neo-analysts are concerned more with the influence of earlier versions on the surviving epics.[44] As for the passage quoted, it has been persuasively argued that the poet is deliberately composing this scene in such a way as to remind the audience of an epic narration of Achilles' own death. The most important points supporting this argument are: (a) the similarity of the expression in line 22 ('the black cloud of sorrow...') to familiar formulae for death, combined with Achilles' prostrate position in the following lines; (b) the lamentation of Thetis and the Nereids, who are listed at considerable length: their intense grief would be appropriate for the death of Thetis' son, rather than the death of the mortal Patroclus; (c) the use of the phrase 'Thetis began the lament' (18.51), language elsewhere

---

[42] Translation from Hammond 1987.

[43] Cf. esp. Achilles himself in Aeschylus' *Myrmidons*, as shown by Ar. *Ran.* 832–4, 912 and scholia, with Taplin 1972. For other cases see N. J. Richardson 1974 on *Hymn to Demeter* 197–201; cf. N. J. Richardson 1980: 281; de Jong 1987b.

[44] Fundamental treatment by J. T. Kakridis 1949, esp. 65–95; the authoritative collection of material is Kullmann 1960. More recent discussions include Kullmann 1981 and 1984 (both reprinted in Kullmann 1992); M. W. Edwards 1991: 15–19; Dowden 1996. M. E. Clark 1986 provides a bibliographical survey; for an excellent synthesis see Willcock 1997. For an attempt at a rapprochement between neo-analysis and oral theory see Burgess 2006.

applied to mourners over a dead man;[45] (d) the way in which Thetis cradles her son's head in her arms, a gesture associated with the mourner at a death-bed (18.71; cf. 23.136, 24.724);[46] (e) the parallels between this scene and the detailed description of Achilles' funeral in the *Odyssey* (24.41–92). A particularly interesting parallel is the use of the phrase in line 26, 'huge and hugely fallen', used in the same passage of the *Odyssey* of Achilles, and elsewhere only of another dead man, Cebriones (*Od.* 24.39–40; *Il.* 16.775–6). All of these points seem to suggest that Achilles' death is foreshadowed here: the reason is obvious, since the decision he is about to make will ensure the death which he has previously been able to avoid. Thetis' words as she prepares to join her son emphasize this inevitable outcome.

If these arguments are accepted, it follows that Achilles' death and funeral had been described in earlier epic, whether by the *Iliad* poet himself or by his predecessors. An important distinction needs to be made, however. The *Iliad* could be making conscious use of (and allusion to) earlier poetry without necessarily drawing on any of the specific epic poems about which we have evidence. The neo-analysts have often marred their case by insisting on the priority of a specific poem in the so-called Epic Cycle: in this case, it was often assumed that the poem which we know to have narrated the death of Achilles, namely the *Aethiopis*, was the 'source' for this passage of the *Iliad*. Sceptics can simply declare that the evidence suggests that the *Aethiopis* is in fact later than Homer, or may insist that the two poems are quite independent. It is preferable to leave the specific relationship between Homer and the Cycle out of the picture, and to think rather in terms of a tradition about the death of Achilles, which the *Iliad* presupposes and exploits. That tradition may well have included many of the elements mentioned by Proclus in his summary of the *Aethiopis*, but it is not necessary to assume that one poem is solely dependent on the other.[47] The important point is that it seems likely that the simpler, more obvious use of these motifs – in a description of Thetis mourning

[45] See 18.316 = 23.17 (Achilles over Patroclus); 24.723, 747, 761 (the women at Hector's funeral).

[46] J. T. Kakridis 1949: 65–6; illustration in Vermeule 1979: 15.

[47] For more extended discussion, see Currie 2012 and Kelly 2012b, the former arguing for allusive intertextuality, the latter strongly opposed to such an approach in dealing with oral poetic tradition. To my mind Currie makes a convincing case that such allusion can indeed exist even between oral poems. Of course, those who accept that the poets were literate do not face the same objections.

for Achilles – came first, whereas the *Iliad*'s more subtle redeployment
of language and situation is a secondary development.[48] Like many
other passages discussed in this Survey, the opening of Book 18 effectively contradicts Erich Auerbach's famous account of Homer's narrative style, according to which everything is on the surface, and there is
no room for complexity, mystery or 'multilayeredness'.[49]

The role of Antilochus as messenger to Achilles is also of interest in
this connection.[50] Even without neo-analytical theories it is clear that
Antilochus, youthful son of Nestor, is a figure of some importance in
the last six or eight books of the poem: he is one of the last to hear
of Patroclus' death, Menelaus breaks the news to him in an emotional
speech, he seems to be the obvious person to take the news to Achilles.
Later he is prominent in the funeral games, a hot-headed competitor
who nevertheless knows when to concede in the face of objections
from his elders. Achilles seems to show him special favour; he smiles
at Antilochus' enthusiastic protestation of his rights – the only place
in the poem where Achilles does smile (23.555–6). It is as though
Achilles responds to Antilochus' impulsiveness: indeed, the latter's
indignation at being deprived of his prize seems to be a small-scale parallel to the great wrath of Achilles (see esp. 1.29 ∼ 23.553).[51] But
whereas Agamemnon's grasping ill-will brought forth the momentous
anger of Achilles, in Book 23 Achilles is the generous peace-maker,
and both Menelaus' bad temper and Antilochus' pique are appeased.

It is not going too far to say that Antilochus is almost becoming a
substitute for Patroclus – and in the *Odyssey* the two men are named
together as part of Achilles' entourage in the underworld (11.468;
24.16, cf. 77–8). Neo-analytic critics see this as having additional significance in view of the parallels between Patroclus' role in the *Iliad*
and Antilochus' role in the *Aethiopis* and possibly in earlier versions
of the same tale. Just as Hector killed Patroclus, so in the lost epic
Memnon killed Antilochus; in both cases Achilles exacted revenge.
Strictly speaking this is difficult to reconcile with the *Iliad*'s version,
since we are told that Achilles' doom awaits him 'immediately after
Hector', and at the end of the poem we assume that his death is

---

[48] Similar argument in Seaford 1994: 154–9, with criticism of the sceptics.
[49] Auerbach's essay 'Odysseus' scar', the first chapter in Auerbach 1953, has often been reprinted. For criticism see Köhnken 1976; de Jong 1987a: 22–3; Lynn-George 1988: 2–27.
[50] See further Willcock 1973 and 1983a. M. L. West 2003c argues against this, because he takes
a different view of the content of the source poem.
[51] Macleod 1982: 28–32, esp. 30.

imminent, at most a few days away. Here again it can be argued that the story-line of the *Iliad* is a later development, that Achilles' revenge on Hector is modelled on Achilles' revenge on Memnon, hard though it is for moderns to accept that so central a part of the plot should be derivative.[52] This argument may well be found less persuasive than the neo-analytic account of Book 18, and its implications for our appreciation of the *Iliad* are less clear. Further explorations of Homer's 'sources', however fascinating, would take us into still more uncertain territory.

6. The pride of Ajax (*Odyssey* 11.543–67)

Other souls of the dead and gone still stood there sorrowfully, each of them questioning me on whatever touched him most. Only the soul of Ajax the son of Telamon kept aloof, nursing anger still at my victory in the contest when beside the ships I made my claim for the armour of Achilles, whose goddess-mother offered the prize. Would I had never won that prize! Because of it, the earth closed over heroic Ajax, who alike in presence and in prowess surpassed all other Danaans after the matchless son of Peleus. To him I now spoke appeasing words:

'Ajax, son of the noble Telamon, is it then a thing beyond all hope that in death at least you should set aside your wrath against me for the winning of those hateful arms? The prize that the gods there offered was to bring distress on all the Argives when the tower of strength that you had been was forever lost to them. Ever since you perished, our grief for you has been like the grief for the son of Peleus, Achilles himself; and no other was the cause of all this but Zeus; he it was who bore hate unbounded against the host of Achaean spearsmen, and because of that decreed your doom. Come to me now, Lord Ajax, and hear the words that I wish to speak; conquer your spirit and pride of heart'.

So I spoke, but he made no answer to me, only followed to Erebus the other souls of men dead and gone.

Then, despite his anger, he might still have spoken to me, or I to him, but my heart was eager to see the souls of the other dead.[53]

In the land of the shades, far from normal human existence, Odysseus has spoken with the ghosts of Agamemnon and Achilles. Other comrades flock around him and speak with him; only Ajax stands aloof, unable to forget or forgive his rival in the contest for Achilles' divine armour. Here Odysseus tries to make amends, not without a few subtle touches of flattery: in particular, by declaring that 'our grief for you has

---

[52] See further Kullmann 1960: 37–8, 311; Seaford 1994: 154–6.
[53] Translation from Shewring 1980, with slight modifications.

been like the grief for the son of Peleus'. Traditionally, in the *Odyssey*
and elsewhere, Ajax is second-best to Achilles.[54] Again, we should
note the way in which Odysseus seeks to slide responsibility for all
the disastrous affair of the arms on to the gods ('no other was the
cause of all this but Zeus...'; 558–9; cf. 555). This speech, like
Priam's words to Helen in *Il.* 3.164, represents delicacy and tact, not
strict theological doctrine. Odysseus' tone is predominantly one of
compassion and regret, but he concludes by inviting Ajax to come closer and listen to his story: as usual, he is eager to be the centre of attention. But Ajax is not to be persuaded, and his silent, unreconciled
withdrawal shows us the kind of hero that he is: it expresses a kind of
resolution and strength which Odysseus will never have and perhaps
does not want. In his famous chapter on Homer, Longinus commented
that Ajax's silence was far more impressive than any words could have
been (*On the Sublime*, 9.2).

The lines which follow, however, may seem startling and incongru-
ous. 'And then nevertheless he would have spoken to me, or I to
him. But my heart in my breast was anxious to see the souls of others
among the dead' (565–7). Editors since antiquity have cut out this conclusion to the episode, wishing to leave Ajax's silent, disdainful exit
unqualified. Surely, they argue, Ajax would not have given in, and in
any case what a shocking attitude for Odysseus to adopt ('well, sorry
Ajax, I really don't have the time...').[55] But we must remember that
it is Odysseus who is telling the story at this point, and that here as elsewhere in the first-person narrative he may be trying to put himself in a
good light. On this reading, the final comment can be seen as bravado
on Odysseus' part. We know, and in his heart he knows, that he could
never have prevailed on Ajax to give way: but he is not prepared to
admit it to the admiring Phaeacian audience. 'Or I to him', an inappropriate alternative in the circumstances, is a stumbling give-away.[56]

This interpretation of the passage in question is reinforced by
detailed study of the narrative technique of Odysseus' account of his
own adventures, in an important paper by Irene de Jong.[57] Her article
establishes that the vocabulary and style of the hero's narrative differs

---

[54] Cf. 470, 550–1, Alcaeus 387, Soph. *Ajax* 1340–1, *PMG* 898. Similarly in the games of *Iliad*
23, Ajax enters three contests and comes first in none of them.

[55] See e.g. Page 1955: 26–7.

[56] So esp. Eisenberger 1973: 184 (independently e.g. A. Parry 1981: 29), endorsed by de Jong
1992: 5 and Sourvinou-Inwood 1995: 85.

[57] De Jong 1992 (cf. already Suerbaum 1968). See also R. B. Rutherford 1986: 150 n. 33.

from the normal manner of the poet, who narrates his tale in less emotional terms and with greater detachment. Thus Odysseus emphasizes the folly of his companions and his own quick wit, and lays stress on the sufferings endured and the ingenuity with which they are surmounted; he is proud of his own foresight in bringing strong wine with him when exploring the Cyclops' territory; he makes sure that the audience do not miss the point about the size of the stag he slew and carried back to his camp (10.168, 171, 180), or the magnitude of the terrible rock that closes off the cave of Polyphemus; and he singles out the loss of six companions to Scylla as 'the most pitiful thing that I saw' (12.258-9; see below). The technique heightens our involvement and establishes the emotional tone of the hero's narrative as distinct from that of the poet's own tale.

7. Monster and man (*Odyssey* 12.243-59)

We had looked that way [i.e. towards the whirlpool Charybdis] with the fear of death upon us; and at that moment Scylla snatched up from inside my ship the six of my crew who were strongest of arm and sturdiest. When I turned back my gaze to the ship in search of my companions, I saw only their feet and hands as they were lifted up; they were calling out to me in their heart's anguish, crying out my name for the last time. As when a fisherman on a promontory takes a long rod to snare little fishes with his bait and casts his ox-hair line down into the sea below, then seizes the creatures one by one and throws them ashore still writhing; so Scylla swung my writhing companions up to the rocks, and there at the entrance began devouring them as they shrieked and held out their hands to me in their extreme of agony. Many pitiful things have met my eyes in my toilings and searchings through the sea-paths, but this was the most pitiful of all.[58]

Scylla, the hideous sea-monster with six heads on long necks, immortal and invulnerable, was described in horrific terms by Circe earlier in the book (73-100), where Odysseus was warned that he could not hope to evade her entirely, but must content himself with losing no more than six men. This inhuman being combines the terrors of nightmares with the tall stories of seafarers: few passages in the poem have a more spine-chilling effect. Odysseus' narration lays stress on the pain he feels at the loss of his comrades: as elsewhere, it is made clear that his homecoming, though in the end successful, involves suffering and loss. The

---

[58] Translation from Shewring 1980.

episode is also used to show Odysseus' continuing efforts to deal with
the weird world of the wanderings in conventional heroic terms: despite
Circe's warnings that any such attempt is futile, he hopes to repel
Scylla, and dons his 'glorious armour' in preparation for her assault.
In fact, not only does he fail even to see her sudden attack, but he
could not slay her if he tried: 'Scylla is not of mortal kind; she is a
deathless monster, grim and baleful, savage, not to be wrestled with'
(Circe's words again, 118–19). He admits in retrospect that he forgot
Circe's advice; but to ignore divine warnings can lead to disaster, as
we see again when his companions kill the cattle of the sun.

There is a double lesson here for Odysseus: he must be prepared to
follow the instructions of the gods (as he follows Athena's in the second
half), and he must also recognize that in some circumstances the old
heroic ethic of confronting one's enemy in open combat is ineffective.
In one respect, however, he already possesses some of the skills he will
need in future: he can keep his own counsel. In giving directions to his
men earlier, 'I had stopped short of mentioning Scylla, an inexorable
horror: the crew in fear might have left their oars and have huddled
down in the hold' (12.223–5). Secrecy and self-restraint will be the key-
notes of his behaviour in the Ithacan narrative which is to follow.

Perhaps the most striking aspect of the passage quoted is the simile
comparing Scylla to a fisherman drawing in his catch. Like many
similes which are applied to supernatural beings, it makes an extraordinary event more vivid and imaginable.[59] More important, it does so by a
kind of inversion of normality: whereas the poet and his audience are
familiar with the sight of a man catching fish, Odysseus witnesses a
creature of the sea 'catching' men. In the strange and remote world
of the wanderings, man is confronted by impossible beings in unnatural
settings: heroic valour, as we have seen, is futile against natural force or
immortal monster.[60] Similarly on land, the gigantic Laestrygonians are
seen spearing men as if they were fish (10.124). Another parallel comes
in Book 5, where the poet is recounting Odysseus' storm-tossed

---

[59] For fuller discussion of Homer's similes, see Fränkel 1921; Scott 1974 (including full lists),
2009; Moulton 1977; Macleod 1982: 48–50; M. W. Edwards 1987a: ch. 12 and 1991: 24–41;
R. B. Rutherford 1992: 73–7; Buxton 2004.

[60] Cf. and contrast Kirk 1970: 162–71, who interprets the Cyclops myth along structuralist lines
as a nature vs. culture story: primitive man-eating monster vs. shrewd intelligent human armed
with a quick wit, wine, and fire. Note also the similes at 9.384–8, 391–4, both applied to
Odysseus as he proceeds with the perilous act of blinding the Cyclops. Both describe his action
in terms of human craftsmanship: ship-building and the work of a bronze-smith, techniques of
a civilized society.

journey from Calypso's island: 'as when many pebbles stick to the suckers of an octopus when he is dragged out of his lair, so the skin was stripped off his [Odysseus'] hands against the rocks' (5.432–5).[61] There Odysseus, out of his element, is helpless and injured whereas the sea-creature is not. Another common feature in the fisherman simile is that it describes something everyday, a timeless scene involving an ordinary man rather than a hero (and indeed the heroes generally do not eat fish except in extreme circumstances).[62] The ordeal of the epic hero is contrasted with the simplicity and order of 'normal' life; at the same time, similes like this also sometimes serve to remind us of the very humanity of the heroes. Especially memorable is the simile which compares Odysseus' nocturnal restlessness with the cooking of a haggis-like dish over a fire (20.22–30) – a startling comparison, but one which reminds us of the emphasis laid elsewhere in the *Odyssey* on the hero's appetite.

The simile in this extract has a further parallel – possibly even a counterpart – in a much later passage, where Odysseus stands triumphantly in his own palace, with the suitors lying dead before him.

He saw the suitors, one and all, lying huddled in blood and dust. They were like the fish that fishermen with their close-meshed nets have drawn out from the whitening sea on to the curving beach; they are all heaped upon the sand, longing for the sea waves, but the sun beats down and takes their lives. So did the suitors lie in heaps, one upon another. (22.384–9)[63]

With Odysseus back in his own rightful place, the 'natural' order is re-established, and the man becomes the fisherman.[64]

There is certainly similarity of subject, but does this count as an echo? As we have seen, much recent criticism of Homer has found extensive cross-reference and interconnection between different parts of the poems, often convincingly; similar attention has been focused on the similes, with rather less success. 'Linked' similes certainly exist, but are perhaps most persuasively identified when they occur in swift succession.[65] Thus, in *Iliad* 2, three similes are used to describe the motion of the Achaean army in terms of the movement of the sea

---

[61] See Macleod 1982: 49.
[62] See Griffin 1980: 19 on heroic diet: add Pl. *Resp* 3. 404b and context; N. J. Richardson 1975: 73 n. 6.
[63] Translation from Shewring 1980.
[64] For other reversals, see R. B. Rutherford 1992 on 20.356–7, and 1986: 152 n. 40.
[65] See further Moulton 1977: ch. 1 and 133–9 (sometimes over-subtle).

(144–7, 209–10, 394–7): it is not necessary, but certainly possible, to see these as planned in a sequence. In Book 16 of the *Odyssey*, we first find Eumaeus' joy at the safe return of Telemachus compared with that of a father tearfully welcoming home his son after many years (this while the true father, Odysseus, is present in disguise). Shortly afterwards, when Odysseus has revealed himself, father and son weep together, and another simile compares them with birds who have lost their young unfledged (*Od.* 16.14–21, 216–19). There is a thematic analogy, but the passages seem too different in subject to speak of a close connection. Other suggestions, however ingenious, are often very implausible. But the possibility of very long-range 'linking' of similes can hardly be denied in view of the famous case describing Odysseus' and Penelope's reunion (23.231–40, quoted on p. 95 above), which recalls the actual experiences of Odysseus in Book 5 and seems also to pick up the themes of a simile there (5.394–9).[66] None of these cases, however, demands actual knowledge of the other passage, and there is never an explicit cross-reference; consequently, it may be better to speak in terms of recurring subject matter or thematic concerns. At a minimum, Homer often shapes his similes for more than mere ornamentation, and linguistic study has suggested that here at least we may see the hand of the individual poet at work, rather than the stock material of the tradition.[67]

8. Travel and adventure (*Odyssey* 14.196–293 [extracts])

I might well enough spend a year recounting the sorrows of my spirit and still not come to an end of them – all the sorrows that I have toiled through because the gods willed it so. Wide Crete is the home I boast of, and I was a rich man's son. He had many other sons as well, bred in the house and born in wedlock. My own mother was a concubine, bought as a slave; yet I, no less than the true-born sons, was given regard by my father, Castor son of Hylax... But the death-spirits carried him down to Hades' home, and his haughty sons divided his substance up, casting lots for it. To me they gave a house and very little besides, but by my own merits I won for wife a daughter of very wealthy parents, because I was no fool and no coward... Work on the land I was never fond of, or such care of the household as brings up children in prosperity. The things that

---

[66] Moulton 1977: 128–9.

[67] Shipp 1972: 208–22, argues on linguistic grounds that the elaborated similes are late in date, and this has been generally accepted (see e.g. Janko 1992: 12, though contrast his p. 9). It is striking, in poems so rich in formulaic material, that similes are so rarely repeated, even when the same subject matter is involved. Is this a sign of Homer's relative independence of the tradition?

I loved were ships and oars and battles and gleaming spears... Even before the sons of the Achaeans ever set foot on the land of Troy, I had nine times had under my command men and swift ships to sail against foreign shores, and hence much booty reached my hands...the people began to urge myself and Idomeneus to lead an expedition of ships to the war at Troy. To deny what they asked was not possible, the people's voice was too compelling... [and after the Trojan War] for a month, no more, I stayed at home and enjoyed myself there with my children and my wedded wife and my possessions; then impulse urged me to fit out vessels and sail to Egypt with my heroic comrades... [but after his comrades recklessly raided Egyptian farms] the Egyptians killed many of us with the keen bronze, others they took inland alive to labour for them in slavery... I dashed the wrought helmet from my head, I threw down the shield from my shoulder, the spear from my hand; I ran to meet the king's chariot and I touched and kissed his knees. He had compassion, and rescued me, gave me a place in his own chariot and took me in tears back to his palace, fearing the wrath of Zeus who protects strangers... In that place I stayed for seven years, and I gathered much wealth among the men of Egypt, because they all made me gifts. But when the eighth year came, there came with it a cunning-witted Phoenician, a rogue who had done harm enough in the world already. He won me over with his craftiness and took me away with him to Phoenicia...then he put me aboard a ship that would sail the sea to Libya. His plan in this was a treacherous one; I was to help him to take the cargo there, but he hoped to sell me myself and get a huge price for me. Though I had misgivings, I had no choice but to go aboard with him...[68]

This is enough to give the flavour of Odysseus' longest lying narrative, the tale he spins to the loyal swineherd, who listens with fascination (see 361–2 and 17.518–21).[69] It is superfluous to comment on the hero's marvellous fluency in invention, but we may note that none of the yarns he spins is precisely the same, though there are common elements. In his lies he regularly portrays himself as a Cretan, and it is tempting to think of the saying 'all Cretans are liars', though that may itself arise partly from the stories in the *Odyssey*! He clearly suits his tale to his addressee: Eumaeus too was carried away by villainous Phoenicians[70] and sold as a slave, as we learn when he recounts his life-story in Book 15 (351–484, esp. 415–84). It is natural to suppose that Odysseus really knows this already;[71] and indeed he draws a comparison later between Eumaeus' experiences and his own tale.

This speech can be studied in various ways. One procedure, now out of favour, is to try to reconstruct from the lies the 'real' adventures of

---

[68] Translation from Shewring 1980.
[69] For bibliography on the lies see above p. 79, n. 9.
[70] There has been a great deal written about the Phoenicians in the archaic period: see e.g. Aubet 1993; López-Ruiz 2011.
[71] For a different view, see Stewart 1976: 90–1.

Odysseus or of some real person on whom he is based; more plausibly, some have argued that parts of the lies preserve valuable clues to other, probably older poetic versions of the travels of Odysseus.[72] An illuminating approach is to study the thematic material, comparing the other lies and the rest of the poem's narrative.[73] What emerges is that a great deal of the speech consists of elements redeployed in various contexts: thus the disastrous raid on the Egyptians resembles the raid by Odysseus' men on the Cicones, the first of his adventures after leaving Troy, and the seven-year stay in Egypt is paralleled by Menelaus' sojourn in the same country. We see also that Odysseus here, as in the longer narrative to the Phaeacians, takes care to build up his own image: he is a fearless and inexhaustible fighter, ever game for adventure; it was his comrades who behaved foolishly in the Egyptian episode and who then panicked, whereas he has the initiative to throw himself on the king's mercy; he is quick-witted enough to suspect the Phoenician's motives, and so forth. The ethical outlook of the false tale also corresponds to that of the *Odyssey* as a whole: compassion and respect for suppliants or strangers are admirable qualities (as the honourable actions of the king of Egypt show); gathering gifts and booty, if it can be done safely, is always desirable; and violent action is not the answer to everything, so that one must sometimes cut one's losses and live to fight another day. In the lies as in the main plot, Odysseus is a survivor.

Finally, there is the historical dimension of the lies, and of the *Odyssey* more generally. We can take it for granted that no wandering sailor ever encountered a Cyclops or visited the land of the dead, but in the lies which Odysseus narrates there is nothing physically impossible or intrinsically improbable. We are not here concerned to recover the actual experiences of a traveller, but to gain some idea of what Homer's audience thought of as 'typical' of sea-voyaging and adventures abroad. Even here we should make some allowance for epic amplification: it is perhaps unlikely that a single leader made nine successful raids, and we may feel sure that an invader-turned-suppliant would have been speared by subordinates before he got anywhere near the physical person of the king of Egypt. Yet many elements of

---

[72] The first approach is pursued with perverse determination by Woodhouse 1930, esp. chs. 17–18; for emphatic rejection see Fenik 1974: 171 n. 69. The second, which concentrates especially on Odysseus' account of his experiences in Thesprotia, is expounded by S. West 1981 (cf. e.g. Danek 1998: 214–20; Malkin 1998: 126–34).

[73] Here the work of Fenik 1974: 167–71 is virtually definitive.

Odysseus' narrative seem entirely realistic: the bastard son of a rich man, favoured by his father but treated less well by the legitimate sons; disgruntlement over inheritance (we naturally think of Hesiod); the bold entrepreneur, scorning the easier life at home and loving the excitement of sea travel.[74]

Thucydides remarked on the way in which Homer treats piracy and looting as normal, almost a familiar profession and certainly not something to which a man might be ashamed to admit (Thuc. 1.5): this was characteristic, as he deduced, of the unstable and warlike conditions of earlier times. Kidnapping and abduction went along with looting, as Herodotus' opening chapters also imply (1.1–4; cf. Eumaeus' tale, *Od.* 15.425–9, 449–53). But it was not only looting which might take a man abroad: the Phoenician trader is sailing all the way to Libya with his unnamed cargo, and Athena, seeking a plausible excuse for her disguised appearance in Ithaca, adopts the identity of Mentes from Taphos, carrying a cargo of iron to the city of Temese which he wishes to exchange for copper. Herodotus mentions a real-life equivalent, the Samian merchant Kolaios, a figure of the mid-600s, who was on his way to Egypt when he was carried off course by storms and ended up in Tartessos, north of Cadiz (Hdt. 4.152).[75] He was renowned as the richest merchant of his time. Trading is normal, though there are signs elsewhere that it is not quite the done thing for an aristocrat (*Od.* 8.159–64). The knowledge in our passage of Egypt and the Nile also anticipates historically attested campaigns: surviving graffiti carved on the colossal statue of Rameses II at Abu Simbel show that Greek mercenaries were in service to the Egyptian king Psammetichus II around 600 BC.[76]

The *Odyssey* thus yields much evidence to the social historian, provided it is recognized that epic narrative needs to be handled with some care. Another aspect is the Greek expansion overseas, as population growth, social dissension, or trading aspirations drove the various communities to establish colonies in far-flung areas of the Mediterranean.[77] According to tradition the process began in Sicily,

---

[74] See Purcell 1990, who touches on Homeric matters only in passing, but presents a stimulating picture of the Mediterranean background. See also Strasburger 1953; Lane Fox 2008 (whose travels take him a long way from Homer: chs. 19–21 are the most relevant).

[75] See Boardman 1999: 114.

[76] ML no. 7; Boardman 1999: 115–16, with illustrations. See also M. L. West 1997a: 617.

[77] Schaefer 1960, Graham 1964, 1982; Boardman 1999 (much-expanded revision of a 1964 book). For a briefer treatment see Jeffery 1976: 50–7.

with Naxos colonized from Euboean Chalcis, and Syracuse from Corinth in about 735, probably within a generation of the *Odyssey* poet's lifetime. It is remarkable that Alcinous assures Odysseus that his people's ships can transport him home with ease, 'even if it is very much further away than Euboea' (*Od.* 7.321).[78] Epic heroes provided precedents and legitimation for these overseas settlements.[79]

Echoes of this movement have been detected elsewhere. In Book 9, Odysseus' description of the island off the Cyclopes' coast gives a strong impression of an opportunity missed: it has woods, vines, arable land, a good harbour, 'but the Cyclopes have no red-cheeked ships, or shipwrights' (*Od.* 9.105–41). Here as in other respects the Cyclopes are defined in opposition to humankind, as primitive and antisocial, unpolitical beings.[80] The opening of Book 6, which describes how Alcinous' father moved to Scheria in order to escape the maraudings of other Cyclopes, lays down the minimal formula for establishing a colony: 'he ringed the city with a wall, built houses, gave the gods temples, apportioned land for tillage' (7–9). Later in the same book the city is described at greater length by Nausicaa (262–9); it is clearly a Greek-style *polis*. The same may be confidently assumed of the community surrounding Odysseus' palace on Ithaca, and is probable even of Troy: arguments that Homer portrays some form of pre-*polis* society are difficult to sustain.[81] Reverting to the passage under discussion, a final point which indicates future political developments occurs in the lines which speak of 'the people's voice', the *dēmou phēmis*, as putting pressure on Idomeneus and others to marshal a force against Troy.[82] Kings and nobles make the decisions, but the people have some influence on their deliberations. This balance of political forces is in accord

[78] Interpretations of this reference vary: Garvie 1994 ad loc. suggests that 'to an Ionian poet Euboea itself seemed to be on the western edge of the known world, so that Scheria must be an unimaginable distance beyond it'. M. L. West 1988: 172 argues that the *Odyssey* may itself have been composed in Euboea; so also Powell 1997.

[79] Malkin 1998; Dougherty 2001. Lane Fox 2008: 382 offers an extended *tour d'horizon* of the Mediterranean world in or around the time of Homer, but strangely insists that the *Odyssey* predates the colonizing movement (suggesting a date of 760–740).

[80] See Vidal-Naquet 1981: 84, 85–7.

[81] Extended argument and bibliography on this debate in Raaflaub 1993. Seaford 1994: chs. 1–2 argues that the *polis* is emergent in Homer, but still weaker and less important than the *oikos*. The subject is also treated by Scully 1990 (somewhat diffuse).

[82] See further Raaflaub 1993: 54–9. On the use of the term *demos* in archaic Greece, see e.g. Donlan 1970, 1973. We note incidentally that here, as in the *Iliad*, there is no trace of the more romantic notion that the Greek leaders, who had all been suitors of Helen, were now bound by an oath to aid her wronged husband. See Taplin 1990: 68–9, who argues that the three possible hints of this oath in the *Iliad* are not significant.

with the 'meritocratic' air of a society in which a bastard son (admittedly, the son of an eminent man, like Archilochus of Paros) with a small inheritance can make a good marriage and rise to wealth and fortune.[83] Archilochus too was a survivor, prepared to drop his shield and fight another day.[84]

Odysseus' account of his expedition to Egypt and his subsequent tale of how he escaped from the Phoenician are a world away from the isle of Calypso and the rock of six-headed Scylla. While they cannot be safely trawled for historical dates and facts, the 'lies' shed indirect light on attitudes, values, and expectations. Something of the pessimistic tone of an authentic beggar sustains the sombre morality found elsewhere in the *Odyssey*, with its emphasis on the instability of fortune and the blindness of men to the future.[85] But there is also a note of exuberance and confidence, which reminds the reader that life is exhilarating, and the world large and full of new surprises, new experiences. It is not too imaginative to see here a reflection of the spirit of some of the Greek settlers and travellers as they set out to explore, sometimes to exploit, the Mediterranean and beyond. Theirs was a simpler world. Yet we can still enjoy and learn from Homer's vision of the greatness, the baseness, the hopes, and the follies of humankind.

---

[83] For a short but lively account of Archilochus' career and poetry, see Jeffery 1976: 181–3; more detail on history in Graham 1978; on poetry in Burnett 1983: part 1.

[84] Fr. 5 West; cf. fr. 114 on the right sort of general.

[85] See e.g. in this speech 14.198, 213–15, 235–6, 243, 274–5, 310, 338. Elsewhere see esp. 18.130–50 (Odysseus to Amphinomus); 19.363–9; 20.194–6.

BIBLIOGRAPHICAL NOTE

Texts

The text most widely used is the Oxford Classical Text (Monro and Allen 1920 for the *Iliad*, Allen 1917–19 for the *Odyssey*), but it is widely agreed that this is deficient (see e.g. Pasquali 1952; Tachinoslis 1984; Janko 1990; N. G. Wilson 1990: 316. The most important new edition of the *Iliad* is that of M. L. West (1998–2000), supplemented by his companion volume (M. L. West 2001b). West's magnificent work provides the reader with more accurate and up-to-date information than any previous edition (especially on the papyri, but also on ancient quotations and testimonia, where West builds on the work of Ludwich). For the *Odyssey* there is P. von der Mühll's edition (1945). H. van Thiel has provided editions of both epics (van Thiel 1991, 1996); his texts are based firmly on the medieval manuscript tradition, setting aside readings from papyri and ancient citations.

Commentaries

The most important change in the period since J. B. Hainsworth's 1969 Survey is that we now have modern commentaries on the whole of Homer's text. Previous work, some of it now over a century old, retains some value (esp. Leaf 1900–2 on the *Iliad*, for his clarity of presentation and firm grammatical grasp; also Stanford 1959 on the *Odyssey*, a sympathetic work though often very brief and selective in annotation); but the new Cambridge *Iliad* (Kirk 1985, 1990; Hainsworth 1993; Janko 1992; M. W. Edwards 1991; N. J. Richardson 1993) and the Oxford *Odyssey* (Heubeck, West, and Hainsworth 1988; Heubeck and Hoekstra 1990; Russo 1992) must now be regarded as standard. For students a good reading text is M. M. Willcock's two-volume *Iliad* (Willcock 1978, 1984).

The *Iliad* commentary is distinguished by its fine introductory essays, and it has been suggested that a list of these would be helpful to students.

Vol. 1 (Kirk 1985): The methods and aims of the commentary; The making of the *Iliad*, preliminary considerations; The structural elements of Homeric verse; Aristarchus and the scholia; The first four books of the *Iliad* in context.

(Note also the long general treatment of the Catalogue of Ships, effectively an independent essay.)

Vol. 2 (Kirk 1990): The Homeric gods: prior considerations (covers oriental influence and cultic 'realities'); Typical motifs and themes; The speech-element in the *Iliad*; History and fiction in the *Iliad*.

Vol. 3 (Hainsworth 1993): Formulas (a long and authoritative treatment); The *Iliad* as heroic poetry.

Vol. 4 (Janko 1992): The gods in Homer: further considerations; The origins and evolution of the epic diction; The text and transmission of the *Iliad*.

Vol. 5 (Edwards 1991): The narrator and the audience; Composition by theme; Similes; Style.

Vol. 6 (Richardson 1993): Structure and themes; Two special problems (book division and the end of the *Iliad* in relation to the *Odyssey*); Homer and his ancient critics.

In addition, all but the first volume provides at least brief introductions to each book (in volume 1 the final part of the introduction serves this purpose). The final volume has a consolidated index of Greek words, but not of other topics. It would be otiose to say much about the relative merits of the various volumes, when such riches are presented in each; I merely note my agreement with those reviewers who find Janko's volume particularly acute and independent, while Edwards perhaps holds the balance most admirably between technical observation and literary sensitivity.

In general the *Odyssey* commentary is less successful and less well integrated. There are general essays of the kind described above only in volume 1 (A. Heubeck, 'General Introduction'; J. B. Hainsworth, 'The Epic Dialect'; and S. West, 'The Transmission of the Text' – all, as one would expect, of high quality). Volume 2, by A. Heubeck and A. Hoekstra, includes a short introduction to the wanderings by the former and an essay by the latter mainly concerned with the poetic dialect. In volume 3, J. Russo gives a general introduction to Books 17–20, and the other contributors (M. Fernadez-Galiano and A. Heubeck) provide short introductions to each of the last four books. There is less cross-referencing and editorial coordination in the project. The effect is peculiar when one passes from Fernandez-Galiano's account of Books 21–22 (severely analyst in tendency) to that of Heubeck on Books 23–24 (unitarian to a fault), and although commentators must of course be allowed to express their views, there is in this case insufficient space given to contrary opinions. The final volume includes cumulative indexes both of words and of subjects. For all of this devoted work generations of scholars and students will be grateful.

Commentaries on individual books continue to appear. The special merits of C. W. Macleod's edition of *Iliad* 24 (Macleod 1982), with its

long and sensitive introduction dealing with the poem as a whole, are well
known. On a similar scale is J. Griffin's edition of *Iliad* 9 (Griffin 1995);
note also S. Pulleyn on *Iliad* 1 (Pulleyn 2001). The Cambridge series
has also issued volumes on *Iliad* 6 (Graziosi and Haubold 2010) and 22
(de Jong 2012), and on *Odyssey* 6–8 (Garvie 1994), 17–18 (Steiner
2010), and 19–20 (R. B. Rutherford 1992). More basic but helpful for
the student are J. T. Hooker's edition of *Iliad* 3 (Hooker 1991), C. H.
Wilson's of *Iliad* 8 and 9 (C. H. Wilson 1996) and J. Watson's of
Odyssey 6 and 7 (Watson 2002, a revision of a much older edition).
Further volumes are in preparation.

Kelly 2007b, on *Iliad* 8, is a work in a different category: enormously
detailed and technical, not a book for the beginner. De Jong 2001 is a narratological commentary on the whole of the *Odyssey*: many insights, but
probably not to be used without a more traditional commentary to hand.
A very different undertaking is the massive project initiated by J. Latacz
and a number of collaborators (Latacz et al. 2000–, in progress), a magisterial text and German commentary on the whole *Iliad*. When completed
this will be an edition even more ambitious than the Cambridge series,
and it makes slow and unpredictable progress (thus far volumes on
Books 1–3, 6, 19, and 24 have appeared); but any specialist will need to
make much use of the work.

Besides the more traditional commentaries, there are smaller and more
modest 'companions' designed for those studying the poems in translation:
e.g. Willcock 1976, Postlethwaite 2000, Jones 2003, all on the *Iliad*; Jones
1988 on the *Odyssey*.

Translations

Translations of Homer become ever more numerous and, with the decline
in wide knowledge of Greek, more important. Alexander Pope's versions,
edited by Maynard Mack in volumes 7–10 of the Twickenham Pope edition (Pope 1967a, 1967b), are dazzling and rhetorical, best read alongside
a more faithful version. Those by Lang, Leaf, and Myers 1882 (*Iliad*) and
by Butcher and Lang 1879 (*Odyssey*), which adopted an archaic prose style
in imitation of the King James Bible, are now probably hard to enjoy reading, though they have a certain dignity. Equally archaic though less distinguished are the old Loeb editions by A. T. Murray (1919, 1924–5): his
Odyssey has now been modernized by G. E. Dimock (A. T. Murray
1995); W. F. Wyatt has performed a similar service for the *Iliad* (A.
T. Murray 1999). The old Penguin Classics by E. V. Rieu were

enormously popular but excessively informal: his *Odyssey* (Rieu 1946) has been revised and on the whole improved by Peter Jones (1991), and the *Iliad* (Rieu 1950) completely replaced by Hammond 1987 (an admirable prose version). An excellent prose *Odyssey* is the rendering by W. Shewring (1980). The most widely used verse translation is by Richmond Lattimore (*Iliad* 1951, *Odyssey* 1965), using a long line which approximates to the rhythm of the hexameter, and translating accurately but occasionally awkwardly. His *Iliad* has been revised and re-issued with a new introduction by R. Martin (2011), though it is a pity that he has dropped Lattimore's own introduction. Other modern verse translations include those by Robert Fitzgerald (*Odyssey* 1961, *Iliad* 1974), Robert Fagles (*Iliad* 1990, *Odyssey* 1996), Stanley Lombardo (*Iliad* 1997, *Odyssey* 2000), and Anthony Verity (*Iliad* 2010). Christopher Logue's *Patrocleia* (1962) was the first and best of a series of very bold adaptations of parts of the *Iliad* into free verse in a modern and cynical mode; while sometimes brilliant, they have also been much criticized (Ezra Pound's adaptations of Propertius are in some ways a parallel case).

Higham and Bowra 1938 contains renderings of fifty-six memorable passages by various translators, and an essay by Higham on the challenge facing the translator of Greek poetry. A more recent anthology is Poole and Maule 1995 (pp. 3–64 on Homer). But pride of place should go to the splendid anthology *Homer in English* (G. Steiner 1996): it is shocking that this has been allowed to go out of print.

Matthew Arnold's classic essay 'On Translating Homer', originally published in 1861 and often reprinted, is still well worth reading. More recent discussions of the problems include: Mason 1972, a polemical but serious study; Shewring's 'epilogue' to his translation of the *Odyssey* (Shewring 1980: 299–330); Silk 1987: 46–54; A. Parry 1989: 39–49 (originally a review published in 1960); Lloyd-Jones 1991 (a review of Fagles' version with extensive comparisons).

Lexica, etc.

The magisterial *Lexicon des frühgriechischen Epos* (Göttingen 1955–2010) has now finally reached completion. Cunliffe 1924 remains extremely useful for easy consultation; Autenrieth 1960 (originally 1877!) is a lesser alternative.

Concordances prepared by computer have been published by J. Tebben 1994 (*Odyssey*) and 1998 (*Iliad*); these are keyed to Van Thiel's texts. The older manmade works by G. Prendergast (1875, revised 1962), and

H. Dunbar (1880), although they omit some of the commonest words, are sufficiently comprehensive for most purposes. Online resources will doubtless be of increasing importance: e.g. the *Thesaurus Linguae Graecae* database, at http://www.tlg.uci.edu, and the Homer Multitext Project at http://www.homermultitext.org. References to websites soon go out of date, but Dué 2011 provides some guidance, and ten minutes' search online will reveal more.

BIBLIOGRAPHY

Adkins, A. W. H. 1960. *Merit and Responsibility. A Study in Greek Ethics.* Oxford, Clarendon Press.

Adkins, A. W. H. 1971. 'Homeric Values and Homeric Society', *JHS* 91: 1–14.

Adkins, A. W. H. 1987. 'Gagarin and the "Morality" of Homer', *CPh* 82: 311–22.

Albinus, L. 2000. *The House of Hades. Studies in Ancient Greek Eschatology.* Aarhus, Aarhus University Press.

Alden, M. 2000. *Homer Beside Himself.* Oxford, Oxford University Press.

Allan, W. 2006. 'Divine Justice and Cosmic Order in Early Greek Epic', *JHS* 126: 1–35

Allan, W. and Cairns, D. 2011. 'Conflict and Community in the *Iliad*', In N. Fisher and H. van Wees (eds.), *Competition in the Ancient World.* Swansea, Classical Press of Wales: 113–46.

Allen, T. W. 1924. *Homer. The Origins and the Transmission.* Oxford, Clarendon Press.

Allen, T. W. (ed.) 1917–19. *Homeri opera. Odyssea.* Oxford Classical Texts. 2 vols. Second edition, Oxford, Clarendon Press.

Allen, T. W., Halliday, W. R., and Sikes, E. E. (eds.) 1936. *The Homeric Hymns.* Oxford, Clarendon Press.

Amory, A. 1963. 'The Reunion of Odysseus and Penelope', In C. H. Taylor (ed.), *Essays on the Odyssey. Selected Modern Criticism.* Bloomington, IN, Indiana University Press: 100–21.

Andersen, Ø. 1978. *Die Diomedesgestalt in der Ilias. Symbolae Osloensis.* Supplement 25. Oslo, Universitetsforlaget.

Andersen, Ø. and Haug, D. (eds.) 2012. *Relative Chronology in early Greek Epic Poetry.* Cambridge, Cambridge University Press.

Apthorp, M. J. 1980a. *The Manuscript Evidence for Interpolation in Homer.* Heidelberg, Winter.

Apthorp, M. J. 1980b. 'The Obstacles to Odysseus' Return', *CQ* 30: 1–22.

Arend, W. 1933. *Die typischen Szenen bei Homer.* Berlin, Weidmann.

Armstrong, J. I. 1958. 'The Arming Motif in the *Iliad*', *AJPh* 79: 337–54.

Aubet, M. E. 1993. *The Phoenicians and the West. Politics, Colonies, and Trade.* Cambridge, Cambridge University Press.

Auerbach, E. 1953. *Mimesis. The Representation of Reality in Western Literature.* Translated by W. R. Trask. Princeton, NJ, Princeton University Press. First published in German, Bern, 1946.

Austin, M. M. 1970. *Greece and Egypt in the Archaic Age.* PCPhS Supplement 2. Cambridge, Cambridge Philological Society.

Austin, N. 1972. 'Name Magic in the *Odyssey*', *California Studies in Classical Antiquity* 5: 1–19.

Austin, N. 1975. *Archery at the Dark of the Moon. Poetic Problems in Homer's Odyssey.* Berkeley, CA, University of California Press.

Autenrieth, G. 1960. *A Homeric Dictionary for Use in Schools and Colleges.* Translated, with additions and corrections, by R. P. Keep. London: Macmillan. First published in German, Leipzig, 1877.

Bakker, E. J. 2005. *Pointing at the Past. From Formula to Performance in Homeric Poetics.* Washington, DC, Center for Hellenic Studies.

Bal, M. 1985. *Narratology. Introduction to the Theory of Narrative.* Toronto, University of Toronto Press.

Bannert, H. 1981. 'Phoinix' Jugend und der Zorn des Meleagros: zur Komposition des neunten Buches der *Ilias'*, *WS* n.s. 15: 69–94.

Bannert, H. 1988. *Formen des Wiederholens bei Homer. Beispiele für eine Poetik des Epos. Wiener Studien* Beiheft 13. Vienna, Verlag der Österreichischen Akademie der Wissenschaften.

Barker, E. 2009. *Entering the Agon.* Oxford, Oxford University Press.

Barrett, W. S. (ed.) 1964. *Euripides. Hippolytos.* Oxford: Clarendon Press.

Bassett, S. E. 1926. 'The So-called Emphatic Position of the Runover Word', *TAPhA* 57: 116–48.

Beck, G. 1964. *Die Stellung des 24. Buches der Ilias in der alten Epentradition.* PhD thesis, Tübingen, Eberhard-Karls-Universität.

Becker, A. S. 1995. *The Shield of Achilles and the Poetics of Ekphrasis.* Lanham, MD, Rowman & Littlefield.

Bennet, J. 1997. 'Homer and the Bronze Age', in Morris and Powell 1997: 511–34.

Bernabé, A. (ed.) 1987. *Poetarum epicorum Graecorum testimonia et fragmenta, pt. 1.* Leipzig: Teubner.

Boardman, J. 1999. *The Greeks Overseas.* Fourth edition, London, Thames and Hudson (first edition, Harmondsworth, 1964).

Boardman, J. and Hammond, N. G. L. (eds.) 1982. *The Expansion of the Greek World, Eighth to Sixth Centuries B.C. Cambridge Ancient History* iii.3². Cambridge, Cambridge University Press.

Bolling, G. M. 1925. *The External Evidence for Interpolation in Homer.* Oxford, Clarendon Press.

Bölte, F. 1934. 'Ein pylisches Epos', *RhM* 83: 319–47.

Bowra, C. M. 1930. *Tradition and Design in the Iliad.* Oxford, Clarendon Press.

Bowra, C. M. 1957. *The Greek Experience.* London, Weidenfeld & Nicolson.

Bowra, C. M. 1961. *Heroic Poetry.* Second edition, London, Macmillan.

Bowra, C. M. 1962. 'Metre', in Wace and Stubbings 1962: 17–25.

Bowra, C. M. 1964. 'The Meaning of a Heroic Age', in Kirk 1964: 22–47.

Braswell, B. K. 1971. 'Mythological Innovation in the *Iliad'*, *CQ* 21: 16–26.

Braswell, B. K. 1982. 'The Song of Ares and Aphrodite: Theme and Relevance to *Odyssey* 8', *Hermes* 90: 129–37.

Braswell, B. K. 1988. *A Commentary on the Fourth Pythian Ode of Pindar.* Berlin, Walter de Gruyter.

Braun, T. F. R. G. 1982. 'The Greeks in Egypt', in Boardman and Hammond 1982: 32–56.

Bremer, J. M. 1987. 'The So-called Götterapparat in Iliad XX–XXII', in Bremer et al. 1987: 31–46.

Bremer, J. M., de Jong, I., and Kalff, J. (eds.) 1987. *Homer. Beyond Oral Poetry.* Amsterdam, B. R. Grüner.

Bremmer, J. N. 1988. 'La plasticité du mythe: Méléagre dans la poésie homérique', in C. Calame (ed.), *Métamorphoses du mythe en Grèce antique.* Geneva, Labor et Fides: 37–56.

Bremmer, J. N. 1994. *Greek Religion. G&R New Surveys 24.* Oxford, Oxford University Press.

Brenk, F. E. 1986. 'Dear Child: The Speech of Phoenix and the Tragedy of Achilles in the Ninth Book of the *Iliad*', *Eranos* 84: 77–86.

Büchner, W. 1940. 'Die Penelopeszenen in der Odyssee', *Hermes* 75: 126–67.

Burgess, J. S. 2001. *The Tradition of the Trojan War in Homer and the Epic Cycle.* Baltimore, MD, Johns Hopkins University Press.

Burgess, J. S. 2006. 'Neoanalysis, Orality and Intertextuality: An Examination of Homeric Motif Transference', *Oral Tradition* 21: 148–89.

Burgess, J. S. 2009. *The Death and Afterlife of Achilles.* Baltimore, MD, Johns Hopkins University Press.

Burkert, W. 1960. 'Das Lied von Ares und Aphrodite: zum Verhältnis von Odyssee und Ilias', *RhM* 103: 130–44 (= Burkert 2001: 105–116). Translated as 'The Song of Ares and Aphrodite: On the Relationship between the *Odyssey* and the *Iliad*', in Wright and Jones 1997: 249–62. Also translated in Doherty 2009: 29–43.

Burkert, W. 1972. 'Die Leistung eines Kreophylos: Kreophyleer, Homeriden und die archaische Heraklesepik', *MH* 29: 74–85 (= Burkert 2001: 138–49).

Burkert, W. 1973. 'Von Amenophis II zur Bogenprobe des Odyssee', *GB* 1: 69–78 (= Burkert 2001: 72–9).

Burkert, W. 1976. 'Das hunderttorige Theben und die Datierung der Ilias', *WS* 89: 5–21 (= Burkert 2001: 59–71).

Burkert, W. 1979. *Structure and History in Greek Mythology.* Berkeley, CA, University of California Press.

Burkert, W. 1985. *Greek Religion.* Oxford, Basil Blackwell. First published in German, Stuttgart, 1977.

Burkert, W. 1987. 'The Making of Homer in the Sixth Century B.C.: Rhapsodes versus Stesichorus', in *Papers on the Amasis Painter and His World*, Malibu, CA, J. Paul Getty Museum: 43–62 (= Burkert 2001: 198–217 = D. Cairns 2001: 92–116).

Burkert, W. 1988. 'Oriental and Greek Mythology: The Meeting of Parallels', in J. Bremmer (ed.), *Interpretations of Greek Mythology.* London, Routledge: 10–40.

Burkert, W. 1992. *The Orientalizing Revolution. Near Eastern Influence on Greek Culture in the Early Archaic Age.* Cambridge, MA, Harvard University Press.

Burkert, W. 1995. 'Lydia between East and West or How to Date the Trojan War: A Study in Herodotus', in Carter and Morris 1995: 139–48 (= Burkert 2001: 218–32).

Burkert, W. 2001. *Kleine Schriften I. Homerica.* Göttingen, Vandenhoeck & Ruprecht.

Burkert, W. 2004. *Babylon, Memphis, Persepolis: Eastern Contexts of Greek Culture.* Cambridge, MA, Harvard University Press.

Burnett, A. P. 1983. *Three Archaic Poets. Archilochus, Alcaeus, Sappho.* London, Duckworth.

Butcher, S. H. and A. Lang. 1879. *The Odyssey of Homer. Done into English Prose.* London, Macmillan.

Butler, S. 1897. *The Authoress of the Odyssey.* London, A. C. Fifield (second edition, 1922).

Buxton, R. 1994. *Imaginary Greece.* Cambridge, Cambridge University Press.

Buxton, R. 2004. 'Similes and Other Likenesses', in R. Fowler 2004: 139–55.

Cairns, D. 1993. *Aidos. The Psychology and Ethics of Honour and Shame in Ancient Greek Literature.* Oxford, Oxford University Press.

Cairns, D. 1996. '*Hybris*, Dishonour, and Thinking Big', *JHS* 116: 1–32.

Cairns, D. (ed.) 2001. *Oxford Readings in Homer's Iliad*. Oxford, Oxford University Press.

Cairns, D. 2003. 'Ethics, Ethology, Terminology: Iliadic Anger and the Crosscultural Study of Emotion', *YClS* 32, 11–49.

Cairns, D. (ed.) 2005. *Body Language in the Greek and Roman World*. Swansea, Classical Press of Wales.

Cairns, D. 2011. 'Honour and Shame: Modern Controversies and Ancient Values', *Critical Quarterly* 53.1: 1–19.

Cairns, D. 2012. '*Atē* in the Homeric Poems', *Papers of the Langford Latin Seminar* 15: 1–52.

Cairns, F. (ed.) 1983. *Papers of the Liverpool Latin Seminar*. Vol. 4. Liverpool, Francis Cairns.

Cairns, F. 1990. *Virgil's Augustan Epic*. Cambridge, Cambridge University Press.

Calhoun, G. M. 1939. 'Homer's Gods: Myth and Märchen', *AJPh* 60: 1–28.

Campbell, D. A. 1991. *Greek Lyric. III. Stesichorus, Ibycus, Simonides and Others*. Loeb Classical Library. Cambridge, MA, Harvard University Press.

Campbell, J. K. 1964. *Honour, Family, and Patronage. A Study of Institutions and Moral Values in a Greek Mountain Community*. Oxford, Clarendon Press.

Carpenter, R. 1946. *Folk Tale, Fiction and Saga in the Homeric Epics*. Berkeley, CA, University of California Press.

Carpenter, T. H. 1991. *Art and Myth in Ancient Greece*. London, Thames and Hudson.

Carroll, M. 1895. *Aristotle's Poetics C. XXV, in the Light of the Homeric Scholia*. Baltimore, MD, John Murphy & Co.

Carter, J. B. and Morris, S. P. (eds.) 1995. *The Ages of Homer. A Tribute to Emily Townsend Vermeule*. Austin, TX, University of Texas Press.

Càssola, F. (ed.) 1975. *Inni Omerici*. Milan, Mondadori.

Cave, T. 1988. *Recognitions. A Study in Poetics*. Oxford, Clarendon Press.

Chadwick, J. 1996. *Lexicographica Graeca. Contributions to the Lexicography of Ancient Greek*. Oxford, Clarendon Press.

Chantraine, P. 1948–53. *Grammaire Homérique*. 2 vols. Paris, Klincksieck.

Clark, G. 1989. *Women in the Ancient World. G&R New Surveys 21*. Oxford, Oxford University Press.

Clark, M. E. 1986. 'Neoanalysis: A Bibliographical Review'. *CW* 79: 379–94.

Clarke, H. W. 1967. *The Art of the Odyssey*. Englewood Cliffs, NJ, Prentice-Hall. Reprinted with additions, Bristol, 1989.

Clarke, H. W. 1981. *Homer's Readers. A Historical Introduction to the Iliad and the Odyssey*. Newark, DE, University of Delaware Press.

Clarke, M. 1999. *Flesh and Spirit in the Songs of Homer. A Study of Words and Myths*. Oxford, Clarendon Press.

Clay, J. S. 1983. *The Wrath of Athena*. Princeton, NJ, Princeton University Press (second edition, Lanham, MD, 1997).

Clay, J. S. 1989. *The Politics of Olympus. Form and Meaning in the Major Homeric Hymns*. Princeton, NJ, Princeton University Press. Reprinted with new preface London, 2006.

Clay, J. S. 1997. 'The Homeric Hymns', in Morris and Powell 1997: 489–507.

Clay, J. S. 2003. *Hesiod's Cosmos*. Cambridge, Cambridge University Press.

Clay, J. S. 2011. 'Heroic Age', in Finkelberg 2011.

Cohen, B. (ed.) 1995. *The Distaff Side. Representing the Female in Homer's Odyssey.* Oxford, Oxford University Press.

Čolaković, Z. 2006. 'The Singer Above Tales: Homer, Međedović and Traditional Epics'. *SemRom* 9: 161–87.

Collins, L. 1988. *Studies in Characterization in the Iliad.* Frankfurt am Main, Athenäum.

Colvin, S. (ed.) 2007. *A Historical Greek Reader. Mycenaean to the Koiné.* Oxford, Oxford University Press.

Combellack, F. M. 1944. 'Homer and Hector', *AJPh* 65: 209–43.

Crane, G. 1988. *Calypso. Backgrounds and Conventions of the Odyssey.* Frankfurt am Main, Athenäum.

Crielaard, J. P. 1995. 'Homer, History and Archaeology: Some Remarks on the Date of the Homeric World', in J. P. Crielaard (ed.), *Homeric Questions. Essays in Philology, Ancient History and Archaeology.* Amsterdam, J. C. Gieben: 201–88.

Crooke, W. 1898. 'The Wooing of Penelope', *Folklore* 9: 97–133.

Crooke, W. 1908. 'Some Notes on Homeric Folk-lore', *Folklore* 19: 52–77, 153–89.

Crotty, K. 1994. *The Poetics of Supplication. Homer's Iliad and Odyssey.* Ithaca, NY, Cornell University Press.

Csapo, E. 2005. *Theories of Mythology.* Oxford, Blackwell Publishing.

Cunliffe, R. J. 1924. *Lexicon of the Homeric Dialect.* London, Blackie & Son.

Currie, B. 2006. 'Homer and the Early Epic Tradition', in M. J. Clarke, B. G. F. Currie and R. O. A. M. Lyne (eds.), *Epic Interactions. Perspectives on Homer, Virgil and the Epic Tradition Presented to Jasper Griffin.* Oxford, Oxford University Press: 1–45.

Currie, B. 2012. 'The *Iliad, Gilgamesh,* and Neoanalysis', in Montanari et al. 2012: 543–80.

Curtius, E. R. 1953. *European Literature and the Latin Middle Ages.* Translated by W. R. Trask. London, Routledge & Kegan Paul. First published in German, Bern, 1948.

Dalley, S. 1989. *Myths from Mesopotamia.* Oxford, Oxford University Press.

Danek, G. 1988. *Studien zur Dolonie.* Vienna, Österreichische Akademie der Wissenschaften.

Danek, G. 1998. *Epos und Zitat. Studien zu den Quellen der Odyssee.* Vienna, Österreichische Akademie der Wissenschaften.

Danek, G. 2002. 'Traditional Referentiality and Homeric Intertextuality', in F. Montanari and P. Ascheri (eds.), *Omero tremila anni dopo.* Rome, Edizioni di Storia e Letteratura: 3–19.

Danek, G. 2010. 'Agamemnon's Ancestors and Ruža's Bridegroom: *Il.* 2.99–109 and a Bosnian Parallel', in C. Tsagalis (ed.), *Homeric Hypertextuality.* Berlin, de Gruyter, 225–38.

Danek, G. 2012. 'The Doloneia Revisited', in Andersen and Haug 2012: 106–121.

Davidson, J. 2007. *The Greeks and Greek Love. A Radical Reappraisal of Homosexuality in Ancient Greece.* London, Weidenfeld and Nicolson, 2007.

Davies, M. (ed.) 1988. *Epicorum Graecorum fragmenta.* Göttingen, Vandenhoeck & Ruprecht.

Davies, M. 1989. *The Greek Epic Cycle.* Bristol, Bristol Classical Press.

Davies, M. 1994. '*Odyssey* 22. 474–7: Murder or Mutilation', *CQ* 44: 534–6.

Davison, J. A. 1955. 'Peisistratos and Homer', *TAPhA* 86: 1–21.

Davison, J. A. 1962a. 'Homeric Criticism: The Transmission of the Text', in Wace and Stubbings 1962: 215–33.

Davison, J. A. 1962b. 'The Homeric Question', in Wace and Stubbings 1962: 234–65.

Dawe, R. D. 1993. *The Odyssey. Translation and Analysis*. Lewes: Book Guild.

de Jong, I. J. F. 1987a. *Narrators and Focalizers. The Presentation of the Story of the Iliad*. Amsterdam, B. R. Grüner. Reprinted with new preface, London, 2004.

de Jong, I. J. F. 1987b. 'Silent Characters in the *Iliad*', in Bremer et al. 1987: 105–21.

de Jong, I. J. F. 1988. 'Homeric Words and Speakers: An Addendum', *JHS* 108: 188–9.

de Jong, I. J. F. 1992. 'The Subjective Style in Odysseus' Wanderings', *CQ* 42: 1–11.

de Jong, I. J. F. 1993. 'Studies in Homeric Denomination', *Mnemosyne* 46: 289–306.

de Jong, I. J. F. (ed.) 1999. *Homer. Critical Assessments*. 4 vols. London, Routledge.[1]

de Jong, I. J. F. 2001. *A Narratological Commentary on Homer's Odyssey*. Cambridge, Cambridge University Press.

de Jong, I. J. F. 2012. *Homer. Iliad 22*. Cambridge, Cambridge University Press.

Detienne, M. and Vernant, J. P. 1974. *Les ruses d'intelligence: la métis des grecs*. Paris, Flammarion. Translated by J. Lloyd as *Cunning Intelligence in Greek Culture and Society*, Brighton, 1978.

di Benedetto, V. 1994. *Nel laboratorio di Omero*. Turin, Einaudi.

Dickey, E. 2007. *Ancient Greek Scholarship*. New York, Oxford University Press.

Dickie, M. 1983. 'Phaeacian Athletes', in F. Cairns 1983: 237–76.

Dietrich, B. C. 1965. *Death, Fate and the Gods*. London, Athlone Press.

Dimock, G. E. 1989. *The Unity of the Odyssey*. Amherst, MA, University of Massachusetts Press.

Dindorf, W. 1855. *Scholia graeca in Homeri Odysseam*. 2 vols. Oxford, Oxford University Press.

Dodds, E. R. 1951. *The Greeks and the Irrational*. Berkeley, CA, University of California Press.

Dodds, E. R. 1968. 'Homer and the Analysts', 'Homer and the Unitarians', 'Homer and Oral Poetry', in M. Platnauer (ed.), *Fifty Years* (and Twelve) of Classical Scholarship (revised edition of *Fifty Years of Classical Scholarship*, 1956). Oxford. Blackwell: 1–8, 8–13, 31–5 (= Kirk 1964: 1–21).

Doherty, L. E. 1995. *Siren Songs. Gender, Audiences and Narrators in the Odyssey*. Ann Arbor, MI, University of Michigan Press.

Doherty, L. E. (ed.) 2009. *Homer's Odyssey*. Oxford Readings in Classical Studies. Oxford, Oxford University Press.

Donlan, W. 1970. 'Changes and Shifts in the Meaning of Demos', *PP* 25: 381–95.

Donlan, W. 1973. 'The Tradition of Anti-aristocratic Thought in Early Greek Poetry', *Historia* 22: 145–54.

Dougherty, C. 2001. *The Raft of Odysseus. The Ethnographical Imagination of Homer's Odyssey*. Oxford, Oxford University Press.

Dover, K. J. 1968. *Lysias and the Corpus Lysiacum*. Berkeley, CA, University of California Press.

Dover, K. J. 1971. *Theocritus. Select Poems*. London, Macmillan.

---

[1] In view of the rarity and high cost of this collection, I have noted only items it includes which are either hard to find elsewhere or are translated, usually for the first time, into English.

Dover, K. J. 1978. *Greek Homosexuality*. London, Duckworth.

Dover, K. J. 1983. 'The Portrayal of Moral Evaluation in Greek Poetry', *JHS* 103: 35–48 (= K. J. Dover, *Greek and the Greeks. Collected Papers I*. Oxford, Basil Blackwell, 1987: 77–96).

Dowden, K. 1996. 'Homer's Sense of Text', *JHS* 116: 47–61.

Dowden, K. 2001. Review of M. L. West 1997, *JHS* 121: 167–75.

Dowden, K. 2004. 'The Epic Tradition in Greece', in R. Fowler 2004: 188–205.

Duckworth, G. E. 1933. *Foreshadowing and Suspense in the Epics of Homer, Apollonius, and Vergil*, Princeton, NJ, Princeton University Press (extract in de Jong 1999: iv.328–38).

Dué, C. 2002. *Homeric variations on a Lament by Briseis*. Lanham, MD, Rowman & Littlefield.

Dué, C. 2011. 'Electronic Homer', in Finkelberg 2011.

Dué, C. and Ebbott, M. 2010, *Iliad 10 and the Poetics of Ambush. A Multitext Edition with Essays and Commentary*. Washington, DC, Center for Hellenic Studies.

Dunbar, H. 1880. *A Complete Concordance to the Odyssey and Hymns of Homer*. Oxford, Clarendon Press.

Easterling, P. E. 1984. 'The Tragic Homer', *BICS* 31: 1–8.

Edwards, A. T. 1985. *Achilles in the Odyssey*. Beiträge zur klassischen Philologie 171. Königstein, A. Hain.

Edwards, G. P. 1971. *The Language of Hesiod*. Oxford, Basil Blackwell.

Edwards, M. W. 1966. 'Some Features of Homeric Craftsmanship', *TAPhA* 97: 115–79.

Edwards, M. W. 1968. 'Some Stylistic Notes on *Iliad* XVIII', *AJP* 89: 257–83.

Edwards, M. W. 1975. 'Type-scenes and Homeric Hospitality', *TAPhA* 105: 51–72.

Edwards, M. W. 1980. 'Convention and Individuality in Iliad 1', *HSPh*, 84:1–28.

Edwards, M. W. 1986. 'Homer and the Oral Tradition: The Formula Part I', *Oral Tradition* 1: 171–230.

Edwards, M. W. 1987a. *Homer, Poet of the Iliad*. Baltimore, Johns Hopkins University Press.

Edwards, M. W. 1987b. 'Topos and Transformation in Homer', in Bremer et al. 1987: 47–60.

Edwards, M. W. 1988. 'Homer and the Oral Tradition: The Formula Part II', *Oral Tradition* 3: 11–60.

Edwards, M. W. 1991. *The Iliad. A Commentary. Vol. 5 Books 17–20*. Cambridge, Cambridge University Press.

Edwards, M. W. 1992. 'Homer and the Oral Tradition: The Type-scene', *Oral Tradition* 7: 284–330.

Eisenberger, H. 1973. *Studien zur Odyssee*. Wiesbaden, Steiner.

Eliot, T. S. 1932. 'Tradition and the Individual Talent', in T. S. Eliot, *Selected Essays*. London, Faber: 13–22.

Ellmann, R. 1974. *Ulysses on the Liffey*. London, Faber (revised edition, London, 1984).

Ellmann, R. 1982. *James Joyce*. Second edition, Oxford, Oxford University Press (first edition, Oxford, 1966).

Emlyn-Jones, C. 1984. 'The Reunion of Odysseus and Penelope', *G&R* 31: 1–18 (=McAuslan and Walcot 1998: 126–43).

Emlyn-Jones, C. 1986. 'True and Lying Tales in the *Odyssey*', *G&R* 33: 1–10 (= McAuslan and Walcot 1998: 144–54).

Emlyn-Jones, C., Hardwick, L., and Purkis, J. (eds.) 1992. *Homer. Readings and Images*. London Duckworth.

Erbse, H. (ed.) 1969–88. *Scholia graeca in Homeri Iliadem scholia vetera*. 7 vols. Berlin: de Gruyter.

Erbse, H. 1972. *Beiträge zum Verstandnis der Odyssee*. Berlin, de Gruyter (pp. 177–229 translated as 'The Ending of the *Odyssey*: Linguistic Problems', in Wright and Jones 1997: 263–320).

Erbse, H. 1978. 'Hektor in der Ilias', in H. G. Beck, A. Kambylis, and P. Moraux (eds.), *Kyklos:Griechisches und Byzantinisches. Rudolf Keydell zum 90. Geburtstag*. Berlin, de Gruyter: 1–19 (=Erbse, *Ausgewählte Schriften zur klassischen Philologie*, Berlin, de Gruyter, 1979: 1–18).

Erbse, H. 1986. *Untersuchungen zur Funktion der Götter im homerischen Epos*. Berlin, de Gruyter.

Fagles, R. 1990. *Homer. The Iliad*. With introduction by B. Knox. New York, Viking (Penguin edition, London, 1991).

Fagles, R. 1996. *Homer. The Odyssey*. With introduction by B. Knox. New York: Viking.

Fairweather, J. 1974. 'Fiction in the Biographies of Ancient Writers', *AncSoc* 5: 234–55.

Fantuzzi, M. 2005, 'The Myths of Dolon and Rhesus from Homer to the "Homeric/ Cyclic: Tragedy *Rhesus*', in F. Montanari and A. Rengakos (eds.), *La poésie épique grecque. Métamorphoses d' un genre littéraire*. Geneva, Fondation Hardt: 135–76.

Faulkner, A. 2008. *The Homeric Hymn to Aphrodite*. Oxford, Oxford University Press.

Faulkner, A. (ed.) 2011. *The Homeric Hymns. Interpretative Essays*. Oxford, Oxford University Press.

Fehling, D. 1977. *Amor und Psyche. Die Schöpfung des Apuleius und ihre Einwirkung auf das Märchen. Eine Kritik der romantischen Märchentheorie*. Mainz, Steiner.

Fehling, D. 1979. 'Zwei Lehrstücke über Pseudo-Nachrichten (Homeriden, Lelantischer Krieg', *RhM* 122: 193–210.

Fehling, D. 1991. *Die ursprüngliche Geschichte vom Fall Trojas, oder, Interpretationen zur Troja-Geschichte*. Innsbrucker Beiträge zur Kulturwissenschaft 75. Innsbruck, Verlag des Instituts für Sprachwissenschaft der Universität.

Felson, N. and L. M. Slatkin. 2004. 'Gender and Homeric Epic', in R. Fowler 2004: 91–114.

Felson-Rubin, N. 1987. 'Penelope's Perspective: Character from Plot', in Bremer et al. 1987: 61–8.

Felson-Rubin, N. (later reprinted as Felson) 1993. *Regarding Penelope. From Character to Poetics*. Princeton, NJ, Princeton University Press.

Fenik, B. 1968. *Typical Battle Scenes in the Iliad*. *Hermes* Einzelchriften 21. Wiesbaden, Steiner.

Fenik, B. 1974. *Studies in the Odyssey*. *Hermes* Einzelschriften 30. Wiesbaden, Steiner.

Fenik, B. (ed.) 1978a. *Homer. Tradition and Invention*. Cincinnati Classical Studies n.s. 2. Leiden, Brill.

Fenik, B. 1978b. 'Stylization and Variety: Four Monologues in the *Iliad*', in Fenik 1978a: 68–90.

Finglass, P. J. 2006. 'The ending of *Iliad* 7', *Philologus* 150: 187–97.

Finglass, P. J., C. Collard, and N. J. Richardson (eds). 2007. *Hesperos. Studies in Ancient Greek Poetry Presented to M. L. West*. Oxford: Oxford University Press.

Finkelberg, M. 1989. 'Formulaic and Nonformulaic Elements in Homer'. *CPh* 84: 179–97.

Finkelberg, M. 2000. 'The Cypria, the Iliad, and the Problem of Multiformity in Oral and Written Tradition', *CPh* 95: 1–11.

Finkelberg, M. (ed.) 2011. *The Homer Encyclopedia*. 3 vols. Oxford, Wiley-Blackwell.

Finkelberg, M. 2012. 'Late Features in the Speeches of the *Iliad*', in Andersen and Haug 2012: 80–95.

Finley, M. I. 1973. *The Use and Abuse of History*. London, Chatto & Windus.

Finley, M. I. 1979. *The World of Odysseus*. Second edition, Harmondsworth, Penguin (first edition, New York, 1954).

Finley, M. I., with Caskey, J. L., Kirk, G. S., and Page, D. L. 1964. 'The Trojan War', *JHS* 84: 1–20.

Finnegan, R. 1977. *Oral Poetry. Its Nature, Significance and Social Context*. Cambridge, Cambridge University Press.

Fisher, N. R. E. 1992. *Hybris. A Study in the Values of Honour and Shame in Ancient Greece*. Warminster, Aris & Phillips.

Fitzgerald, R. (trans.). 1961. *Homer. The Odyssey*. Garden City, NY, Anchor Press/ Doubleday.

Fitzgerald, R. (trans.). 1974. *Homer. Iliad*. Garden City, NY, Anchor Press.

Foley, H. 1978. '"Reverse Similes" and Sex Roles in the *Odyssey*', *Arethusa* 11: 7–26 (= Peradotto and Sullivan 1984: 59–78; = Doherty 2009: 189–207).

Foley, H. (ed. and trans.) 1994. *The Homeric Hymn to Demeter*. Princeton, NJ, Princeton University Press.

Foley, J. M. 1988. *The Theory of Oral Composition.: ?History and Methodology*. Bloomington, IN, Indiana University Press.

Foley, J. M. 1991. *Immanent Art. From Structure to Meaning in Traditional Oral Epic*. Bloomington, IN, Indiana University Press.

Foley, J. M. 1997. 'Oral Tradition and its Implications', in Morris and Powell 1997: 146–73.

Foley, J. M. 1999. *Homer's Traditional Art*. University Park, PA, Pennsylvania State University Press.

Foley, J. M. (ed.) 2005. *A Companion to Ancient Epic*. Oxford, Wiley-Blackwell.

Ford, A. 1992. *Homer: Poetry of the Past*. Ithaca, NY, Cornell University Press.

Ford, A. 2002. *The Origins of Criticism*. Princeton, NJ, Princeton University Press.

Foster, B. R. 2005. *Before the Muses. An anthology of Akkadian Literature*. Third edition, Bethesda, MD, CDL Press (first edition, 1993).

Fowler, D. P. 1989. 'First Thoughts on Closure: Problems and Perspectives', *MD* 22: 75–122 = D. P. Fowler 2000: 239–83.

Fowler, D. P. 1997. 'Second Thoughts on Closure', in Roberts *et al.* 1997: 3–22 (= Fowler 2000: 284–307).

Fowler, D. P. 2000. *Roman Constructions. Readings in Postmodern Latin*. Oxford, Oxford University Press.

Fowler, R. L. 1998. 'Genealogical Thinking, Hesiod's *Catalogue*, and the Creation of the Hellenes', *PCPhS* 44: 1–19.

Fowler, R. L. (ed.) 2004. *The Cambridge Companion to Homer*. Cambridge, Cambridge University Press.

Foxhall, L. and Davies, J. K. (eds.) 1984. *The Trojan War. Its Historicity and Context*. Papers of the First Greenbank Colloquium, Liverpool. Bristol, Bristol Classical Press.

Fraenkel, E. (ed.), 1950. *Aeschylus. Agamemnon*. Oxford: Clarendon Press.

Frame, D. 2010. *Hippota Nestor*. Washington, DC, Center for Hellenic Studies.

France, P. (ed.) 2001. *The Oxford Guide to Literature in English Translation*. Oxford, Oxford University Press.

Fränkel, H. 1921. *Die homerischen Gleichnisse*. Göttingen, Vandenhoeck & Ruprhecht (pp. 98–114 translated in Wright and Jones 1997: 103–23; pp. 16–35 translated in de Jong 1999: iii.301–21).

Fränkel, H. 1975. *Early Greek Poetry and Philosophy*. Translated by M. Hadas and J. Willis. Oxford, Basil Blackwell.

Fraser, P. M. 1972. *Ptolemaic Alexandria*. Oxford, Clarendon Press.

Fredericksmeyer, H. C. 1997. 'Penelope polutropos: The Crux at *Odyssey* 23.218–24', *AJPh* 118: 487–97.

Friedrich, R. 1987. 'Thrinakia and Zeus' Ways to Men in the Odyssey'. *GRBS* 28: 375–400.

Friedrich, W. H. 1956. *Verwundung und Tod in der Ilias. Homerischen Darstellunsgweisen*. Göttingen, Vanderhoeck & Ruprecht (translated by G. Wright and P. Jones as *Wounding and Death in the Iliad*. London, Duckworth, 2003).

Gagarin, M. 1987. 'Morality in Homer'. *CPh* 82: 285–306.

Gainsford, P. 2003. 'Formal Analysis of Recognition Scenes in the Odyssey', *JHS* 123: 41–59.

Gantz, T. 1993. *Early Greek Myth. A Guide to Literary and Artistic Sources*. Baltimore, MD, Johns Hopkins University Press.

Garvie, A. F. (ed.) 1986. *Aeschylus. Choephori*. Oxford, Clarendon Press.

Garvie, A. F. (ed.) 1994. *Homer. Odyssey 6–8*. Cambridge, Cambridge University Press.

Gaskin, R. 1990. 'Do Homeric Heroes Make Real Decisions?', *CQ* 40: 1–15 (= D. Cairns 2001: 147–69).

Genette, G. 1980. *Narrative Discourse*. Translated by J. E. Lewis. Oxford, Basil Blackwell.

George, A. R. 1999. *The Epic of Gilgamesh*. London, Allen Lane (Penguin edition, 2003).

George, A. R. 2003. *The Babylonian Gilgamesh Epic*. Oxford, Oxford University Press.

Goldhill, S. 1986. *Reading Greek Tragedy*. Cambridge, Cambridge University Press.

Goldhill, S. 1990. 'Supplication and Editorial Comment in the *Iliad*: *Iliad* Z 61–2', *Hermes* 118: 273–6.

Goldhill, S. 1991. *The Poet's Voice. Essays on Poetics and Greek Literature*. Cambridge, Cambridge University Press.

Gould, J. 1973. '*Hiketeia*', *JHS* 93: 74–103 (= Gould 2001: 22–73).

Gould, J. 1994. 'Herodotus and Religion', in Hornblower 1994: 91–106 (= Gould 2001: 359–77).

Gould, J. 2001. *Myth, Ritual, Memory, and Exchange. Essays in Greek Literature and Culture*. Oxford, Oxford University Press.

Grafton, A., Most, G. W., and Settis, S. (eds.) 2010. *The Classical Tradition*. Cambridge, MA, Belknap Press of Harvard University Press.

Graham, A. J. 1964. *Colony and Mother City in Ancient Greece*. Manchester, Manchester University Press.

Graham, A. J. 1978. 'The Foundation of Thasos', *ABSA* 73: 61–98.

Graham, A. J. 1982. 'The Western Greeks', in Boardman and Hammond 1982: 163–95.

Graves, R. 1955. *Homer's Daughter*. London, Cassell; Garden City, NY, Doubleday.

Graziosi, B. 2002. *Inventing Homer. The Early Reception of Epic*. Cambridge, Cambridge University Press.

Graziosi, B. and Greenwood, E. (eds.) 2007. *Homer in the Twentieth Century. Between World Literature and the Western Canon*. Oxford, Oxford University Press.

Graziosi, B. and Haubold, J. 2005. *Homer. The Resonance of Epic*. London, Duckworth.

Graziosi, B. and Haubold, J. 2010. *Homer. Iliad 6*. Cambridge, Cambridge University Press.

Greene, W. C. 1944. *Moira. Fate, Good and Evil in Greek Thought*. Cambridge, MA, Harvard University Press.

Greenhalgh, P. A. L. 1972. 'Patriotism in the Homeric World', *Historia* 21: 528–37.

Griffin, J. 1977. 'The Epic Cycle and the Uniqueness of Homer', *JHS* 97: 39–53 (= D. Cairns 2001: 365–84).

Griffin, J. 1980. *Homer on Life and Death*. Oxford, Oxford University Press.

Griffin, J. 1986. 'Homeric Words and Speakers', *JHS* 106: 36–57.

Griffin, J. 1987. *Homer. The Odyssey*. Landmarks of World Literature. Cambridge, Cambridge University Press.

Griffin, J. 1991. Review of Usener 1990, *CR* 41: 288–91.

Griffin, J. (ed.) 1995. *Homer. Iliad IX*. Oxford, Clarendon Press.

Griffin, J. and Hammond, M. 1982. 'Critical Appreciations VI: Homer, *Iliad* 1.1–52', *G&R* 29: 126–42 (= McAuslan and Walcot 1998: 65–82).

Griffith, M. 1990. 'Contest and Contradiction in Early Greek Poetry', in M. Griffith and D. Mastronarde (eds.), *Cabinet of the Muses*. Atlanta, GA, Scholars Press: 185–207.

Grossart, P. 1998. *Die Trugreden in der Odyssee und ihre Rezeption in der antiken Literatur*. *Sapheneia* 2. Bern, Peter Lang.

Hägg, J. 1983. *The Novel in Antiquity*. Oxford, Blackwell.

Hainsworth, J. B. 1962. 'The Homeric Formula and the Problem of its Transmission', *BICS* 9: 57–68.

Hainsworth, J. B. 1968. *The Flexibility of the Homeric Formula*. Oxford, Clarendon Press.

Hainsworth, J. B. 1969. *Homer. G&R* New Surveys 3. Oxford, Clarendon Press (revised with additional bibl. 1979).

Hainsworth, J. B. 1970. 'The Criticism of an Oral Homer', *JHS* 90: 90–8 (= Wright 1978: 28–40; = Emlyn-Jones et al. 1992: 65–75).

Hainsworth, J. B. 1978. 'Good and Bad Formulae', in Fenik 1978a: 41–50.

Hainsworth, J. B. 1984. 'The Fallibility of an Oral Heroic Tradition', in Foxhall and Davies 1984: 111–35.

Hainsworth, J. B. 1993. *The Iliad. A Commentary. Vol. 3 Books 9–12*. Cambridge, Cambridge University Press.

Hall, E. 1989. *Inventing the Barbarian. Greek Self-definition through Tragedy*. Oxford, Clarendon Press.

Hall, E. 2008. *The Return of Ulysses. A Cultural History of Homer's Odyssey.* London, I. B. Tauris.

Hall, J. 2007. *A History of the Archaic Greek World ca. 1200–479 BCE.* Oxford, Blackwell.

Haller, B. 2011. 'Geography, the *Odyssey*', in Finkelberg 2011.

Halliwell, S. (trans.) 1986. *Aristotle's Poetics.* London, Duckworth.

Halliwell, S. 1990. 'Traditional Greek Conceptions of Character', in Pelling 1990: 32–59.

Halliwell, S. 2008. *Greek Laughter. A Study of Cultural Psychology from Homer to Early Christianity.* Cambridge, Cambridge University Press.

Halliwell, S. 2012. *Between Ecstasy and Truth.* Oxford, Oxford University Press.

Halperin, D. M. 1990. *One Hundred Years of Homosexuality.* London, Routledge.

Hammer, D. C. 2002. *The Iliad as Politics. The Performance of Political Thought.* Norman, OK, University of Oklahoma Press.

Hammond, M. 1987. *Homer. The Iliad. A New Prose Translation.* Harmondsworth, Penguin.

Hankey, R. 1990. '"Evil" in the *Odyssey*', In E. Craik (ed.), *Owls to Athens. Essays on Classical Culture Presented to Sir Kenneth Dover.* Oxford, Clarendon Press: 87–96.

Hansen, W. 1997. 'Homer and the Folktale', in Morris and Powell 1997: 442–62.

Hansen, W. 2002. *Ariadne's Thread. A Guide to International Tales Found in Classical Greek Literature.* Ithaca, NY, Cornell University Press.

Hardie, P. 1986. *Virgil's Aeneid. Cosmos and Imperium.* Oxford, Clarendon Press.

Hardwick, L. and Stray, C. (eds.) 2008. *A Companion to Classical Receptions.* Oxford, Blackwell.

Harris, W. V. 2001. *Restraining Rage. The Ideology of Anger Control in Classical Antiquity.* Cambridge, MA, Harvard University Press.

Harsh, P. W. 1950. 'Penelope and Odysseus in *Odyssey* XIX', *AJPh* 71: 1–21.

Hartmann, A. 1917. *Untersuchungen über die Sagen vom Tod des Odysseus.* Munich, C. H. Beck.

Haslam, M. 1997. 'Homeric Papyri and Transmission of the Text', in Morris and Powell 1997: 55–100.

Haslam, M. 2011. 'Text and Transmission', in Finkelberg 2011.

Hatto, A. T. (ed.) 1980. *Traditions of Heroic and Epic Poetry. Vol. 1. The Traditions* London, Modern Humanities Research Association.

Haubold, J. 2000. *Homer's People. Epic Poetry and Social Formation.* Cambridge, Cambridge University Press.

Haubold, J. 2002. 'Greek Epic: A Near Eastern Genre?', *PCPhS* 48: 1–19.

Heath, M. 1989. *Unity in Greek Poetics.* Oxford, Clarendon Press.

Heiden, B. 2008. *Homer's Cosmic Fabrication. Choice and Design in the Iliad.* American Classical Studies 52. New York, Oxford University Press.

Henige, D. P. 1974. *The Chronology of Oral Tradition. Quest for a Chimera.* Oxford, Clarendon Press.

Herington, J. 1985. *Poetry into Drama. Early Tragedy and the Greek Poetic Tradition.* Berkeley, CA, University of California Press.

Heubeck, A. 1954. *Der Odyssee-Dichter und die Ilias.* Erlangen, Palm & Enke.

Heubeck, A. 1974. *Die homerische Frage. Ein Bericht über die Forschung der letzten Jahrzehnte.* Darmstadt, Wissenschaftliche Buchgesellschaft.

Heubeck, A. 1979. *Schrift.* Archaeologia Homerica 10. Göttingen, Vandenhoeck & Ruprecht.

Heubeck, A. and Hoekstra, A. 1990. *A Commentary on Homer's Odyssey. Volume II. Books IX-XVI.* Oxford, Clarendon Press.

Heubeck, A., West, S. R., and Hainsworth, J. B. 1988. *A Commentary on Homer's Odyssey. Volume I. Introduction and Books I-VIII.* Oxford, Clarendon Press.

Higbie, C. 1990. *Measure and Music: Enjambement and Sentence Structure in the Iliad.* Oxford, Clarendon Press.

Higham, T. E. and Bowra, C. M. (eds.) 1938. *The Oxford Book of Greek Verse in Translation.* Oxford, Oxford University Press.

Hirschberger, M. 2004. *Gynaikōn katalogos und Megalai ēhoiai. Ein Kommentar zu den Fragmenten zweier hesiodeischer Epen.* Munich, K. G. Saur.

Hoekstra, A. 1965. *Homeric Modifications of Formulaic Prototypes. Studies in the Development of Greek Diction.* Amsterdam, Noord-Hollandsche Uitg. Mij.

Hölscher, U. 1939.*Untersuchungen zur Form der Odyssee.* Hermes Einzelschriften 6. Berlin, Weidmann.

Hölscher, U. 1989. *Die Odyssee. Epos zwischen Märchen und Roman.* Munich, C. H. Beck.

Hooker, J. T. 1980. *Homer. Iliad III.* Bristol, Bristol Classical Press.

Hornblower, S. (ed.) 1994. *Greek Historiography.* Oxford, Clarendon Press.

Horrocks, G. 1997. 'Homer's Dialect', in Morris and Powell 1997: 193–217.

Hubbard, M. (trans.) 1972. 'Aristotle.*Poetics*', in Hubbard, M. *Ancient Literary Criticism. The Principal Texts in New Translations.* Oxford, Clarendon Press: 90–132.

Hunter, R. L. (ed.) 2005. *The Hesiodic Catalogue of Women. Constructions and Reconstructions.* Cambridge, Cambridge University Press.

Hutchinson, G. O. (ed.) 1985. *Aeschylus. Septem contra Thebas.* Oxford, Clarendon.

Irwin, T. H. 1989. *Classical Thought.* Oxford, Oxford University Press.

Jacoby, F. 1933. 'Die geistige Physiognomie der Odyssee', *Der Antike* 9: 159–94 (= F. Jacoby, *Kleine philologische Schriften.* 2 vols. Berlin, Akademie-Verlag, 1961: i.107–38).

Janko, R. 1982. *Homer, Hesiod and the Hymns. Diachronic Development in Epic Diction.* Cambridge, Cambridge University Press.

Janko, R. 1986. 'The *Shield of Heracles* and the Legend of Cycnus', *CQ* 36: 38–59.

Janko, R. 1990. 'The *Iliad* and its Editors: Dictation and Redaction', *ClAnt.* 9: 324–34.

Janko, R. 1992. *The Iliad. A Commentary. Vol. 4 Books 13–16.* Cambridge, Cambridge University Press.

Janko, R. 1998. 'The Homeric Poems as Oral Dictated Texts', *CQ* 48: 1–13.

Janko, R. 2012. 'πρῶτόν τε καὶ ὕστατον αἰὲν ἀείδειν: Relative Chronology and the Literary History of the Greek Epos', in Andersen and Haug 2012: 20–43.

Jeffery, L. H. 1961. *The Local Scripts of Archaic Greece.* Oxford, Clarendon Press (second edition revised by A. Johnston, Oxford, 1990).

Jeffery, L. H. 1976. *Archaic Greece. The City-states.* London, Benn.

Jensen, M. S. 1980. *The Homeric Question and the Oral-formulaic Theory.* Copenhagen, Museum Tusculanum Press.

Jones, P. 1988. *Homer's Odyssey. A Companion to the English Translation of Richard Lattimore*. Bristol, Bristol Classical Press.

Jones, P. (trans.) 1991. *Homer. Odyssey 1 and 2*. Warminster, Aris & Phillips.

Jones, P. 2003. *Homer's Iliad. A Commentary on Three Translations*. Bristol, Bristol Classical Press.

Jörgensen, O. 1904. 'Das Auftreten der Götter in den Büchern ι–μ der Odyssee', *Hermes* 39: 357–82.

Kakridis, J. T. 1949. *Homeric Researches*. Lund, Gleerup.

Kakridis, J. T. 1971. *Homer Revisited*. Lund, Gleerup.

Kakridis, P. J. 1961. 'Achilles' Rüstung', *Hermes* 89: 288–97.

Katz, M. A. 1991. *Penelope's Renown. Meaning and Indeterminacy in the Odyssey*. Princeton, NJ, Princeton University Press.

Kavanagh, P. J. 1964. *Collected Poems*. London, MacGibbon & Kee (reprinted New York and London, 1973).

Kearns, E. 1982. 'The Return of Odysseus: A Homeric Theoxeny', *CQ* 32: 2–8.

Kearns, E. 2004. 'The Gods in the Homeric Epics', in R. Fowler 2004: 59–73.

Kearns, E. 2011. 'Religion', in Finkelberg 2011.

Kelly, A. 2006. 'Homer and History: *Iliad* 9.381–4', *Mnemosyne* 59: 321–33.

Kelly, A. 2007a. 'How to End an Orally-derived Epic Poem', *TAPhA* 131: 371–402.

Kelly, A. 2007b. *A Referential Commentary and Lexicon to Homer, Iliad VIII*. Oxford, Oxford University Press.

Kelly, A. 2008a. 'The Babylonian Captivity of Homer: The Case of the *Dios Apate*', *RhM* 151: 259–304.

Kelly, A. 2008b. 'The Ending of *Iliad* 7: A Response', *Philologus* 152: 5–17.

Kelly, A. 2008c. 'Performance and Rivalry: Homer, Odysseus, and Hesiod', in M. Revermann and P. Wilson (eds.), *Performance, Iconography, Reception. Studies in Honour of Oliver Taplin*. Oxford, Oxford University Press: 177–203.

Kelly, A. 2012a. 'The Audience Expects: Odysseus and Penelope', in E. Minchin (ed.), *Orality, Literacy, and Performance in the Ancient World*. Leiden, Brill: 3–24.

Kelly, A. 2012b. 'The Mourning of Thetis: "Allusion" and the Future in the *Iliad*', in Montanari et al. 2012: 221–68.

Kenner, H. 1980. *Ulysses*. London, Allen & Unwin (revised edition, Baltimore, MD, 1987).

Kirk, G. S. 1960. 'Objective Dating Criteria in Homer'. *MH* 17: 189–205 (= Kirk 1964: 174–90).

Kirk, G. S. 1962. *The Songs of Homer*. Cambridge, Cambridge University Press (abridged as *Homer and the Epic*, Cambridge, 1965).

Kirk, G. S. (ed.) 1964. *The Language and Background of Homer. Some Recent Studies and Controversies*. Cambridge, Heffer.

Kirk, G. S. 1970. *Myth. Its Meaning and Function*. Berkeley, CA, University of California Press; Cambridge, Cambridge University Press.

Kirk, G. S. 1974. *The Nature of Greek Myths*. Harmondsworth, Penguin.

Kirk, G. S. 1976. *Homer and the Oral Tradition*. Cambridge, Cambridge University Press.

Kirk, G. S. 1985. *The Iliad. A Commentary. Vol 1. Books 1–4*. Cambridge, Cambridge University Press.

Kirk, G. S. 1990. *The Iliad. A Commentary. Vol. 2 Books 5–8.* Cambridge, Cambridge University Press.

Klingner, F. 1940. 'Über die Dolonie', *Hermes* 75: 337–68 (= Klingner 1964: 7–39).

Klingner, F. 1944. *Über die vier ersten Bücher der Odyssee. Berichter über die Verhandlungen der Sächsischen Akademie der Wissenschaften. Philologisch-historische Klasse* 96.1. Leipzig, S. Hirzel (= Klingner 1964: 40–79; English translation in Wright and Jones 1997: 192–216).

Klingner, F. 1964. *Studien zur griechischen und römischen Literatur.* Zürich, Artemis Verlag.

Kohl, J. G. 1917. *De Chorizontibus.* Darmstadt, Bender. (PhD thesis, University of Giessen).

Köhnken, A. 1976. 'Die Narbe des Odysseus', *A&A* 22: 101–114 (= J. Latacz [ed.], *Homer. Die Dichtung und ihre Deutung.* Wege der Forschung 634. Darmstadt, Wissenschaftliche Buchgesellschaft, 1991: 491–513).

Krischer, T. 1971. *Formale Konventionen der homerischen Epik. Zetemata* 56. Munich, C. H. Beck.

Kullmann, W. 1960. *Die Quellen der Ilias. Hermes* Einzelschriften 14. Wiesbaden, F. Steiner.

Kullmann, W. 1981. 'Zur Methode der Neoanalyse in der Homerforschung'. *WS* n.s. 15: 5–42 (= Kullmann 1992: 67–99).

Kullmann, W. 1984. 'Oral Poetry and Neoanalysis in Homeric Research'. *GRBS* 25: 307–23 (= Kullmann 1992: 140–55).

Kullmann, W. 1985. 'Gods and Men in the *Iliad* and the *Odyssey*', *HSPh* 89: 1–23.

Kullmann, W. 1992. *Homerische Motive. Beiträge sur Enstehung, Eigenart und Wirkung von Ilias und Odyssee.* Stuttgart, Franz Steiner.

Kullmann, W. 2012. 'The Relative Chronology of the Homeric Catalogue of Ships and of the Lists of Heroes and Cities within the Catalogue', in Andersen and Haug 2012: 210–23.

Laird, A. (ed.) 2006. *Ancient Literary Criticism.* Oxford Readings in Classical Studies. Oxford, Oxford University Press.

Lamberton,, R. and Keaney,, J. (eds.) 1992. *Homer's Ancient Readers.* Princeton, NJ, Princeton University Press.

Lane Fox, R. 1986. *Pagans and Christians.* Harmondsworth, Viking.

Lane Fox, R. 2008. *Travelling Heroes. Greeks and Their Myths in The Epic Age of Homer.* London, Allen Lane.

Lang, A., Leaf, W., and Myers, E. 1882. *The Iliad of Homer. Done into English Prose.* London, Macmillan.

Lang, M. 1983. 'Reverberation and mythology in the *Iliad*', in Rubino and Shelmerdine 1983: 140–64.

Latacz, J. 1974. 'Zur Forschungsarbeit an den direkten Reden bei Homer', *Gräzer Beiträge* 2: 395–422.

Latacz, J. 1977. *Kampfparänese, Kampfdarstellung und Kampfwirklichkeit in der Ilias, bei Kallinos und Tyrtaios. Zetemata* 66. Munich, C. H. Beck.

Latacz, J. (ed.) 1991. *Zweihundert Jahre Homer-forschung. Rückblick und Ausblick.* Stuttgart, B. G. Teubner.

Latacz, J. 1996. *Homer. His Art and His World.* Translated by J. P. Holoka. Ann Arbor, MI, University of Michigan Press.

Latacz, J. 2004. *Troy and Homer. Towards a Solution of an Old Mystery*. Translated by K. Windle and R. Ireland. Oxford, Oxford University Press.

Latacz, J. et al. (2000–). *Homer, Ilias. Gesamtkommentar*. Basel, de Gruyter.

Lateiner, D. 1995. *Sardonic Smile. Nonverbal Behaviour in Homeric Epic*. Ann Arbor, MI, University of Michigan Press.

Lattimore, R. (trans.) 1951. *The Iliad of Homer*. Chicago, University of Chicago Press (revised edition, Chicago, 2011).

Lattimore, R. 1965. *The Odyssey of Homer*. New York, Harper & Row.

Leaf, W. 1900–2. *Homer. The Iliad*. 2 vols. London, Macmillan.

Lefkowitz, M. R. 1981. *The Lives of the Greek Poets*. London, Duckworth (second edition, London, 2012).

Lendle, O. 1968. 'Paris, Helena und Aphrodite: zur Interpretation des 3. Gesanges der Ilias', *A&A* 14: 63–71.

Lesky, A. 1961. *Göttliche und menschliche Motivation im homerischen Epos*. Sitzungberichte der Heidelberger Akadamie der Wissenschaften, Phil.-hist. Klasse 1961.4. Heidelberg, Winter (partly translated in D. Cairns 2001: 170–202; pp. 22–44 translated in de Jong 1999: ii.384–403).

Leumann, M. 1950. *Homerische Wörter*. Basel, Reinhardt.

Lewis, D. M. 1988. 'The Tyranny of the Pisistratidae', in J. Boardman, N. G. L. Hammond, D. M. Lewis, and M. Ostwald (eds.), *Persia, Greece and the Western Mediterranean c.525 to 479 B.C. Cambridge Ancient History iv²*. Cambridge, Cambridge University Press: 287–302.

Lloyd-Jones, H. 1971. *The Justice of Zeus*. Berkeley, CA, University of California Press (second edition, Berkeley, 1983).

Lloyd-Jones, H. 1987. 'A Note on Homeric Morality', *CPh* 82: 307–310.

Lloyd-Jones, H. 1990. 'Honour and Shame in Ancient Greek Culture', in H. Lloyd-Jones, *Greek Comedy, Hellenistic Literature, Greek Religion, and Miscellanea. The Academic Papers of Sir Hugh Lloyd-Jones*. Oxford, Clarendon Press: 253–80 (originally published in German, 1987).

Lloyd-Jones, H. 1991. 'Translating Homer'. *New York Review of Books, 14 February 1991* (= H. Lloyd-Jones, *Greek in a Cold Climate*. London, Duckworth, 1991: 1–17).

Logue, C. 1962. *Patrocleia*. Lowestoft, Scorpion Press.

Lohmann, D. 1970. *Die Komposition der Reden in der Ilias*. Berlin, de Gruyter (English translation of pp. 12–40 in Wright and Jones 1997: 71–102; of pp. 12–30 in de Jong 1999: iii.239–57).

Lohmann, D. 1988. *Die Andromache-Szenen in der Ilias*. Hildesheim, G. Olms.

Lombardo, S. (trans.) 1997. *Homer. Iliad*. Indianapolis, IN, Hackett.

Lombardo, S. (trans.). 2000. *Homer. Odyssey*. Indianapolis, IN, Hackett Pub. Co.

Long, A. A. 1970. 'Morals and Values in Homer', *JHS* 90: 121–39.

López-Ruiz, C. 2010. *When the Gods Were Born. Greek Cosmogonies and the Near East*. Cambridge, MA, Harvard University Press.

López-Ruiz, C. 2011. 'Phoenicians', in Finkelberg 2011.

Lord, A. B. 1953. 'Homer's Originality: Oral Dictated Texts', *TAPhA* 84: 124–33 (=Lord 1991: 38–48; = de Jong 1999: i.228–36).

Lord, A. B. 1960. *The Singer of Tales*. Cambridge, MA, Harvard University Press (reprinted with CD, 2000).

Lord, A. B. 1991. *Epic Singers and Oral Tradition*. Ithaca, NY, Cornell University Press.

Louden, D. B. 1999. *The Odyssey. Structure, Narration, and Meaning*. Baltimore, MD, Johns Hopkins University Press.

Louden, D. B. 2006. *The Iliad. Structure, Myth, and Meaning*. Baltimore, MD, Johns Hopkins University Press.

Louden, D. B. 2011. *Homer's Odyssey and the Near East*. Cambridge, Cambridge University Press.

Lowe, N. J. 2000. *The Classical Plot and the Invention of Western Narrative*. Cambridge, Cambridge University Press.

Lynn-George, M. 1988. *Epos. Word, Narrative and the Iliad*. Basingstoke, Macmillan.

McAuslan, I. and Walcot, P. (eds.) 1998. *Homer. G&R* Studies 4. Oxford, Oxford University Press.

Mackie, H. 1996. *Talking Trojan. Speech and Community in the Iliad*, Lanham, MD, Rowman & Littlefield.

Macleod, C. W. (ed.) 1982. *Homer. Iliad Book XXIV*. Cambridge, Cambridge University Press.

Macleod, C. W. 1983. 'Homer on Poetry and the Poetry of Homer', in C. W. Macleod, *Collected Essays*. Oxford, Clarendon Press: 1–15 (= D. Cairns 2001: 294–310).

Mactoux, M. 1975. *Pénélope. Legende et mythe*. Paris, Les Belles Lettres.

Maehler, H. 1963. *Die Auffassung des Dichterberufs im frühen Griechentum bis zur Zeit Pindars*. Göttingen, Vandenhoeck & Ruprecht (English translation of pp. 21–34 in de Jong 1999: iv.6–20).

Malkin, I. 1998. *The Returns of Odysseus. Colonization and Ethnicity*. Berkeley, CA, University of California Press.

March, J. 1987. *The Creative Poet. Studies on the Treatment of Myths in Greek Poetry. BICS* Supplement 47. London, University of London, Institute of Classical Studies.

Marg, W. 1956. 'Das erste Lied des Demodokos', in *Navicula Chiloniensis. Studia philologa Felici Jacoby professori Chiloniensi emerito octogenario oblata*. Leiden, E. J. Brill: 16–29.

Marincola, J. 2007. 'Odysseus and the Historians', *SyllClass* 18: 1–79.

Martin, R. P. 1989. *The Language of Heroes. Speech and Performance in the Iliad*. Ithaca, NY, Cornell University Press.

Martin, R. P. 2005. 'Pulp Epic: The *Catalogue* and the *Shield*', in Hunter 2005: 153–75.

Mason, H. A. 1972. *To Homer through Pope*. London, Chatto and Windus.

Mattes, W. 1958. *Odysseus bei den Phäaken. Kritisches zur Homeranalyse*. Würzburg, K. Triltsch.

Meijering, R. 1987. *Literary and Rhetorical Theories in Greek Scholia*. Groningen, E. Forsten.

Mellink, M. J. (ed.) 1986. *Troy and the Trojan War. A Symposium Held at Bryn Mawr College, October 1984*. Bryn Mawr, PA, Bryn Mawr College.

Merkelbach, R. 1952. 'Die Pisistratische Redaktion der homerischen Gedichte', *RhM* 95: 23–47 (= R. Merkelbach, *Untersuchungen zur Odyssee*. Second edition, Munich, Beck, 1969: 239–62).

Meuli, K. 1921. *Odyssee und Argonautika*. Berlin, Weidmann.

Mikalson, J. D. 1983. *Athenian Popular Religion*. Chapel Hill, NC, University of North Carolina Press.

Millett, P. 1984. 'Hesiod and his world', *PCPhS* n.s. 30: 84–115.

Minchin, E. 2001. *Homer and the Resources of Memory. Some Applications of Cognitive Theory to the Iliad and the Odyssey*. Oxford, Oxford University Press.

Monro, D. B. 1891. *A Grammar of the Homeric Dialect*. Second edition, Oxford, Clarendon Press (first edition, Oxford, 1882).

Monro, D. B. and Allen, T. W. (eds.) 1920. *Homeri Opera. Ilias*. Oxford Classical Texts. 2 vols. Third edition, Oxford, Clarendon.

Montanari, F., Rengakos, A., and Tsagalis, C. (eds.) 2009. *Brill's Companion to Hesiod*. Leiden, Brill.

Montanari, F., Rengakos, A., and Tsagalis, C. (eds.) 2012. *Homeric Contexts. Neoanalysis and the Interpretation of Oral Poetry*. Trends in Classics, Supplementary Volumes 12. Berlin, de Gruyter.

Morgan, C. 1990. *Athletes and Oracles. The Transformation of Olympia and Delphi in the Eighth Century B.C.* Cambridge, Cambridge University Press.

Morris, I. 1986. 'The Use and Abuse of Homer', *ClAnt* 5: 81–138 (= D. Cairns 2001: 57–91).

Morris, I. 1997. 'Homer and the Iron Age', in Morris and Powell 1997: 535–60.

Morris, I. and Powell, B. (eds.) 1997. *A New Companion to Homer*. Mnemosyne Supplement 163. Leiden, E. J. Brill.

Morrison, J. M. 1992. *Homeric Misdirection. False Predictions in the Iliad*. Ann Arbor, MI, University of Michigan Press.

Most, G. W. 1989. 'The Structure and Function of Odysseus' *Apologoi*', *TAPhA* 119: 15–30 (= de Jong 1999: iii.486–503).

Most, G. W. 2003. 'Anger and Pity in Homer's *Iliad*', in S. Braund and G. W. Most (eds.), *Ancient Anger. Perspectives from Homer to Galen*. Cambridge, Cambridge University Press, 2003: 50–75.

Motzkus, D. 1964. *Untersuchungen zum 9. Buch der Ilias unter besonderer Berücksichtigung der Phoinixgestalt*. Hamburg (PhD thesis, Hamburg).

Moulton, C. 1974. 'The End of the Odyssey', *GRBS* 15: 139–52.

Moulton, C. 1977. *Similes in the Homeric Poems*. Hypomnemata 49. Göttingen, Vandenhoeck & Ruprecht.

Moulton, C. 1979. 'Homeric Metaphor', *CPh* 74: 279–93.

Mueller, M. 1984. *The Iliad*. Unwin Critical Library. London, G. Allen & Unwin.

Muellner, L. C. 1996. *The Anger of Achilles. Mēnis in Greek Epic*. Ithaca, NY, Cornell University Press.

Mühll, P. von der 1945. *Homeri Odyssea*. Basel, Helbing & Lichtenhahn.

Müller, M. 1966. *Athene als göttliche Helferin in der Odyssee*. Heidelberg, C. Winter.

Murnaghan, S. 1987. *Disguise and Recognition in the Odyssey*. Princeton, NJ, Princeton University Press.

Murnaghan, S. 1995. 'The Plan of Athena', in Cohen 1995: 61–80.

Murray, A. T. (ed. and trans.) 1919. *The Odyssey. Homer*. Loeb Classical Library. 2 vols. Cambridge, MA, Harvard University Press.

Murray, A. T. (ed. and trans.) 1924–5. *The Iliad. Homer.* Loeb Classical Library. 2 vols. Cambridge, MA, Harvard University Press.

Murray, A. T. (ed. and trans.). 1995. *The Odyssey. Homer.* Loeb Classical Library. 2 vols. Second edition, revised by G. E. Dimock. Cambridge, MA, Harvard University Press.

Murray, A. T. (ed. and trans.) 1999. *The Iliad. Homer.* Loeb Classical Library. 2 vols. Second edition, revised by W. F. Wyatt. Cambridge, MA, Harvard University Press.

Murray, G. 1934. *The Rise of the Greek Epic.* Oxford, Oxford University Press (first edition, Oxford, 1907).

Murray, O. 1980. *Early Greece.* Brighton, Harvester Press (second edition, London, 1993).

Murray, O. 2001. 'Herodotus and Oral History', in N. Luraghi (ed.), *The Historian's Craft in the Age of Herodotus.* Oxford, Oxford University Press: 16–44, with afterword, 'Herodotus and Oral History Reconsidered', 314–25 (original article in H. Sancisi-Weerdenburg and A. Kuhrt [eds.], *Achaemenid History. II. The Greek Sources.* Leiden, Nederlands Instituut voor het Nabije Oosten, 1987: 93–115).

Myres, J. L. 1958. *Homer and His Critics.* Edited D. Gray. London, Routledge & Kegan Paul.

Nagy, G. 1979. *The Best of the Achaeans. Concepts of the Hero in Archaic Greek Poetry.* Baltimore, MD, Johns Hopkins University Press.

Nagy, G. 1990. *Pindar's Homer. The Lyric Possession of an Epic Past.* Baltimore, MD, Johns Hopkins University Press.

Nagy, G. 1992. 'Homeric Questions', *TAPhA* 122: 17–60.

Nagy, G. 1995. 'An Evolutionary Model for the Making of Homeric Poetry: Comparative Perspectives', in Carter and Morris 1995: 163–79.

Nagy, G. 1996. *Poetry as Performance. Homer and Beyond.* New York, Cambridge University Press.

Nagy, G. 2001. 'Homeric Poetry and Problems of Multiformity: The "Panathenaic Bottle-neck"', *CPh* 96: 109–19.

Nagy, G. 2003. *Homeric Responses.* Austin, TX, University of Texas Press.

Nagy, G. 2010. *Homer the Preclassic.* Berkeley, CA, University of California Press.

Naiden, F. S. 2006. *Ancient Supplication.* Oxford, Oxford University Press.

Nesselrath, H.-G. 1992. *Ungeschehenes Geschehen. Beinahe-Episoden im griechischen und römischen Epos von Homer bis zur Spätantike.* Stuttgart, Teubner.

Nilsson, M. P. 1932. *The Mycenaean Origins of Greek Mythology.* Cambridge, Cambridge University Press (revised edition, with new introduction and bibliography, Berkeley, CA, 1972).

Notopoulos, J. A. 1949. 'Parataxis in Homer: A New Approach to Homeric Literary Criticism', *TAPhA* 80: 1–23 (= de Jong 1999: iv.94–112).

Notopoulos, J. A. 1950. 'The Generic and Oral Composition in Homer', *TAPhA* 81: 28–36.

Notopoulos, J. A. 1964. 'Studies in Early Greek Oral Poetry', *HSPh* 68: 1–77.

Nünlist, R. 2010. *The Ancient Critic at Work.* Cambridge, Cambridge University Press.

Olson, S. D. 1990. 'The Stories of Agamemnon in Homer's *Odyssey*', *TAPhA* 120: 57–71.

Olson, S. D. 1995. *Blood and Iron. Story and Storytelling in Homer's Odyssey. Mnemosyne* Supplement 148. Leiden, Brill.

Osborne, R. 1993. 'À la grecque', *JMA* 6: 231–7.

Osborne, R. 2004. 'Homer's Society', in R. Fowler 2004: 206–19.

Oswald, R. 1993. *Das Ende der Odyssee. Studien zu Strukturen epischen Gestaltens.* Graz, Teschnische Universität Graz (dissertation, Karl-Franzens-Universität Graz).

Page, D. L. 1955. *The Homeric Odyssey.* Oxford, Clarendon Press.

Page, D. L. 1959. *History and the Homeric Iliad* (Berkeley, CA, University of California Press.

Page, D. L. 1973a. *Folktales in Homer's Odyssey.* Cambridge, MA, Harvard University Press.

Page, D. L. 1973b. 'Stesichorus, *Geryoneis*', *JHS* 93: 138–54.

Palmer, L. R. 1962. 'The Language of Homer', in Wace and Stubbings 1962: 75–178.

Palmer, L. R. 1980. *The Greek Language.* London, Faber and Faber.

Parker, R. 1983. *Miasma. Pollution and Purification in Early Greek Poetry.* Oxford, Clarendon Press.

Parker, R. 1985. 'Homer's War Music', *Omnibus* 10: 17–21.

Parker, R. 1991. 'The Hymn to Demeter and the Homeric Hymns', *G&R* 38: 1–17.

Parker, R. 1998. 'Pleasing Thighs: Reciprocity in Greek Religion', in C. Gill, N. Postlethwaite, and R. Seaford (eds.), *Reciprocity in Ancient Greece.* Oxford, Oxford University Press: 105–25.

Parks, W. 1990. *Verbal Dueling in Heroic Narrative. The Homeric and Old English Traditions.* Princeton, NJ, Princeton University Press.

Parry, A. 1956. 'The Language of Achilles', *TAPhA* 87: 1–7 (= Kirk 1964: 48–54; = A. Parry 1989: 1–7).

Parry, A. 1966. 'Have We Homer's *Iliad*?', *YClS* 20: 177–216 (= A. Parry 1989: 104–40).

Parry, A. 1971. 'Introduction', in M. Parry 1971: ix–lxii (reprinted in A. Parry 1989: 195–264).

Parry, A. 1972. 'Language and Characterization in Homer', *HSPh* 76: 1–22 (= A. Parry 1989, 301–26).

Parry, A. 1981. *Logos and Ergon in Thucydides.* New York, Arno Press.

Parry, A. 1989. *The Language of Achilles and Other Papers.* Edited with foreword by H. Lloyd-Jones. Oxford, Clarendon Press.

Parry, M. 1971. *The Making of Homeric Verse. The Collected Papers of Milman Parry.* Edited by Adam Parry. Oxford, Clarendon Press.

Pasquali, G. 1942. 'Arte allusiva', *Italia che Scrive* 25: 185–7 (reprinted in G. Pasquali, *Stravaganze quarte e supreme.* Venice, Neri Pozza, 1951: 11–20).

Pasquali, G. 1952. *Storia della tradizione e critica del testo.* Second edition, Florence, F. Le Monnier.

Patzer, H. 1952. 'Rhapsodos', *Hermes* 80: 314–24.

Pease, A. S. (ed.) 1955–8. *Cicero. De Natura Deorum.* Loeb Classical Library. 2 vols. Cambridge, MA, Harvard University Press.

Pelling, C. B. R. (ed.) 1990. *Characterization and Individuality in Greek Literature.* Oxford, Clarendon Press.

Penglase, C. 1994. *Greek Myths and Mesopotamia.* London, Routledge.

Peradotto, J. and Sullivan, J. P. (eds.) 1984. *Women in the Ancient World. The Arethusa Papers.* Albany, NY, State University of New York Press.

Peristiany, J. (ed.) 1965. *Honour and Shame. The Values of a Mediterranean Society*. London, Weidenfeld and Nicolson.

Petersmann, G. 1974. 'Die Entscheidungsmonologe in den Homerischen Epen', *GB* 2: 147–69.

Petersmann, H. 1981. 'Homer und das Märchen', *WS* 15: 43–68.

Petzl, G. 1969. *Antike Diskussionen über die beiden Nekyiai*. Meisenheim am Glan, A. Hain.

Pfeiffer, R. 1968. *History of Classical Scholarship from the Beginnings to the End of the Hellenistic Age*. Oxford, Clarendon Press.

Pontani, F. (ed.) 2007. *Scholia graeca in Odysseam i. Scholia ad libros a–b*. Rome, Edizioni di Storia e Letteratura.

Poole, A. and Maule, J. 1995. *The Oxford Book of Classical Verse in Translation*. Oxford, Oxford University Press.

Pope, A. 1967a. *The Iliad of Homer*. Edited by M. Mack. 2 vols. London, Routledge.

Pope, A. 1967b. *The Odyssey of Homer*. Edited by M. Mack. 2 vols. London, Routledge.

Pope, M. W. M. 1963. 'The Parry–Lord Theory of Homeric Composition', *AClass* 6: 1–21.

Porter, D. H. 1972. 'Violent Juxtaposition in the Similes of the *Iliad*', *CJ* 68: 11–21 (= de Jong 1999: iii.338–50).

Postlethwaite, N. 1995. 'Agamemnon Best of Spearmen', *Phoenix* 49: 95–103.

Postlethwaite, N. 2000. *Homer's Iliad. A Commentary on the Translation by Richmond Lattimore*. Exeter, University of Exeter Press.

Powell, B. B. 1977. *Composition by Theme in the Odyssey*. Meisenheim am Glan, Hain.

Powell, B. B. 1991. *Homer and the Origins of the Greek Alphabet*. Cambridge, Cambridge University Press.

Powell, B. B. 1997. 'Homer and Writing', in Morris and Powell 1997: 3–32.

Powell, B. B. 2004. *Homer*. Oxford, Blackwell.

Pratt, L. H. 1993. *Lying and Poetry from Homer to Pindar. Falsehood and Deception in Archaic Greek Poetics*. Ann Arbor, MI, University of Michigan Press.

Prendergast, G. 1875. *A Complete Concordance to the Iliad of Homer*. London, Longmans, Green, and Co. (revised by B. Marzullo, Hildesheim, 1962).

Pulleyn, S. 1997. *Prayer in Greek Religion*. Oxford, Clarendon Press.

Pulleyn, S. (ed.) 2001. *Homer. Iliad Book One*. Oxford, Oxford University Press.

Purcell, N. 1990. 'Mobility and the *Polis*', In O. Murray and S. Price (eds.), *The Greek City from Homer to Alexander*. Oxford, Clarendon Press: 29–58.

Raaflaub, K. 1991. 'Homer und die Geschichte des 8. Jh.s v. Christ', in Latacz 1991: 205–56.

Raaflaub, K. 1993. 'Homer to Solon: The Rise of the *Polis*, The Written Sources', in M. H. Hansen (ed.), *The Ancient Greek City-state*. Copenhagen, Munksgaard: 41–105.

Rabel, R. J. 1988. 'Chryses and the opening of the *Iliad*', *AJPh* 109: 473–81.

Radermacher, L. 1915. *Erzählungen der Odyssee*. *SAWW* 178. Vienna, A. Hölder.

Radermacher, L. (ed.) 1951. *Artium Scriptores. Reste der voraristotelischen Rhetorik*. *SAWW* 227. Vienna, Rohrer.

Reckford, K. J. 1964. 'Helen in the *Iliad*', *GRBS* 5: 5–20.

Redfield, J. M. 1975. *Nature and Culture in the Iliad. The Tragedy of Hector*. Chicago, University of Chicago Press (new edition, Durham, NC, 1994, with additional chapter on the gods).

Redfield, J. M. 1983. 'The Economic Man', in Rubino and Shelmerdine 1983: 218–47.

Reece, S. 1993. *The Stranger's Welcome: Oral Theory and the Aesthetics of the Homeric Hospitality Scene*. Ann Arbor, MI, University of Michigan Press.

Reeve, M. D. 1973. 'The Language of Achilles', *CQ* 23: 193–5.

Reichel, M. 1990. 'Retardationstechniken in der Ilias', in W. Kullmann and M. Reichel (eds.), *Der Übergang von der Mündlichkeit zur Literatur bei den Griechen*. Tübingen, Gunter Narr: 125–51.

Reichel, M. 1994. *Fernbeziehungen in der Ilias. ScriptOralia* 62 A, Bd. 13. Tübingen, Gunter Narr.

Reinhardt, K. 1938. *Das Parisurteil. Wissenschaft und Gegenwart* 11. Frankfurt am Main, V. Klostermann (reprinted in Reinhardt, 1960: 16–36; English translation, 'The Judgement of Paris', in Wright and Jones 1997: 170–91).

Reinhardt, K. 1948. 'Die Abenteuer des Odysseus', in K. Reinhardt, *Von Werken und Formen*. Godesburg, H. Küpper, 52–162 (reprinted in Reinhardt 1960: 47–124; English translation, 'The Adventures in the *Odyssey*', in Schein 1996: 63–132).

Reinhardt, K. 1960. *Tradition und Geist*. Göttingen, Vandenhoeck & Ruprecht.

Reinhardt, K. 1961. *Die Ilias und ihr Dichter*. Göttingen, Vandenhoeck & Ruprecht.

Reynolds, L. D. and Wilson, N. G. 1991. *Scribes and Scholars. A Guide to the Transmission of Greek and Latin Literature*. Third edition, Oxford, Clarendon Press (first edition, 1968).

Richardson, N. J. (ed.) 1974. *The Homeric Hymn to Demeter*. Oxford, Clarendon Press.

Richardson, N. J. 1975. 'Homeric Professors in the Age of the Sophists', *PCPhS* n.s. 21: 65–81 (= Laird 2006: 62–86).

Richardson, N. J. 1980. 'Literary Criticism in the Exegetical Scholia to the *Iliad*', *CQ* 30: 265–87 (= Laird 2006: 176–210).

Richardson, N. J. 1983. 'Recognition Scenes in the *Odyssey* and Ancient Criticism', in F. Cairns 1983: 219–35.

Richardson, N. J. 1985. 'Pindar and Later Literary Criticism in Antiquity', in F. Cairns (ed.), *Papers of the Liverpool Latin Seminar*, vol. 5. Liverpool, Francis Cairns: 383–401.

Richardson, N. J. 1987. 'The Individuality of Homer's Language', in Bremer et al. 1987: 165–84.

Richardson, N. J. 1993. *The Iliad. A Commentary. Vol. 6 Books 21–24*. Cambridge, Cambridge University Press.

Richardson, N. J. 2007. 'The Homeric Hymn to Hermes', in Finglass et al. 2007: 83–91.

Richardson, N. J. 2010. *Three Homeric Hymns*. Cambridge, Cambridge University Press.

Richardson, S. 1990. *The Homeric Narrator*. Nashville, TN, Vanderbilt University Press.

Rieu, E. V. (trans.). 1946. *Homer. The Odyssey*. Harmondsworth, Penguin (revised edition, London, 1991, by D. C. H. Rieu in consultation with P. Jones).

Rieu, E. V. (trans.). 1950. *Homer. The Iliad*. Harmondsworth, Penguin.

Roberts, D. H., Dunn, F. M., and Fowler, D. P. (eds.) 1997. *Classical Closure. Reading the End in Greek and Latin Literature*. Princeton, NJ, Princeton University Press.

Rohde, E. 1925. *Psyche. The Cult of Souls and Belief in Immortality among the Ancient Greeks.* Translated by W. B. Hillis. London, Routledge & Kegan Paul (first published in German, Freiburg, 1894).

Romm, J. 1992. *The Edges of the Earth in Ancient Thought. Geography, Exploration, and Fiction.* Princeton, NJ, Princeton University Press.

Rosen, R. 1997. 'Homer and Hesiod', in Morris and Powell 1997: 463–88.

Rosner, J. A. 1976. 'The Speech of Phoenix: *Iliad* 9.434–605', *Phoenix* 30: 314–27.

Rowe, C. J. 1983. 'The Nature of Homeric Morality', in Rubino and Shelmerdine 1983: 248–75.

Rubino, C. A. and Shelmerdine, C. W. (eds.) 1983. *Approaches to Homer.* Austin, TX, University of Texas Press.

Russo, C. F. 1965. *Hesiodi Scutum.* Second edition, Florence, La Nuova Italia.

Russo, J. 1968. 'Homer Against His Tradition' *Arion* 7: 275–95 (= de Jong 1999: iv.125–41; = J. Latacz [ed.], *Homer. Tradition und Neuerung. Wege der Forschung* 463. Darmstadt, Wissenschaftliche Buchgesellschaft, 1979: 403–26 [German version]).

Russo, J. 1992. *A Commentary on Homer's Odyssey. Volume 3 Books XVII–XXIV.* With M. Fernandez-Galiano and A. Heubeck. Oxford, Clarendon Press.

Russo, J. 1997. 'The Formula', in Morris and Powell 1997: 238–60.

Rüter, K. 1969. *Odysseeinterpretationen. Untersuchungen zum ersten Buch und zur Phaiakis. Hypomnemata* 19. Göttingen, Vandenhoeck & Ruprecht.

Rutherford, I. C. 2012. 'The *Catalogue of Women* within the Greek Epic Tradition: Allusion, Intertextuality and Traditional Referentiality', in Andersen and Haug 2012: 152–67.

Rutherford, R. B. 1982. 'Tragic Form and Feeling in the *Iliad*', *JHS* 102: 145–60 (= D. Cairns 2001: 260–93, with afterword).

Rutherford, R. B. 1985. 'At Home and Abroad: Aspects of the Structure of the *Odyssey*', *PCPhS* n.s. 31: 133–50.

Rutherford, R. B. 1986. 'The Philosophy of the *Odyssey*', *JHS* 106: 145–62 (= Doherty 2009: 155–88, with afterword).

Rutherford, R. B. 1991. Review of Dimock 1989, *CR* 41: 9–10.

Rutherford, R. B. 1991–3. 'From the *Iliad* to the *Odyssey*', *BICS* 38: 37–54 (= D. Cairns 2001: 117–46, with afterword).

Rutherford, R. B. 1992. *Homer. Odyssey. Books 19 and 20.* Cambridge, Cambridge University Press.

Saïd, S. 2011. *Homer and the Odyssey.* Oxford, Oxford University Press.

Sale, W. M. 1963. 'Achilles and Heroic Values', *Arion* 2: 86–100.

Sale, W. M. 1989. 'The Trojans, Statistics, and Milman Parry', *GRBS* 30: 341–410.

Sammons, B. 2010. *The Art and Rhetoric of the Homeric Catalogue.* Oxford, Oxford University Press.

Saunders, K. B. 1999. 'The Wounds in *Iliad* 13–16', *CQ* 49: 346–63.

Schadewaldt, W. 1938. *Iliasstudien.* Leipzig, S. Hirzel (third edition, Darmstadt, 1966; English version of Chapter 1 in de Jong 1999: i.67–95).

Schadewaldt, W. 1965. *Von Homers Welt und Werk.* Fourth edition, Stuttgart, Koehler (first edition, Leipzig, 1944; extracts in English translation as Schadewaldt 1997a and 1997b).

Schadewaldt, W. 1997a. 'Achilles' Decision'. Translated by G. M. Wright and P. Jones in Wright and Jones 1997: 143–69 (previously published in German in Schadewaldt 1965).

Schadewaldt, W. 1997b. 'Hector and Andromache'. Translated by G. M. Wright and P. Jones in Wright and Jones 1997: 124–42 (previously published in German in Schadewaldt 1965).

Schaefer, H. 1960. 'Eigenart und Wesenszüge der griechischen Kolonisation', *Heidelberger Jahrbücher* 4: 77–93.

Schein, S. L. 1984. *The Mortal Hero. An Introduction to Homer's Iliad*, Berkeley, CA, University of California Press.

Schein, S. L. (ed.) 1996. *Reading the Odyssey. Selected Interpretative Essays*. Princeton, NJ, Princeton University Press.

Schein, S. L. 2002. 'The Horses of Achilles in Book 17 of the *Iliad*', in M. Reichel and A. Rengakos (eds.), *Epea Pteroenta. Beiträge zur Homerforschung. Festschrift für Wolfgang Kullmann*. Stuttgart, F. Steiner: 193–205.

Schofield, M. 1986. 'Euboulia in the *Iliad*', *CQ* 36: 6–31 (= D. Cairns 2001: 220–59).

Schwartz, E. 1940. 'Der Name Homeros', *Hermes* 75: 1–9.

Schwinge, E.-R. 1991. 'Homerische Epen und Erzählforschung', in Latacz 1991: 482–512.

Scodel, R. 1982. 'The Autobiography of Phoenix: *Iliad* 9.444–95', *AJPh* 103: 128–36.

Scodel, R. 1999. *Credible Impossibilities. Conventions and Strategies of Verisimilitude in Homer and Greek Tragedy*. Stuttgart, Teubner.

Scodel, R. 2002. *Listening to Homer. Tradition, Narrative, and Audience*. Ann Arbor, MI, University of Michigan Press.

Scodel, R. 2004. 'The Story-teller and his Audience', in R. Fowler 2004: 45–55.

Scodel, R. 2008. *Epic Facework. Self-presentation and Social Interaction in Homer*. Swansea, Classical Press of Wales.

Scott, W. C. 1974. *The Oral Nature of the Homeric Simile. Mnemosyne* Supplement 58. Leiden, Brill.

Scott, W. C. 2009. *The Artistry of the Homeric Simile*. Hanover, NH, University Press of New England.

Scully, S. R. 1990. *Homer and the Sacred City*. Ithaca, NY, Cornell University Press.

Seaford, R. 1994. *Reciprocity and Ritual. Homer and Tragedy in the Developing City-state*. Oxford, Clarendon Press.

Sealey, R. 1957. 'From Phemius to Ion', *REG* 70: 17–46.

Segal, C. 1962. 'The Phaeacians and the Symbolism of Odysseus' Return', *Arion* 1: 17–64 (revised in Segal 1995: 12–64).

Segal, C. 1967. 'Transition and Ritual in Odysseus' Return', *PP* 22: 321–42 (revised in Segal 1995: 65–85).

Segal, C. 1968. 'The Embassy and the Duals of *Iliad* 9.182–89', *GRBS* 9: 101–14.

Segal, C. 1971a. 'Andromache's Anagnorisis', *HSPh* 75: 33–57.

Segal, C. 1971b. *The Theme of the Mutilation of the Corpse in the Iliad. Mnemosyne* Supplement 17. Leiden, Brill.

Segal, C. 1983. 'Kleos and its Ironies in the *Odyssey*', *AC* 52: 22–47 (= Segal 1995: 85–109; = Schein 1996: 201–22).

Segal, C. 1992. 'Divine Justice in the Odyssey: Cyclops, Helios and Poseidon', *AJPh* 113: 89–518 (= Segal 1995: 195–227).

Segal, C. 1995. *Singers, Heroes and Gods in the Odyssey*. Ithaca, NY, Cornell University Press.

Sharples, R. 1983. '"But why has my spirit spoken with me thus?" Homeric Decision-making', *G&R* 30: 1–7 (= McAuslan and Walcot 1998: 164–70).

Sherratt, E. S. 1990. 'Reading the Texts: Archaeology and the Homeric Poems', *Antiquity* 64: 807–24 (= Emlyn-Jones 1992: 145–65; = de Jong 1999: ii.77–101).

Shewring, W. 1980. *Homer. The Odyssey*. With introduction by G. S. Kirk. Oxford, Oxford University Press.

Shipp, G. P. 1972. *Studies in the Language of Homer*. Second edition, Cambridge, Cambridge University Press (first edition, Cambridge, 1953).

Shive, D. 1987. *Naming Achilles*. New York, Oxford University Press.

Silk, M. S. 1987. *Homer. The Iliad*. Landmarks in World Literature. Cambridge, Cambridge University Press.

Simon, E. 1985. *Die Götter der Griechen*. Third edition, Munich, Hirmer (first edition, Munich, 1969).

Slatkin, L. M. 1991. *The Power of Thetis. Allusion and Interpretation in the Iliad*. Berkeley, CA, University of California Press.

Smith, B. H. 1968. *Poetic Closure. A Study of How Poems End*. Chicago, University of Chicago Press.

Smith, P. M. 1981. 'Aineiadai as Patrons of *Iliad* XX and the Homeric Hymn to Aphrodite', *HSPh* 85: 17–58.

Snell, B. 1953. *The Discovery of the Mind. The Greek Origins of European Thought*. Oxford, Blackwell.

Snipes, K. 1988. 'Literary Interpretation in the Homeric Scholia: The Similes of the *Iliad*', *AJPh* 109: 196–222.

Snodgrass, A. M. 1998. *Homer and the Artists. Text and Picture in Early Greek Art*. Cambridge, Cambridge University Press.

Sourvinou-Inwood, C. 1986. 'Crime and Punishment: Tityos, Tantalos and Sisyphos in Odyssey 11', *BICS* 33: 37–58.

Sourvinou-Inwood, C. 1995. *'Reading' Greek Death. To the End of the Classical Period*. Oxford, Clarendon Press.

Stanford, W. B. (ed.) 1959. *Homer. Odyssey*. Stanford, W. B. London, Macmillan.

Stanford, W. B. 1963. *The Ulysses Theme*. Second edition, Oxford, Blackwell.

Stanford, W. B. and Luce, J. V. 1974. *The Quest for Ulysses*. London, Phaidon Press.

Stanley, K. 1993. *The Shield of Homer. Narrative Structure in the Iliad*. Princeton, NJ, Princeton University Press.

Steiner, D. 2010. *Homer. Odyssey. Books XVII and XVIII*. Cambridge, Cambridge University Press.

Steiner, G. 1967. 'Homer and the Scholars', in G. Steiner, *Language and Silence*. London, Faber: 197–213.

Steiner, G. (ed.) 1996. *Homer in English*. London, Penguin Books.

Stewart, D. J. 1976. *The Disguised Guest. Rank, Role, and Identity in the Odyssey*. Lewisberg, PA, Bucknell University Press.

Stoevesandt, M. 2004. *Feinde – Gegner – Opfer. Zur Darstellung der Troianer in den Kampfszenen der Ilias.* Basel, Schwabe.

Stössel, H.-A. 1975. *Der letzte Gesang der Odyssee.* Erlangen (PhD thesis, Friedrich-Alexander-Universität).

Strasburger, G. 1953. 'Der soziologische Aspekt der homerischen Epen', *Gymnasium* 60: 97–114 (reprinted in G. Strasburger, *Studien zur alten Geschichte*, vol. 1. Hildesheim, G. Olms, 1982: 491–518; English translation, 'The Sociology of the Homeric Epics', in Wright and Jones 1997: 47–70).

Strasburger, G. 1954. *Die kleinen Kämpfer der Ilias.* Frankfurt am Main, n.p.

Suerbaum, W. 1968. 'Die Ich-Erzählungen des Odysseus', *Poetica* 2: 150–77 (= de Jong 1999: iii.431–59).

Sutton, D. n.d. *Homer and the Papyri.* Second edition ed. N. Gagy. Center for Hellenic Studies, Harvard University. http://chs.harvard.edu/wa/pageR?tn=ArticleWrapper& bdc=12&mn=1168 (last visited 15 November 2012).

Swain, S. R. C. 1988. 'A Note on *Iliad* 9.524–99: The Story of Meleager', *CQ* 38: 271–76.

Tachinoslis, N. 1984. *Handschriften und Ausgaben der Odyssee.* Frankfurt am Main, Lang.

Taplin, O. 1972. 'Aeschylean Silences and Silences in Aeschylus', *HSPh* 76: 57–97.

Taplin, O. 1980. 'The Shield of Achilles within the *Iliad*', *G&R* 27: 1–21 (= McAuslan and Walcot 1998: 96–115; = D. Cairns 2001: 342–64).

Taplin, O. 1990. 'Agamemnon's Role in the *Iliad*', in Pelling 1990: 60–92.

Taplin, O. 1992. *Homeric Soundings. The Shaping of the Iliad.* Oxford, Clarendon Press.

Tebben, J. 1994. *Concordantia Homerica I. Odyssea.* Hildesheim, Olms-Weidmann.

Tebben, J. 1998. *Concordantia Homerica II. Ilias.* Hildesheim, Olms-Weidman.

Thalmann, W. G. 1984. *Conventions of Form and Thought in Early Greek Epic Poetry.* Baltimore, MD, Johns Hopkins University Press.

Thalmann, W. G. 1988. 'Thersites: Comedy, Scapegoat, and Heroic Ideology in the *Iliad*', *TAPhA* 118: 1–28.

Thalmann, W. G. 1998. *The Swineherd and the Bow. Representations of Class in the Odyssey,* Ithaca, NY, Cornell University Press.

Thomas, R. 1989. *Oral Tradition and Written Record in Classical Athens.* Cambridge, Cambridge University Press.

Thomas, R. 1993. *Literacy and Orality in Ancient Greece.* Cambridge, Cambridge University Press.

Thompson, S. 1955–8. *Motif Index of Folk Literature.* Copenhagen, Rosenkild & Bagger.

Thomson, J. A. K. 1962. 'Introduction: Homer and His Influence', in Wace and Stubbings: 1–15.

Thornton, A. 1970. *People and Themes in Homer's Odyssey.* London, Methuen.

Thornton, A. 1984. *Homer's Iliad. Its Composition and the Motif of Supplication. Hypomnemata* 81. Göttingen, Vandenhoeck & Ruprecht.

Tracy, S. V. 1990. *The Story of the Odyssey.* Princeton, NJ, Princeton University Press.

Tsagarakis, O. 1969. 'The Achaean Wall and the Homeric Question', *Hermes* 97: 129–35.

Tsagarakis, O. 1982. *Form and Content in Homer.* Hermes Einzelschriften 46. Wiesbaden, Franz Steiner.

Tsagarakis, O. 2000. *Studies in Odyssey 11.* Hermes Einzelschriften 82. Stuttgart, F. Steiner.

Turner, E. J. 1968. *Greek Papyri.* Oxford, Clarendon Press (second edition, Oxford, 1980).

Turner, F. M. 1981. *The Greek Heritage in Victorian Britain.* New Haven, CT, Yale University Press.

Usener, K. 1990. *Beobachtungen zum Verhältnis der Odyssee zur Ilias.* ScriptOralia 21. Tübingen, G. Narr.

van Thiel, H. 1982. *Ilias und Iliaden.* Basel, Schwabe.

van Thiel, H. 1988. *Odysseen.* Basel, Schwabe.

van Thiel, H. (ed.) 1991. *Homeri Odyssea.* Hildesheim, G. Olms.

van Thiel, H. (ed.) 1996. *Homeri Ilias.* Hildesheim, G. Olms.

van Thiel, H. 2000. *Scholia D in Iliadem.* http://www.uni-koeln.de/phil-fak/ifa/vanthiel/scholiaD.pdf (last visited 20 November 2012).

van Thiel, H. 1992a. 'Kings in Combat: Battles and Heroes in the *Iliad*', *CQ* 38: 1–24.

van Thiel, H. 1992b. *Status Warriors. War, Violence, and Society in Homer and History.* Amsterdam, J. C. Gieben.

van Thiel, H. 1994. 'The Homeric Way of War: The *Iliad* and the Hoplite Phalanx', *G&R* 41: 1–18, 131–55.

van Thiel, H. 2004. *Greek Warfare. Myths and Realities.* London, Duckworth.

Vansina, J. 1965. *Oral Tradition. A Study in Historical Methodology.* Translation by H. M. Wright. London, Routledge and Kegan Paul (first published in French, Tervuren, 1961).

Vansina, J. 1985. *Oral Tradition as History.* London, Currey.

Verity, A. (trans.) 2010. *Homer. The Iliad.* Introduction and notes by B. Graziosi. Oxford, Oxford University Press.

Vermeule, E. 1979. *Aspects of Death in Early Greek Art and Poetry.* Berkeley, CA, University of California Press.

Vernant, J.-P. 1965. *Mythe et pensée chez les grecs.* Paris, Maspero (English version, *Myth and Thought among the Greeks*, London, 1983).

Versnel, H. 2011. *Coping with the Gods. Wayward Readings in Greek Theology.* Leiden, Brill.

Vester, H. 1968. 'Das 19. Buch der Odyssee', *Gymnasium* 75: 417–34.

Vidal-Naquet, P. 1981. 'Land and Sacrifice in the *Odyssey*', in R. Gordon (ed.), *Myth, Religion and Society.* Cambridge, Cambridge University Press, 1981: 80–94 (originally published as 'Valeurs religieuses et mythiques de la terre et du sacrifice dans l'Odyssée', *Annales (ESC)* 25 [1970]: 1278–97; also in English in Schein 1996: 33–54).

Visser, E. 1987. *Homerische Versificationstechnik.* Frankfurt am Main, P. Lang.

Visser, E. 1988. 'Formulae or Single Words? Towards a New Theory on Homeric Verse-making', *WJA* 14: 21–37 (= de Jong 1999: i.364–81).

Visser, E. 1997. *Homers Katalog der Schiffe.* Stuttgart, Teubner.

Wace, A. J. B., and Stubbings, F. H. (eds.) 1962. *A Companion to Homer.* London, Macmillan.

Wachter, R. 2012. 'The Other View: Focus on Linguistic Innovations in the Homeric Epics', in Andersen and Haug 2012: 5–79.

Wade-Gery, H. T. 1952. *The Poet of the Iliad*. Cambridge, Cambridge University Press.

Wade-Gery, H. T. 1959. 'Hesiod', in H. T. Wade-Gery, *Essays on Greek History*. Oxford, Blackwell: 1–16.

Walbank, F. W. 1979. *A Historical Commentary on Polybius. Vol. 3, Commentary on Books XIX–XL*. Oxford, Clarendon Press.

Walcot, P. 1966. *Hesiod and the Near East*. Cardiff, Wales University Press.

Walcot, P. 1977. 'Odysseus and the Art of Lying', *AncSoc* 8: 1–19 (= Emlyn-Jones et al. 1992: 49–62).

Watson, J. (ed.) 2002. *Homer. Odyssey VI & VII*. London, Bristol Classical Press.

Webster, T. B. L. 1958. *From Mycenae to Homer*. London, Methuen.

Weil, S. 1940–1. 'L'Iliade ou le poème de force', *Cahiers du Sud* 230 and 231 (under the pseudonym Émile Novis) (English translation in S. Weil, *Intimations of Christianity among the Greeks*. London, Routledge & Kegan Paul, 1957: 24–55.

Weiler, L. 1974. *Der Agon im Mythos*. Darmstadt, Wissenschaftliche Buchgesellschaft.

Wender, D. 1978. *The Last Scenes of the Odyssey*. Mnemosyne Supplement 52. Leiden, Brill.

West, M. L. 1966. *Hesiod. Theogony*. Oxford, Clarendon Press.

West, M. L. 1969. 'The Achaean Wall', *CR* 19: 255–60 (= West 2011b: 233–41).

West, M. L. 1973a. 'Greek Poetry 2000–700 BC', *CQ* 23: 179–92 (= West 2011b: 1–21).

West, M. L. 1973b. *Textual Criticism and Editorial Technique*. Stuttgart, Teubner.

West, M. L. (ed.) 1978. *Hesiod. Works and Days*. Oxford, Clarendon Press.

West, M. L. 1981. 'The Singing of Homer and the Modes of Early Greek Music,' *JHS* 101: 113–29 (partly reprinted in West 2011b: 128–40).

West, M. L. 1982. *Greek Metre*. Oxford, Clarendon Press.

West, M. L. 1985. *The Hesiodic Catalogue of Women*. Oxford, Clarendon Press.

West, M. L. 1987. *Introduction to Greek Metre*. Oxford, Clarendon Press.

West, M. L. 1988. 'The Rise of the Greek Epic', *JHS* 108: 151–72 (= West 2011b: 35–73).

West, M. L. 1995. 'The Date of the Iliad', *MH* 52: 203–19 (= West 2011b: 188–208).

West, M. L. 1997a. *The East Face of Helicon*. Oxford, Clarendon Press.

West, M. L. 1997b. 'Homer's Meter', in Morris and Powell 1997: 218–37.

West, M. L. 1998–2000. *Homeri Ilias*. Stuttgart, Teubner.

West, M. L. 1999. 'The Invention of Homer', *CQ* 49: 364–82 (= West 2011b: 408–36).

West, M. L. 2001a. 'The Fragmentary Homeric Hymn to Dionysus', *ZPE* 134: 1–11 (= West 2011b: 313–28).

West, M. L. 2001b. *Studies in the Text and Transmission of the Iliad*. Munich, K. G. Saur.

West, M. L. (ed.) 2003a. *Greek Epic Fragments from the Seventh to the Fifth Centuries BC*. Loeb Classical Library. Cambridge, MA, Harvard University Press.

West, M. L. (ed.) 2003b. *Homeric Hymns. Homeric Apocrypha. Lives of Homer*. Loeb Classical Library. Cambridge, MA, Harvard University Press.

West, M. L. 2003c. '*Iliad* and *Aethiopis*', *CQ* 53: 1–14 (= West 2011b: 242–64).

West, M. L. 2005. '*Odyssey and Argonautica*', *CQ* 55: 39–64 (= West 2011b: 277–312).

West, M. L. 2007a. *Indo-European Poetry and Myth*. Oxford, Oxford University Press.

West, M. L. 2007b. Review of Hirschberger 2004, *Gnomon* 79: 289–94.

West, M. L. 2010. 'Rhapsodes at Festivals', *ZPE* 173: 1–13.

West, M. L. 2011a. 'The First *Homeric Hymn* to Dionysus', in Faulkner 2011: 29–43.

West, M. L. 2011b. *Hellenica. Selected Papers on Greek Literature and Thought I. Epic.* Oxford, Oxford University Press.

West, M. L. 2011c. *The Making of the Iliad*. Oxford, Oxford University Press.

West, M. L. 2012. 'Towards a Chronology of Early Greek Epic', in Andersen and Haug 2012: 224–41.

West, M. L. 2013. *The Epic Cycle. A Commentary on the Lost Troy Epics*. Oxford, Oxford University Press.

West, S. 1967. *The Ptolemaic Papyri of Homer*. Cologne and Opladen, Westdeutscher Verlag.

West, S. 1981. 'An Alternative Nostos for Odysseus', *LCM* 6: 169–75.

West, S. 1988: refers to her contributions to Heubeck, West, and Hainsworth 1988.

West, S. 1989. 'Laertes Revisited', *PCPhS* n.s. 35: 113–43.

West, S. 2001. 'Phoenix's Antecedents: A Note on *Iliad* 9', *SCI* 20: 1–15.

West, S. 2007. 'Terminal Problems', in Finglass et al. 2007: 3–21.

West, S. 2012a. 'Odyssean Stratigraphy', in Andersen and Haug 2012: 122–37.

West, S. 2012b. 'Some Reflections on *Alpamysh*', in Montanari et al. 2012: 531–42.

Whallon, W. 1969. *Formula, Character and Context*. Washington, DC, Center for Hellenic Studies.

Whitman, C. 1958. *Homer and the Heroic Tradition*. Cambridge, MA, Harvard University Press.

Whitman, C. and Scodel, R. 1981. 'Sequence and Simultaneity in *Iliad* N, Ξ, and O', *HSPh* 85: 1–15.

Whitmarsh, T. 2002. 'What Samuel Butler Saw: Classics, Authorship and Cultural Authority in Victorian England', *PCPhS* n.s. 48: 66–86.

Willcock, M. M. 1964. 'Mythological Paradeigmata in the *Iliad*', *CQ* 14: 141–51.

Willcock, M. M. 1970. 'Some Aspects of the Gods in the *Iliad*', *BICS* 17: 1–10 (= Wright 1978: 58–69; = de Jong 1999: ii.404–15).

Willcock, M. M. 1973. 'The Funeral Games of Patroclus', *BICS* 20: 1–11.

Willcock, M. M. 1976. *A Companion to the Iliad*. Chicago, University of Chicago Press.

Willcock, M. M. 1977. '*Ad hoc* Invention in the *Iliad*', *HSPh* 81: 41–53.

Willcock, M. M. 1978. *The Iliad of Homer. Books I–XII*. Basingstoke, Macmillan.

Willcock, M. M. 1983a. 'Antilochus in the *Iliad*', in M. Willcock (ed.), *Mélanges Édouard Delebecque*. Aix-en-Provence, Université de Provence: 479–85.

Willcock, M. M. 1983b. 'Battle Scenes in the *Aeneid*', *PCPhS* n.s. 29: 87–99.

Willcock, M. M. 1984. *The Iliad of Homer. Books XII–XXIV*. Basingstoke, Macmillan Education.

Willcock, M. M. 1997. 'Neoanalysis', in Morris and Powell 1997: 174–89.

Willi, A. 2011. 'Language', in Finkelberg 2011.

Williams, B. 1993. *Shame and Necessity*. Berkeley, CA, University of California Press.

Williams, F. 1978. *Callimachus. Hymn to Apollo*. Oxford, Clarendon Press.

Wilson, C. H. (ed.) 1996. *Homer. Iliad Books VIII and IX*. Warminster, Aris & Phillips.

Wilson, N. G. 1990. 'Thomas William Allen, 1862–1950'. *PBA* 76: 311–19.

Winkler, J. J. 1990. *The Constraints of Desire. The Anthropology of Sex and Gender in Ancient Greece*. London, Routledge.

Winterbottom, M. 1989. 'Speaking of the Gods', *G&R* 26: 33–41.

Wolf, F. A. 1985. *Prolegomena to Homer*. Edited and translated by A. Grafton, G. W. Most, and J. E. G. Zetzel. Princeton, NJ, Princeton University Press (from edition of R. Peppmüller, Halle, 1884; first published 1795).

Wolf, H.-H. and Wolf, A. 1968. *Der Weg des Odysseus. Tunis, Malta, Italien in den Augen Homers*. Tübingen, Wasmuth.

Woodard, R. D. 1997. *Greek Writing from Knossos to Homer. A Linguistic Interpretation of the Origin of the Greek Alphabet and the Continuity of Ancient Greek Literacy*. Oxford, Oxford University Press.

Woodhouse, W. J. 1930. *The Composition of Homer's Odyssey*. Oxford, Clarendon Press.

Wright, G. M. and Jones, P. (eds.) 1997. *Homer. German Scholarship in Translation*. Oxford, Clarendon Press.

Wright, J. (ed.) 1978. *Essays on the Iliad. Selected Modern Criticism*. Bloomington, IN, Indiana University Press.

Wyatt, W. F. 1985. 'The Embassy and the Duals in *Iliad* 9', *AJPh* 106: 399–408.

Yamagata, N. 1994. *Homeric Morality. Mnemosyne* Supplement 131. Leiden, Brill.

Young, D. 1967. 'Never Blotted a Line? Formula and Premeditation in Homer and Hesiod', *Arion* 6: 279–324 (= N. Rudd [ed.], *Essays on Classical Literature Selected from Arion*. Cambridge, Heffer, 1972: 33–78).

Zanker, G. 1994. *The Heart of Achilles. Characterization and Personal Ethics in the Iliad*. Ann Arbor, MI, University of Michigan Press.

Zeitlin, F. I. 1995. 'Figuring Fidelity in Homer's Odyssey', in Cohen 1995: 117–52.

Zhirmunsky, W. 1966. 'The Epic of "Alpamysh" and the Return of Odysseus', *PBA* 52: 267–86.

Zielinski, T. 1901. 'Die Behandlung gleichzeitiger Ereignisse im antiken Epos', *Philologus* Supplement 8: 407–49 (translated as 'The Treatment of Simultaneous Events in Ancient Epic' in de Jong 1999: iv.317–38).

ABOUT THE AUTHOR

Richard Rutherford was born in 1956 and educated at Robert Gordon's College, Aberdeen, and at Worcester College, Oxford. Since 1982 he has been Tutor in Greek and Latin Literature at Christ Church, Oxford, and has written books and articles on a wide variety of authors. Among his publications are *The Meditations of Marcus Aurelius. A Study* (Oxford, 1989), *Homer. Odyssey 19 and 20* (Cambridge, 1992), *The Art of Plato* (London, 1995), *Classical Literature. A Concise History* (London, 2005), and *Greek Tragic Style. Form, Language and Interpretation* (Cambridge, 2012).

INDEX

This index is deliberately selective; it is intended mainly to help readers find the principal discussion of a given topic.

Regular subscribers to the journal *Greece & Rome* receive a volume in the New Surveys in the Classics series as part of their subscription. The following volumes are also available to purchase as books.

Volume 41 *Homer*, Second Edition (ISBN 9781107670167)
Volume 40 *Greek Art*, Second Edition (ISBN 9781107601505)
Volume 39 *Roman Landscape: Culture and Identity* (ISBN 9781107400245)
Volume 38 *Epigram* (ISBN 9780521145701)
Volume 37 *Comedy* (ISBN 9780521706094)
Volume 36 *Roman Oratory* (ISBN 0521687225)
Volume 35 *The Second Sophistic* (ISBN 0198568819)
Volume 34 *Roman Art* (ISBN 9780198520818)
Volume 33 *Reception Studies* (ISBN 0198528655)
Volume 32 *The Invention of Prose* (ISBN 0198525234)
Volume 31 *Greek Historians* (ISBN 019922501X)
Volume 30 *Roman Religion* (ISBN 0199224331)
Volume 29 *Greek Science* (ISBN 0199223955)
Volume 28 *Virgil* (ISBN 0199223424)
Volume 27 *Latin Historians* (ISBN 0199222932)
Volume 26 *Homer* (ISBN 0199222096)
Volume 25 *Greek Thought* (ISBN 0199220743)
Volume 24 *Greek Religion* (ISBN 0199220735)

Lightning Source UK Ltd.
Milton Keynes UK
UKHW022138141219
355412UK00016B/380/P